UNIX Systems for Microcomputers

UNIX Systems for Microcomputers
ROSS BURGESS

BSP PROFESSIONAL BOOKS
OXFORD LONDON EDINBURGH
BOSTON PALO ALTO MELBOURNE

Copyright © **Ross Burgess** 1988

All rights reserved. No part of this
publication may be reproduced, stored
in a retrieval system, or transmitted,
in any form or by any means, electronic,
mechanical, photocopying, recording
or otherwise without the prior
permission of the copyright owner.

First published 1988

British Library
Cataloguing in Publication Data

Burgess, Ross
   Unix systems for microcomputers. —
   (Professional and industrial computing
   series).
   1. UNIX (Computer operating systems)
   I. Title II. Series
   005.4'46   QA76.76.063

ISBN 0-632-02036-9

BSP Professional Books
A division of Blackwell Scientific
   Publications Ltd
Editorial Offices:
Osney Mead, Oxford OX2 0EL
   (Orders: Tel. 0865 240201)
8 John Street, London WC1N 2ES
23 Ainslie Place, Edinburgh EH3 6AJ
Three Cambridge Center, Suite 208,
   Cambridge, MA 02142, USA
667 Lytton Avenue, Palo Alto,
   California 94301, USA
107 Barry Street, Carlton, Victoria 3053,
   Australia

Set by Setrite Typesetters Ltd

Printed and bound in Great Britain
by Billing & Sons Limited, Worcester.

UNIX is a registered trademark of AT&T in the USA and other countries.
IBM is a trademark of International Business Machines Corporation.
POSIX is a trademark of the Institute of Electrical and Electronic Engineers Inc.
XENIX is a trademark of Microsoft Inc.
X/Open is a trademark of the X/Open Group Members.
DEC, PDP, and VAX are trademarks of Digital Equipment Corp.

Contents

Preface, vi

Part I – Introducing UNIX
1. What is UNIX? 3
2. UNIX and its Development 12
3. UNIX and Microcomputers 20
4. UNIX Computers – the Hardware 30
5. Introducing the Software 42
6. Concepts and Features 54
7. Disks and Files 63

Part II – Putting UNIX to Work
8. Personal computing 73
9. Text Processing and Word Processing 82
10. UNIX and Office Automation 91
11. Database Management 98
12. More about SQL and Database Management 111
13. Graphics 119
14. Communications 126
15. Accounting and Business Systems 133
16. UNIX with a Friendly Face 141

Part III – Behind the Scenes
17. How UNIX works 155
18. Controlling a UNIX system 169
19. Getting More from the Shell 181
20. Writing Your Own Software 191
21. Networking 205

Part IV – UNIX Today and Tomorrow
22. Varieties of UNIX Systems 219
23. Standards and the Future 230
24. UNIX in the Wider Context 240

Part V – Appendices
A. Keyboards and Characters 251
B. Standard Commands and Utilities 257
C. System Calls and Library Routines 265
D. Standard File Formats 270
E. Glossary 271

Index 284

Preface

In the forty years since computers were invented, they have caused enormous changes to the way companies and organisations of all sorts carry out their business. But future changes will be still more dramatic, as the new generation of microcomputers make real computing power affordable for even the smallest company or department, and available on every office worker's desk.

In the new age of universal computing power, it will no longer be feasible for each user to have programs specially written; the emphasis will be almost entirely on packaged software, bought off the shelf. Already this has happened with personal computers: PC-based software packages are remarkable in their diversity and their quality compared to traditional computer systems, despite the severe restrictions imposed by PC hardware. The new generation of microcomputers is overcoming the hardware restrictions of the past, and has the potential to make computing much more powerful, more flexible, and above all easier to use, than ever before. But the potential will only be realised if there is a standard for computer systems, that all types of software package can be designed to work with. At last that standard is attainable, in the shape of UNIX.

UNIX itself was not always a standard — at one time many different versions existed. The key to the future success of UNIX is that the different versions have now come together. AT&T, the originators of UNIX, have promoted System V as a common standard. Microsoft's Xenix (the most widely used version of UNIX up to now) is being absorbed into System V on the new generation of 32-bit microcomputers. IBM, the world's leading computer company, have promised that their own AIX will be compatible with the emerging standards, and available on IBM machines from the personal system to the largest mainframe. The X/Open Group, embracing another eleven of the most important computer manufacturers, have launched a standard for portability, such that the same programs can run on computers supplied by any of the eleven. Most important of all, the POSIX standard, produced by a committee including IBM, AT&T, and the other major players, is now a standard UNIX, no longer the property of any single manufacturer.

Preface vii

POSIX is important because an organisation can now specify UNIX as a standard for its computing, and be free from dependence on any particular supplier. The US Government have already standardised in this way; the British Government are doing the same, as are bodies as diverse as General Motors and the European Community. The combined purchasing power that this represents will provoke an enormous range of software packages, and will ensure that UNIX is from now on the mainstream of computing, for all but very specialised applications.

What this book is about

This is not just a book about UNIX — there are plenty of those already. Rather it is a book about *UNIX systems* — that is, the way UNIX can be used to construct a complete solution, including the computer hardware, UNIX itself, and the wide range of software packages which are now available.

It is important to understand that UNIX operates on two levels. The operating system itself offers you excellent basic facilities, which can be used as they stand, or extended by the use of packages sold by specialist software companies. A bare UNIX system allows you to create and edit text files, to perform calculations, to write your own programs, to keep a diary, and to send messages to other users. But you can increase the usefulness of the computer enormously by purchasing database management systems, office automation packages, word processors, spreadsheets, and software for specific applications such as accounting. I have therefore attempted to cover both what UNIX itself will do for you, and also what you can expect from current third-party software packages.

Part I gives an introduction to UNIX, aimed at those with no previous experience of UNIX systems. Part II describes the way UNIX can be put to work, in the main application areas such as accounting, office automation, graphics, and personal productivity. Two chapters are devoted to database management, which for many companies will be the central hub of their computer systems. Part III looks behind the scenes, for the benefit of those with a little more interest in technical aspects, or who are considering writing their own software. Finally, Part IV covers some wider aspects such as the future of UNIX, its use as a standard within an organisation, and the areas in which it still needs to be improved.

The world of computers moves quickly; especially is this so in an area such as UNIX, which has been receiving so much interest from both suppliers and users of computer systems. Inevitably by the time these words appear in print UNIX will have moved on a little, and the features of the various software packages will have been yet further refined and expanded. This book is therefore merely a starting point for your exploration of UNIX and the software it supports; before purchasing any hardware or software you should contact the suppliers, or a reputable systems house, to check what is currently available and appropriate for your particular requirements.

Acknowledgements

My thanks are due to colleagues who assisted by reading my drafts and giving their comments. Olivier Saurin corrected my English as well as supplying many useful observations. Bob Balderson detected and corrected several areas of confusion on UNIX internals. Nigel Fox supplied some invaluable points on the commercial background to UNIX, while Simon Edwards gave me the benefit of his extensive experience with UNIX-based accounting packages. Figures 1 and 5 are reproduced by courtesy of IBM (UK) Ltd. Figures 2 and 3 were produced on a plotter using software from Pacific Basin Graphics on an AT&T 3B2 microcomputer; thanks to Nick Brown of Digitus for his assistance.

This book would have been quite impossible without the extremely varied experience I have gained working for Digitus. I would like to thank Alan Wood for directing my attention to the market aspects of UNIX, and Steve Feldman for the many insights he has provided, both during and after our collaboration on *The UNIX Report*.

Finally, I would like to thank Joseph St. John Bate who helped to launch me on the road to authorship, and Anthony Crook who has helped with the index to this book and in many other ways.

Ross Burgess

Part I
Introducing UNIX

Chapter 1
What is UNIX?

The computer is one of the most important inventions of the twentieth century, with enormous power to make life easier in science, in business, and in many other fields of human activity. And yet in many organisations the computer is regarded as a necessary evil, as an impediment and a constraint, as a machine for consuming money and effort with little to show for it. Too many companies have an uneasy relationship to the computer — they can no longer do without it, but it is not really doing what is required. The computer should be a means to solving a problem, but often it brings new problems instead.

But it need not be like this. Ever since computers began, some organisations have succeeded in making a real success of using them. Today, a new breed of computers is available, with the potential to provide really effective information processing within the reach of the smallest organisation. The key factor is the microcomputer, and UNIX is a vital part of the picture.

Microcomputers — that is, computers whose central processor is a single silicon chip — have been around since the late 1970s, but today's micros are very different to their predecessors. A microcomputer is no longer the poor relation of the big computers. Today's microcomputers, costing a few thousand pounds, can have equivalent processing power to a mainframe previously costing millions. A microcomputer may be a single-user workstation for personal computing, computer-aided design, or scientific processing — or a multi-user computer, supporting a whole team of people working on common data and common applications, in a department or small business — or perhaps a node in a network serving a major international company. The microcomputer, in its various forms, will be the most widely used form of computer power for the rest of this century, leaving the old mainframes and minis in the shade.

The importance of the microcomputer lies partly in its low cost. Computer power is no longer an expensive commodity, and the power can be harnessed to build systems that are much easier to use, and easier to modify to meet changing requirements, than the systems of the past. But cost is only part of the picture. Previous generations of computers worked in a way that was specific to a particular make and

4   *Chapter 1*

Fig. 1. The IBM 6150 Microcomputer. (Courtesy IBM (UK) Ltd.)

model. An IBM computer could not run ICL software, and vice versa. But today's microcomputers run standard software, based on standard operating systems such as UNIX.

Computers need a standard

If you have had any contact with computers, you may be well aware that what works on one does not necessarily work on another. If you go from machine A to machine B you find that the commands you have to use are different, the programming language is different, the programs that run on one will not run on the other, a disk on which you have stored some data will be unreadable by another machine. Part of the reason is in the hardware — perhaps the keyboards have different layouts, the disks are different sizes, and so on. But a great part of the problem is that the standards and conventions for the *software* are different from one machine to another.

This is not just a problem for the particular organisation — it has held up the advance of computers generally. As long as the computer industry was made up of many small islands of incompatibility, there was little incentive for hardware and software suppliers to produce high quality, low price products. The existence of standards in the personal computer market has given that sector an enormous range of excellent products; the coming UNIX standard is beginning to have the same effect for machines one step up in power from the personal computer. The small and medium-sized multi-user computer for general business use and the powerful single-user workstation for the specialist together make up the market sector in which the UNIX operating system is becoming the dominant force.

What is an operating system?

The phrase 'operating system' is one of those technical terms which are taken for granted by computer professionals, and guaranteed to confuse those for whom a computer is a means to a end rather than a subject of interest in itself.

As with so many other key terms, it is easier to describe what an operating system is than attempt to give a definition. But fundamentally the operating system is that layer of software, that series of programs, that looks after the actual running of the computer, so that you as a user, or the programs that you buy or have written, do not have to deal directly with the details of the hardware. An operating system typically comprises several different elements:
- a supervisory program that looks after the running of the computer — in UNIX this is called the 'kernel';
- a language in which users can give commands directly to the system — in UNIX this is called the 'shell';
- a set of standard programs which you can call by typing commands;
- some facilities for writing your own programs and thus creating additional commands;
- a series of 'system calls' — in other words standard routines which programmers can incorporate into programs, and which will make use directly of the services that the kernel offers.

It is the operating system which gives each computer system its particular characteristics — so we can talk about 'UNIX systems' meaning a wide range of computers of very different shapes and sizes, from many different manufacturers, which all work in a very similar fashion.

Types of operating system

Any business computer — and pretty well any other sort of computer — must have an operating system if it is actually to do any work. Of course the computer will be used to run various programs — sales ledgers, word processors, spreadsheets, games, scientific calculations. But underneath all these pieces of 'application software' there is always some 'system software' which takes over when your application program comes to an end, or sits in the background while the application is running, and quietly gets on with the computer's own housekeeping. System software can include database management systems, user interface programs, transaction processing monitors, programming languages, and networking packages, but the fundamental element is the operating system.

The majority of microcomputers today are single-user machines, devoted to one task at a time. They often have rather simple operating systems — MS-DOS, PC-DOS, CP/M, for example. But there is another big class of computers which can have several users 'logged in' at once, each sitting at his or her own terminal. Computers today — or at least their central processors — run so fast that they can switch their attention in a fraction of a second between one user and another, so that although the computer can fundamentally do only one thing at a time, it can appear to a particular user as if he has a computer entirely to himself. To talk of single-user and multi-user *computers* is in a sense not correct — there are single-user and multi-user *operating systems*, and most computer hardware will allow you to run either sort. UNIX is a prime example of a multi-user operating system.

Multi-user operating systems need to be far more active and complex, to allow the various users to access the computer and its data without interfering with one another. If you have used a personal computer, you probably have had occasions when the software has crashed, or the machine has come to a complete halt, and nothing will make it go again except turning it off and on, or 'rebooting'. On a single-user system, this is unfortunate, particularly if you lose your data in the process. On a multi-user system it would be totally unacceptable for an error by one user, or one program, to bring down the whole system and all the other users with it. So a multi-user system has to be much more resilient, and insulate the users from one another, by ensuring that whatever difficulties a program may get into, other users are not affected.

Multi-user computers come in various shapes and sizes – the big 'mainframes', the middle-sized 'minis', and the fast-growing 'micros'.

The older makes of minis and mainframes each came with their own operating system, designed specially by the manufacturer to get the best performance out of the particular hardware design. As long as computer hardware was very expensive, it was natural to design operating systems so as to use it as efficiently as possible, and therefore to design them with a particular machine in mind. As a result the computer market became divided up into separate camps following each of the big suppliers. One software company would concentrate on programs written for the IBM 370 range, another for the DEC VAX. The software market was fragmented, and a particular package could only sell in small numbers. As a result, software was over-priced and of mediocre quality.

Today the situation is different – computer hardware has become incredibly cheap by comparison with a few years ago, while the cost of writing software has gone up year by year. Where there were just a few computer manufacturers selling million pound machines, today new computer companies are springing up all the time, producing machines that sell for thousands or even hundreds of pounds, but in very large quantities.

Two things, then, have revolutionised the computer business – the microprocessor has made computers available to even the smallest business, or the home user; and the growth of industry standard software such as that based on UNIX has ensured that the users have worthwhile programs to run on their machines.

The growth of standards

Computer users today are calling as never before for standards. Standardisation, in such a fast-moving industry, is difficult to achieve. The computer industry, in the countries in which it has thrived (the USA, Europe, Japan), has been a product of the market economy, of manufacturers competing to offer the best, the cheapest and the most attractive product. Each manufacturer needs to differentiate his product from the rest of the market, which means being (to an extent) non-standard. The standardisation bodies come along later and try to tidy things up.

Most industries go through several phases. First of all there are many manufacturers, each developing their products in isolation and working out their own standards. Later, the pressure of the market drives out all but a few, and defines their products as standards which the rest of the industry follow. In the mature phase of the industry, the standards have been accepted and there is still room for new firms to compete on price, on quality and on new features.

When the first motor-cars came out, each manufacturer had to decide on his own arrangement of the controls, and there were many variations. Eventually a consensus emerged that the accelerator pedal should be on the right, so that one less design decision had to be made. In fact without some such standardisation of the basic controls, the sales of cars would have grown much more slowly. The standardisation process has gradually extended to cover more and more details: modern cars now have the indicator stalk on the left, the windscreen wiper control on the right.

Standardisation thus helps the customer enormously, since he can easily switch from one car to another. It may not benefit every supplier, since they are selling into a bigger and more competitive market, but ultimately it is in the interests of the industry as a whole.

Computers particularly need standards. For instance, at one time different computers used different ways of representing the various numbers and letters of the alphabet. All computers fundamentally use not letters or decimal digits, but 'bits' or binary digits, with the two values 0 and 1. For real life purposes, however, they need to represent not just numbers of all sorts and sizes, but also letters, punctuation marks and so on. Just as the Morse code defines a standard way of building up the 26 letters of the alphabet from dots and dashes, so the ASCII code (see Appendix A) defines a standard way of representing letters by 0s and 1s.

Standard codes like ASCII make it possible for computers to exchange data at a very basic level. But standardisation today needs to go much further. Most companies nowadays use more than one make of computer – no doubt often for very good reasons – but they are wasting money and resources if the programs, the skills, and the data, which have been built up on one make or model, cannot be transferred to another.

So, computing desperately needs standards, and it needs them in two particular areas – standardisation of program formats, so that a program written for one machine will run on another, and standardisation of data formats, so that a disk created on one machine can be read by another. These two areas are a large part of what constitutes the difference between one operating system and another.

Industry-standard operating systems

Producing an operating system is not an everyday activity, even for computer professionals. The big mainframe operating systems took years to develop, and had enormous teams of programmers working on them. Nonetheless, from time to time small groups of people, outside the main computer companies, have decided that the operating system supplied by the computer manufacturer did not suit them, and have set about devising one of their own. UNIX arose in this way; it owes much of its success to the fact that it was written by a small team who knew exactly what they wanted, rather than by an army of programmers working to a specification designed by a committee.

UNIX was designed for a specific machine, but designed in such a way that it could be moved in due course to other machines. Today, UNIX runs on far more makes of computers than any other operating system.

The nature of UNIX

What sort of an operating system is UNIX? First of all, as already mentioned, it is a multi-user operating system. But there are several sorts of these. Some are intended for intensive use by large numbers of people keying in data, all working on the same basic files; others are designed to keep the various users isolated from each other, so that each can forget that there are other users on the system. UNIX falls somewhere between these two extremes. As an individual using a UNIX system you have your own identity, and can create your own files to store your own data, privately from everyone else, if that is what you want. But you can also look at what your colleagues are doing, if they let you; you can share files with them, send messages to them, and generally interact with them as much or as little as you wish.

UNIX is also a 'multi-tasking' system. In other words you are not restricted to running one program at a time – you can run several at a time, and they can pass messages to one another. This is perhaps not something that most computer users consciously wish to do, but it gives the software developer the ability to build up effective solutions to complex problems, in a way that is just not possible on more primitive operating systems.

In the case of UNIX, the multi-tasking aspects are really more fundamental than the multi-user aspects. The original design of UNIX was a single-user system, but allowed multiple tasks or processes to be loaded in memory and to share the time of the central processor. Once its creators had achieved this, it was relatively easy to extend the concept so that different tasks could be assigned to different users and different terminals.

UNIX is a general-purpose operating system. Actually it has achieved a remarkable success in two quite distinct areas. One is the small-to-medium sized multi-user system, for a department or small company, handling accounts, office automation, and databases. The other is the high-performance single-user workstation for graphics, scientific or engineering computation, and computer-aided design.

Why is UNIX important?

UNIX is important first of all because it is a standard. It is a standard for *user organisations:* major government and private organisations have begun insisting on UNIX when they invite tenders for computer systems. It is a standard for *computer manufacturers:* more and more new firms are springing up, using UNIX as a quick way of getting into the market, while existing suppliers are turning to UNIX because of pressure from their customers. It is a standard for *software houses,* who are increasingly aiming their software packages at the UNIX market as it becomes bigger and less fragmented.

Most important of all, UNIX has succeeded in becoming an accepted industry standard *independent of any one supplier.* In the past the UNIX standard was set partly by software houses and hardware manufacturers, partly by user groups, partly by universities, and very largely by AT&T, the owners of the system. But the new standard UNIX, under the new name of POSIX, has been defined by the Institute of Electrical and Electronics Engineers, and is becoming part of the common body of standards maintained by independent international organisations.

Of course UNIX will not succeed in ousting the proprietary operating systems — at least those running on major makes of hardware such as the IBM mainframes and the DEC minis. But the crucial point to remember is that mainframes and minis will be a smaller proportion of the computers actually in use, for very simple economic reasons. A mainframe, or even a mini, is a very expensive way to buy computer power. A microcomputer, or a network of microcomputers, can provide the same power as a mainframe for a fraction of the cost. In the future, the overwhelming majority of computers in use will be microcomputers, based on one of the standard microprocessors. These microcomputers will come in many shapes and sizes; some will be the equivalent of the personal computers of today, running either UNIX, or a simpler system such as MS-DOS or OS/2; but a large class of microcomputers — 'super-micros' we should call them — will be multi-user machines, designed for the co-operative sharing of data and resources. The vast majority of these will have UNIX as their main operating system.

Chapter 2
UNIX and its Development

The origins of UNIX were very far removed from the worldwide standard that it has since become. Today the UNIX operating system is one of the key assets of its proprietor, AT&T. Back in 1969, it was developed by a group of people within AT&T purely for their own purposes, and without any thought that it would one day achieve astounding worldwide success.

AT&T

AT&T is a household name in the USA but little known in the rest of the world. American Telephone and Telegraph was for many years the telephone company for most parts of the United States, roughly the equivalent of British Telecom, a private organisation with a monopoly position, and therefore very closely regulated by the US Government. It provided individual telephones, the local exchanges, and the long-distance lines linking all parts of the country.

A key factor in the success of AT&T was its continued research and development effort, with Bell Telephone Laboratories at its heart. Bell Labs has always been a centre of excellence, in pure research as well as specific applications, attracting Nobel prize-winners and many of the best brains in science and technology. Bell Labs was always primarily concerned with telephones and communications, but research went on in many other areas, some of which have been important for the development of computers and information processing: particularly the invention of the transistor, from which the microchip age has sprung.

The origins of UNIX

In the 1960s, there was much interest in developing standard operating systems, particularly systems designed for on-line terminals, as compared to the traditional mainframe operating systems which were largely batch oriented. Bell Labs collaborated with other organisations, including General Electric and the Massachusetts Institute of

Technology (MIT), on a project called Multics, intended to produce a powerful multi-user, multi-processing operating system. The AT&T contribution to the project was the input/output system. Eventually Bell Labs pulled out, but the project continued without them and later formed the basis of Honeywell GE's timesharing system.

Back at Bell Labs, Ken Thompson, an astronomer by training, continued working on his own, using many of the ideas that had come out of Multics, but adapting them to a much simpler environment. He had at his disposal a PDP-7 made by DEC (Digital Equipment Corporation). The PDP-7 was a minicomputer, but a very primitive one compared to today's minis and even micros. Thompson's aims were not ambitious — he wanted an environment basically for his own use which would provide good facilities for programming, and some text processing utilities, including a sort of primitive word processor. Among the early programs developed was a game called 'Space Travel', reflecting Thompson's astronomical interests. At first the new system had no name, but Thompson's colleague Brian Kernighan invented the name 'UNIX' in sharp distinction to 'Multics', to emphasise its simplicity. Some say that the word 'UNIX' was to reflect the idea of a *unified* environment for a team of programmers working together, as opposed to Multics in which users were separated from one another.

Operating systems up to that time were always written in the specific assembler language of the machine concerned, and the PDP-7 version of UNIX was no exception. However, soon Thompson's group acquired a new computer, a PDP-11. Compared to the PDP-7, this was a considerably more powerful machine, although it hardly bears comparison to today's microcomputers. Although made by DEC, this machine was different in many ways to the PDP-7, and UNIX had to be substantially rewritten to run it. This set the team thinking about ways of writing operating systems in portable languages, so that moving them to a different machine would be much easier in future. Unfortunately, none of the programming languages in common use was really suitable for such an undertaking.

Thompson was joined about this time by Dennis Ritchie. Ritchie was unhappy with the various programming languages available, and decided to produce a new one. This language was eventually called 'C'. In 1973 the key step was taken: UNIX was rewritten almost entirely in C, and from then on it became much easier to move it onto new makes of computer.

UNIX continued to develop, and was adopted by various groups within AT&T. New versions appeared: Version 5 in 1973, Version 6 in 1975, Version 7 in 1979. As well as the regular numbered series, other versions also appeared within AT&T: for instance, the Programmer's Work Bench (PWB), which pioneered a number of features later ported to other versions.

UNIX and its users

To understand the development of UNIX, one needs to be aware of the various licensing arrangements that have existed from time to time. UNIX is a proprietary product of AT&T, and no one can obtain or use a copy without paying AT&T for the privilege. UNIX is also a computer program — or, rather, a collection of a large number of programs. Like any program, it exists in two forms: as source code, and as object code.

Source code is the original program, written by human beings in a programming language such as COBOL, BASIC, or FORTRAN. Generally speaking, it will look a little like English text, or perhaps a little like algebra — C, the language used for nearly all of UNIX, is at the algebraic end of the spectrum — but a programmer who knows the language can work out what it is doing, and can make changes to it. Object code, on the other hand, is the program in a language that the machine can understand: a special utility called a compiler will have input source code at one end, and output object code at the other. Object code is essentially a series of binary numbers (it is often referred to as a 'binary program') and it is extremely difficult for a human being to work out how it was written, or how to amend it, except on a very restricted scale.

Object code by its nature is specific to a particular type of computer. Machine languages are not at all standardised, so if you have the object code of a program intended for, say, the IBM Personal computer, it may just possibly run on other computers based on the Intel 8086 family of microprocessors, but there is no way it will run on a computer which has a Motorola 68000 as its central processor. Source code on the other hand is — or at least can be — portable between one machine and another, provided that each has a compiler for the language in question.

When AT&T first made UNIX available to the wider world, about 1975, they supplied it in source language form. The licence fee was very cheap to educational establishments, but very expensive to the few commercial users who were subsequently allowed to have it. Moreover, the UNIX system of those days had many gaps and a number of bugs, and came with no support or guarantee whatever. Because of AT&T's position as a regulated monopoly, they were actually not permitted by law to offer UNIX — or any other computer system — as a 'product' for sale.

UNIX, in its unsupported form, appealed to university departments; it was cheaper than equivalent DEC operating systems, and since the source code was supplied, it could be used as a basis for teaching students about operating system design. Not surprisingly, those who bought licences were inclined to make changes to the system to suit their own needs — and since they had the source code, they were well able to do so. So the first UNIX community grew up, mainly in the universities: a community who not merely used UNIX, but produced their own utilities, and their own enhanced versions of the Bell Labs programs. Not only did they produce such enhancements, but they were also obliged by the terms of their licence to make them available to other users.

In the academic world, the most important institution with an interest in UNIX was the University of California at Berkeley (UCB), who rewrote a large part of the UNIX kernel (the main controlling program of the system) and also provided a number of additional utilities and other programs. The Berkeley versions, such as BSD 4.2 and 4.3 (standing for 'Berkeley Software Distribution') were in many respects superior to the original Bell UNIX, particularly for larger computers and technical applications.

Binary licences

The original unsupported versions of UNIX would have been quite unacceptable for the ordinary business computer user. But as UNIX developed, various software companies produced strengthened and enhanced versions suitable for commercial use, and provided support to their customers. This led to the introduction of binary licences. A binary licence allows you to receive the binary version of UNIX — that is, the object code for a particular type of computer — but not the source. Binary licences are not supplied by AT&T directly, but by third parties such as software houses and computer manufacturers, who pay AT&T for the privilege.

The cost of a binary licence for UNIX has generally depended on the number of users — i.e. the number of terminals connected to the machine. However, from System V Release 3 onwards, there is a fixed licence fee of $150, a price increase for the most common categories (up to eight users) but a very substantial reduction for the very large UNIX installation.

A source licence for System V Release 3.1 costs $71,000.

The AT&T versions

UNIX within Bell Labs, and within AT&T generally, has gone through quite a few changes and revisions. Some were released outside AT&T,

but not all, which accounts for the apparent gaps in the numbering of the successive versions.

Earlier versions of UNIX were given numbers corresponding to the edition of the Programmer's Manual issued with them, culminating in Version 7. At some stage, however, AT&T decided that their current revision was sufficient of a step forward to be called UNIX System II. This never appeared outside AT&T, but System III was released in 1981.

The next major version of UNIX was System V (again no System IV was released). System V is much more powerful and more standardised, and has absorbed many of the enhancements produced by Berkeley and other sources. But the real importance of System V should be sought in the changes that have taken place in AT&T itself. AT&T has been split up and deregulated by the American courts. It no longer owns the local telephone organisations, which have been hived off to 'Regional Bell Operating Companies' (RBOCs). It still has the long trunk lines, but is diversifying its activities into other areas. No longer a monopoly, and therefore no longer subject to the old legal constraints, it is actively pursuing new markets which were previously barred to it. In particular it is marketing its own range of computers (in conjunction with its European associate, Olivetti) and is promoting UNIX System V as the only operating system worth bothering with.

System V itself has continued to evolve, the most recent versions at the time of writing being Release 3 (1986), and Release 3.1 (1987). System V Release 3 (or V.3 for short) includes a number of very important enhancements, particularly Remote File Sharing (RFS) to enable multiple computers to work closely together.

Other versions of UNIX

AT&T and UCB have not by any means been the only organisations contributing to the growth of UNIX. In particular the software company, Microsoft, were in the market very early with a commercial version of UNIX, including features to make it suitable for business computing. The Microsoft version, called Xenix, has far exceeded all the others in terms of the number of binary licences sold. Other software houses with an important contribution have been Unisoft (now owned by the UK software house Root Computers) whose version called Uniplus+ has been ported to very many makes of computer, and Interactive Systems, who in conjunction with IBM have produced versions such as PC/IX, AIX, and IX/370, to run on IBM computers ranging from the PC to the mainframe.

Moves to standardisation

As long as AT&T was not permitted to promote UNIX commercially, different and incompatible versions flourished: a number of AT&T versions were current at one time, as well as Berkeley, Xenix, and other implementations. System III was a step towards rationalisation — and Xenix, for instance, although based on Version 7, was brought into outward compatibility with System III. But the big push to standardisation has come with System V.

Clearly one of the main advantages of UNIX is that it is a standard available on many different types of computer. But this does not count for much if in fact there are many different versions, all more or less incompatible. It is very much in AT&T's interest to standardise UNIX, and the company has been taking active steps to achieve this, notably the publication of the *System V Interface Definition* (SVID) and the writing of a set of programs called the *System V Validation Suite* (SVVS) which software companies can buy to test out their operating systems to make sure that they are really System V-compatible.

Virtually all suppliers of UNIX systems have now brought them in line with AT&T. Only the Berkeley versions show any sign of surviving as alternatives to System V. And there are moves to harmonise System V and Berkeley in the future; Sun Microsystems and AT&T are working together on this.

Other standardisation attempts

UNIX, it might be said, is now too important to be left to AT&T. There are obvious objections to a standard being set by a particular manufacturer, with its own very definite interests in the market. Many of AT&T's competitors would be happier following a standard defined by a more impartial body. Several moves are in fact being made in this direction. One example is the X/Open group, formed by a number of European computer manufacturers, and subsequently expanded to include some American suppliers, as well as AT&T themselves.

The X/Open standard relies heavily on the System V Interface Definition, but with additional standards to define the format of data and programs on floppy disk, and other areas not covered by System V as such.

Another influential body was the UNIX User Group in the USA, known as */usr/group* (the reason for the spelling will become clear later), who published various standardisation proposals of their own. This led on to the POSIX standard, being developed by the IEEE –

the Institute of Electrical and Electronics Engineers, who have defined important US (and eventually international) standards in several areas of computing and data communications. Chapter 23 looks in a little more detail at these developments.

Pressure from users for standardisation

It is all very well the suppliers, and organisations such as the IEEE, producing standard operating systems; the standards will lead nowhere if customers are unwilling to buy the product. It is the mounting pressure of an educated user community that will determine the success or failure of UNIX. A few major organisations have such dominant buying power that they can set standards that the rest of the market will follow. Already some of the most influential customers − leading industrial companies such as General Motors, and governmental organisations in the USA, the UK, and the European Community − are demanding UNIX as a standard. In future, suppliers bidding for contracts with such organisations will more and more have to demonstrate UNIX or POSIX compatibility.

The IBM factor

Only one computer manufacturer today can afford to swim against the tide. IBM (International Business Machines) has always been big enough to define its own standards, no matter what the rest of the world may do. In 1985, IBM was the most profitable company in the world, and it certainly far outstrips any other company in the computer business.

IBM has dominated mainframe computers from almost the start of the computer age. The company has also dominated the personal computer market since about 1981. However, in the middle range machines − the segment in which UNIX is strongest − IBM's offerings have been confused.

For a long time, IBM ignored UNIX. Then it half-heartedly issued a variety of UNIX-based systems on different types of computers. But soon IBM recognised that in the critical price range of $15,000 to $50,000, half of new computer sales were going to non-proprietary operating systems − in other words, to UNIX. Despite its considerable technical strengths, IBM was always predominantly a marketing-based company, and the UNIX market was one it could no longer afford to ignore. Accordingly, IBM launched a new range of microcomputers − the 6150, or RT PC, with AIX, an enhanced version of UNIX, as its only operating system. The 6150, originally aimed at the scientific and engineering market, was almost immediately repositioned as a multi-user business computer.

Finally IBM have committed to a common UNIX approach based on AIX. It is clear that UNIX will never supplant IBM's own proprietary operating systems, which have now been brought together in SAA (Systems Application Architecture). But there is room within IBM for other standards alongside SAA, and AIX as an important subsidiary IBM standard will from now on be available on small machines (Personal System/2), middle sized machines (6150), and large machines (the various mainframes).

The size of the UNIX market

One measure of the success of an operating system is the number of computers on which it is installed. Precise figures are not easy to come by − some colleagues and I discovered this in the course of the research into the UNIX market in the United Kingdom. Our conclusion, embodied in *The UNIX Report*, published by Digitus, was that by the end of 1984, about 5,500 UNIX licences had been sold in the UK, 20,000 in Europe as a whole, and 145,000 in the world. Since then the figures have at least doubled, to around 300,000 by 1986, of which perhaps 15,000 were in the UK. Some authorities estimated worldwide cumulative sales of about a million by the end of 1987.

These figures are certainly impressive, although at first sight small compared to the much larger numbers of personal computers with MS-DOS/PC-DOS. But remember that an MS-DOS licence is for a single user only, whereas each UNIX licence on average (according to the Digitus figures) represents about six users. On this basis, the number of workstations attached to UNIX machines, and therefore the number of people actually using UNIX systems, is a very respectable fraction of the MS-DOS figure.

In the future, the growth of UNIX will continue to feed upon itself, as increased hardware sales generate a new wave of software products, and these make UNIX more attractive, leading in turn to further hardware sales. The problems that have held UNIX back in the past have included the lack of software, and the incompatibility of different versions of UNIX itself. These problems are now very largely overcome, and the dramatic expansion in sales of UNIX systems that people have been predicting for so long is at last set to take place.

Chapter 3
UNIX and Microcomputers

> *Note: Some of this chapter may seem rather technical to those not familiar with computer hardware. If your interest does not lie in this area, you may prefer to move on to later chapters, which are almost entirely concerned with software.*

Processors and microprocessors

The most important piece of hardware in any computer — and the one that to a very large extent defines its capabilities — is the processor, also known as the central processing unit (cpu). A cpu is an extremely complex device, made up of thousands of components, but today's semiconductor technology, using VLSI (very large scale integration) can make these devices exceedingly small, and combine vast numbers of them on each silicon chip. We can thus make an important distinction — we can define a 'microprocessor' as a processor which consists of a single chip. A 'microcomputer' (as opposed to a mainframe or a minicomputer) is a computer whose cpu is a microprocessor.

What a microprocessor does in essence is simple. It takes in a small chunk of data, typically from the computer's memory, it performs some manipulation, and it sends out a chunk of data, usually back to memory. It has a small number of internal storage areas, known as 'registers', and a means of deciding which register, or which location in memory, its data is to be taken from or sent to. The chunk of data processed at a time is referred to as a 'word', and processors are classified by their word size, typically 8, 16, or 32 bits.

A microprocessor is not impressive to look at. The actual silicon chip is hidden from view inside the familiar packaging of an integrated circuit — a black plastic (or sometimes ceramic) casing a few centimetres long, surrounded by pins to enable it to be inserted into its socket on a printed circuit board.

Each of the pins has a specific function in conveying signals between the processor and the outside world, but two groups of pins are particularly important. One group represents the data bus — 8, 16, or

32 pins used to bring in or send out a word of data. The other represents the address bus — a set of pins which give the location in memory where the word of data is to be taken from or sent to.

Computing at the speed of light

When a microprocessor is at work, all its components are very closely synchronised by a 'clock', which ticks millions of times a second. At each tick, or 'processor cycle', the processor carries out a complete stage in the execution of an instruction.

The speed of a processor is measured in two ways — its clock speed, measured in megahertz (MHz), that is millions of cycles per second, and its overall throughput rate, measured in Mips (millions of instructions per second). To carry out a particular instruction will take several cycles, perhaps one or two to fetch the instruction itself from memory, one to fetch the data, and one to do the calculation and write the results out. Some instructions, such as multiplication and division, take more cycles than others. Clearly, if a processor is running at 18 MHz, and takes 6 cycles on average per instruction, then its throughput rate is 3 Mips. Some processors use special tricks such as 'pipelining' to speed things up; for example, reading the next instruction while the previous one is being processed.

The Mips rating of a processor is thus a first approximation to an assessment of its speed. But other measures may be more relevant, depending on the use that is to be made of it. For scientific calculations, 'megaflops' (millions of floating point instructions per second), or Whetstone units, are often quoted rather than Mips, while for commercial multi-user systems the speed of the processor is only one aspect of the speed of the computer system; much will depend on the speed of the memory, the disk, and the various input/output channels.

The instruction set

The different families of processors differ considerably in the range of instructions at their disposal. Typical instructions include:
- moving data from one part of memory to another;
- moving data between memory and one of the internal registers;
- adding a number from memory to a number held in a register;
- shifting bits left or right;
- jumping to a different part of the program;
- comparing the contents of a register to that of a location in memory;

- conditionally jumping, depending whether the last comparison was found to be true or false;
- executing a subroutine;
- changing to a different privilege level (for instance, executing a system call to the operating system).

Modern microprocessors often have several hundred different instructions — indeed, there is a natural tendency for microprocessors, like other electronic devices, to become more and more complex, with larger and larger instruction sets. But if the instruction set becomes very large, it may not be practicable to implement all the instructions directly in the basic circuitry of the chip; instead the chip internally translates each instruction into a series of still lower-level instructions, using a sort of language known as 'microcode'. If a processor has a very large instruction set, some of the instructions may be used rather seldom. Indeed, an initial batch of Intel 80386 processors was found to have a fault which none of its users had ever noticed — because the instruction affected had never been used!

There has been something of a reaction against the increasing size of instruction sets — a number of designers have adopted the idea of a 'reduced instruction set computer' (RISC). Examples include the 'ROMP' microprocessor used in the IBM 6150, while other RISC designs have been produced by Hewlett Packard, Pyramid, and the British firm, Acorn (now part of AT&T's Italian associate, Olivetti).

Measuring the micro

Other factors determining the power of a microprocessor include:
- the number and size of its internal registers;
- the size of the address bus, that is the length of address that can be used to specify a location in memory;
- the size of the data bus, that is the number of bits of data that can be moved at one go, either within the chip itself, or to or from memory or other devices.

When people talk about the various generations and categories of microprocessor, the size of the data bus is the measure that is most often mentioned, and is what categorises '8-bit', '16-bit', and '32-bit' computers. Even this is not a simple matter, since some processors have a smaller data bus externally than internally — for instance, the Intel 8088 is an 8/16-bit processor in this sense.

The size of the data bus clearly defines the maximum chunk of data which the processor can deal with at one bite. How important this is depends on the type of data in question. On a 16-bit computer, the data bus size by definition is 16 bits, enough to cope with numbers up to 2^{16} — about 65,000, or half this size if negative numbers need to be catered for as well.

Table 3.1 shows the number of combinations that can be expressed in different numbers of bits.

Table 3.1 Bits and numbers.

Number of bits	Number of combinations
1	2
2	4
3	8
4	16
5	32
6	64
8	256
9	512
10	1,024
16	65,536
32	4,294,967,295

It should be apparent from the table that for integers, that is whole numbers representing such everyday quantities as the price of an article in pence or cents, a 16-bit computer 'word' is somewhat restrictive, but 32 bits are sufficient for most purposes. Thus for everyday arithmetic, a 32-bit processor is a lot more effective than a 16-bit one, but the benefit of moving to a 64-bit processor, the logical next step, is much less obvious. This is one reason why the 32-bit micro has at last become the the main vehicle for UNIX-type systems: the 8-bit micro is obsolete except as a home computer for playing games, while 16-bit micros are today essentially limited to single-user personal computers.

Despite the move from 8 to 16 to 32 bits, an 8-bit unit (the byte) is still of fundamental importance in computer systems, the reason being that when dealing with alphabetic data as opposed to pure numbers, each byte contains one letter or character (256 combinations being quite enough for most purposes).

The address bus

Another key aspect of modern microcomputers is the size of the address bus. The address of an area in memory can be likened to a telephone number. London telephone numbers (excluding the 01 prefix) are seven-digit numbers, so the maximum number of lines that can be accommodated is 10^7 or ten million. In fact, some of the possible numbers are reserved for various purposes, so that the actual capacity of the system is substantially less than ten million, and British Telecom are investigating ways of increasing the numbers to eight digits to allow for an increased number of subscribers. In a similar way, most 8-bit computers, and many 16-bit ones, had a 16-bit address bus, allowing them to address up to 10^{16}, or 65,536, different locations (that is bytes) in memory.

Table 3.2 shows the memory size that can be addressed by different sizes of address bus.

Table 3.2 Address length and addressable memory sizes.

Address length (bits)	Addressable memory size (bytes)
10	1,024 = 1k
16	65,536 = 64k
20	1,048,576 = 1 megabyte (Mb)
24	16,777,216 = 16 Mb
30	1,073,741,824 = 1 gigabyte (Gb)
32	4,294,967,295 = 4 Gb
40	1,099,511,627,776 = 1 terabyte (Tb)

Notice that there are special names for some of the memory sizes, where one of the powers of 2 happens to approximate to a round number of thousands or millions. Hence the frequent use in computing of terms such as 'k' to mean 2^{10}, or approximately a thousand.

The size of the address bus has become more important as memory has become cheaper. Often computer designers have had to find ways of getting round the limitations of the address bus size. At the time UNIX was invented, a 16-bit address bus, and thus a memory of 64k, might have been reasonable for the 'core store' of a small mainframe. Indeed the PDP-11 on which UNIX was largely developed had 16k of memory available for use by the operating system plus 8k for the user. Today 16k, or even 64k, is considered insufficient even for a home computer.

The first generation of 16-bit personal computers (typified by the IBM PC) could address up to a megabyte, of which 640k was available to the Disk Operating System (DOS). The 640k limit soon came to be regarded as one of the shortcomings of DOS. For UNIX, virtually no machines are sold today with less than a megabyte of memory. In fact it has been said that a UNIX machine should ideally have enough memory so that each user on the system at any one time can have half a megabyte to himself, with half a megabyte over for the system.

Virtual memory

In a multi-tasking operating system such as UNIX, there are a number of processes active at one time — that is, a number of programs residing in different parts of memory, each one in turn having a go at using the processor. The memory areas used by the various processes need to be kept strictly segregated (apart from some areas specifically designated as 'shared memory') so that one process does not interfere with another.

A microprocessor can help in a multi-tasking environment by enforcing protection between one task and another, so that a task can only access those areas of memory which it ought to.

A computer program always relies on knowing that its data, the next instruction to be executed, and so on, are at specific addresses in memory. But in UNIX, because memory is shared between many processes, there is no guarantee where a particular process will actually be loaded in memory, and therefore where any piece of data will actually be located. To get round this problem, UNIX, like most modern operating systems, uses 'virtual memory'. In other words a process does not need to know where the various data items are physically located: instead, it works on a 'virtual' address space private to itself. It thinks, for instance, that variable *xyz* is at address location 500, and the operating system converts this virtual address to a real address, transparently to the program.

There are two ways this translation can be carried out: by segmentation, or by paging.

Segmentation means that each process consists of one or more large chunks of memory (typically three for UNIX). The system keeps track of where each segment is physically loaded in memory, so that if the program tries to access virtual address 500, and the segment was loaded starting from physical address 20000, the system will actually look for the data at physical address 20500.

The alternative approach is paging. In this case the memory is divided up into relatively small 'pages' of a fixed size: typical sizes are 512 bytes, 1k (1024 bytes), 2k, or 4k. A page of virtual memory can be associated to a page of real memory, and the system maintains a 'page table' which it can look up to find which page is where when it needs to translate addresses. With 'demand paging', the system only allocates real memory to pages of a process when they are actually used, and pages not recently used may be stored away to a special area of disk until needed again. In this way, a process can use an address space that is actually much larger than the entire memory of the machine.

Segmentation is fairly simple to organise, on all types of computers, and can be implemented entirely in software. Demand paging, on the other hand, gives greater speed and more economical use of memory, but it is much more complex for the operating system to manage. Demand paging is really only a practical proposition if it is organised by the hardware. To meet this need, most current 32-bit microcomputers have built-in paging facilities, or else a memory management unit (MMU) on a separate chip to look after these functions.

Families of microprocessors

An 8-bit microprocessor is really not suitable for running UNIX, and there is therefore no need to dwell on the various 8-bit families — the Intel 8080, the similar Zilog Z80, and the 6502.

The first 16-bit microprocessors appeared in the late 1970s, and paved the way for the big expansion of UNIX. There were three main families of 16-bit chips, made by three of the major American 'merchant semiconductor houses':
- the Zilog Z8000, used in the Onyx — one of the first commercial UNIX systems — and in Zilog's own 16-bit range of UNIX-based computers;
- the Intel 8088, 8086, 80186, and 80286, used in the IBM Personal Computer and its various clones;
- the Motorola 68000, used in the Apple Macintosh and also a very large number of UNIX machines.

The 16-bit micros provided the larger address space necessary for running a system such as UNIX, but in some ways they were rather restrictive. For instance they had little in the way of memory management facilities, and the 8086 in particular had its memory divided up into chunks of 64k, making it difficult to have segments larger than this size. The 80286 overcame this problem to an extent, but it was not entirely successful as a multi-tasking machine. Altogether, the 16-bit generation of micros were still inferior to the more established minicomputers as vehicles for running UNIX.

The 32-bit generation of micros are in a very different class, and can support UNIX much better — indeed, most of the manufacturers say they designed their 32-bit processors specifically with UNIX in mind. Already 32-bit microprocessors are comparable in power with minicomputers, and the next generation will have the power of today's mainframes.

UNIX and the 32-bit chip

What does a processor need to run UNIX efficiently? Clearly it needs to be able to provide memory protection between one task and another; that is, the processor itself must know which segments and pages are assigned to which process, and prevent unauthorised processes from accessing them. It also needs to have an efficient method of dealing with 'context switching' — that is, the processor turning its attention from one process to another — which happens many times a second on large UNIX systems. And it needs to have a large 'linear' address space (not broken up into 64k chunks) and to support demand paging.

At the time of writing, there are four main families of 32-bit microprocessors:
- the Motorola 68020: essentially a more powerful version of the 68000, but with demand paging;
- the Intel 80386;
- the National Semiconductor 32032;
- the Western Electric 32000.

Other 32-bit processors will appear as time goes on — the heyday of 16-bit chips lasted only a few years, but the 32-bit era will last much longer, giving much more time for new designs to appear. Other companies already have 32-bit processors, which could yet challenge the more established models.

The Western Electric chip is particularly important for UNIX, as Western Electric is part of AT&T, and this range of processors is used in the AT&T 3B computers, on which new official versions of UNIX first appear. However, AT&T also work closely with Intel and the other main microprocessor manufacturers, to ensure that good, official, versions of System V are available on the most important processors as soon as possible.

The 80386

The Intel 80386 is particularly interesting. The IBM PC and other machines based on Intel's previous chips were extremely successful, and generated a vast amount of good 16-bit single-user software. The 80386 therefore had to have some way of keeping faith with the company's loyal users, by emulating the 8086 range, as well as providing far superior facilities in its native 32-bit mode.

Thus the 80386 is able to protect one task's memory from another, but can lay this feature aside if it needs to emulate an 8086. Like the earlier 80286, it can switch from one mode to the other; unlike the 286, however, the 386 can do the switch very quickly, so that with a little help from special software, it becomes possible to run a mix of UNIX and MS-DOS tasks.

The 386 is an impressive piece of silicon, packing over 275,000 transistors into a single chip. Running at 16 MHz, it is rated at 3 to 4 MIPs. It makes extensive use of pipelining – that is loading the next instruction while the current one is being executed.

The memory management unit (MMU) is incorporated into the chip. Unusually, it supports both segmentation and paging. A task or process can have up to six segments addressable at once: a code segment, a stack segment, and up to four data segments; segments can be either private to a single task, or shared between one or more tasks. All this corresponds very closely to the way that UNIX organises its processes. Each segment can be up to 2^{32} bytes, that is 4 gigabytes, as a single linear address space, while the total virtual memory space is 2^{46}, or 64 terabytes. Needless to say, most 386-based computers for a long time to come will have physical memory far smaller than these theoretical limits. Paging is optional, using pages of 4k bytes each.

Any 32-bit processor needs a large number of pins to carry the signals in and out of the chip – typically 32 for the data bus, and 32 for the address bus, plus a variety of others. Earlier processors, like other integrated circuits, were generally oblong, with a single set of pins down each of the longer sides – the so-called DIP-arrangement (dual in-line package). The 80386 on the other hand has 132 pins altogether, arranged in three rows all round the package, at intervals of a tenth of an inch. The entire package is 1.45 inches square (about 37 mm) which makes it very large as integrated circuits go.

The ROMP

In addition to the 'industry standard' chips, a number of computer manufacturers make their own proprietary microprocessors. The most important of these, as far as UNIX is concerned, must be IBM's ROMP, used in the 6150 (known outside Europe as the RT PC).

The origins of IBM's ROMP chip go back to 1977, when IBM Office Products Division (OPD) in Texas decided to produce a new type of high-performance microprocessor. Meanwhile IBM Research in New York State were working on a new type of minicomputer, the IBM 801, based on RISC technology (Reduced Instruction Set Computer). The two projects came together and the resulting chip is therefore known as the Research/OPD Microprocessor, or ROMP for short. The main difference between the 801 and the ROMP is that the ROMP is a true microprocessor – in other words, the central processing unit is a single chip, with a second chip used as the memory management unit (MMU).

The 6150 can support up to 16 Mb of real memory, but the MMU allows much larger virtual addresses to be used within programs. The basic address length is 32 bits, so that a program can have a 4 gigabyte address space, consisting of up to 16 segments of up to 256 megabytes each. In fact the MMU itself translates the 32-bit address to a 40-bit address, giving a theoretical total address space of 1 terabyte. The MMU maintains a table relating virtual addresses to real addresses in memory. Real memory is divided into 'pages', each of 2k bytes. If a program refers to a virtual address which has no corresponding real address in memory, a 'page fault' occurs, and the MMU will load the page in question from disk, clearing out other pages if necessary to make room.

The ROMP is a true 32-bit micro, although it has a number of 16-bit instructions. There are actually 118 separate instructions, a relatively small number by today's standards, and limited to those which the processor can carry out very efficiently – typically in one tick of the system clock – thus justifying the 'RISC' designation.

Compared to the 80386, the ROMP is not so closely aimed at a UNIX-type environment; the fundamental software that has been designed to run on the 6150 is a special IBM system called VRM (Virtual Resource Manager). But the VRM itself does very little, except to provide the basic environment on which true operating systems can be supported – in particular AIX, IBM's proprietary version of UNIX.

The significance of the new processors

With the arrival of 32-bit processors such as the ROMP, the 80386, or the 68020, the potential power of microcomputers has taken a major leap forward. We now have micros essentially freed from the old limitations of address space, and powerful enough to support multiple users efficiently, or to provide extremely fast and complex systems in a single-user workstation. The 32-bit micro is without doubt *the* computer of the coming decade – further than that is too long to predict in the computer industry. It will take the place of today's personal computers (except perhaps at the very low end) and minicomputers. All it needs is the software.

When the first 80386-based computers appeared they were merely faster versions of the IBM PC, with most of their power going to waste. To make full use of that power, as a single-user or a multi-user machine, a substantial operating system is required. For single-user purposes, systems such as OS/2 (the multi-tasking replacement for MS-DOS) may compete with UNIX; for multi-user applications, UNIX is the only possible choice.

Chapter 4
UNIX computers – the Hardware

What you get with a UNIX system

If you are familiar with personal computers, a UNIX system may seem a much more formidable piece of equipment. For a start, most UNIX computers are multi-user systems, so the computer itself is no longer (in most cases) on the user's desk – it may well be out of sight somewhere in a computer room, or at least a special area of the office. Unlike the big computers of the past, however, it usually does not need its own air-conditioning.

The computer itself – that is, the system unit containing the processor and other central components – these days takes the form of a rather anonymous-looking box, either standing on the floor, or in some cases sitting on a desk. There may be an indicator light or two, and an on-off switch, but certainly nothing like the arrays of buttons and flashing lights that appeared on older computers. There will certainly be one or two slots at the front, one for loading diskettes and/or one for cartridge tapes. Diskettes or tapes are used regularly (perhaps once a day) for taking backup copies of the main data files, and less frequently for loading new software, or other data that the organisation may have acquired in disk or tape form. The main disks, that the machine uses continuously for storing and retrieving data, are out of sight, inside the system unit.

At the back of the system unit there will certainly be a number of sockets, or 'ports' to use the technical term, for plugging in terminals or other devices. Most of these will be 'serial ports', following the standard which is known as 'RS232' or 'V.24'. The number of ports provided on a computer is quite an important measure of its capability, since it determines how many terminals you can connect, and hence the maximum number of people who can use the computer simultaneously. It should be pointed out, however, that (on most models of computer) if the maximum number of terminals are in use all at once, each user may find a noticeable falling off in performance.

Inside the box

If you take the cover off a modern computer, you will see a number of printed circuit boards, many of them holding large numbers of little black integrated circuits. For maintenance purposes, and to expand the capacity of the machine, it is usually easy to take out boards and replace them or add new ones. There are a number of established standards for the electrical and mechanical connections to the 'bus' or main data highway to which the boards are attached, and third-party boards may be available to be slotted in, to complement those supplied by the manufacturer.

The processor

The most important part of any computer is the processor, which controls all that goes on, and carries out all the various instructions given to it by the software, one at a time. In bigger computers, the processor may be one or more boards, containing many separate devices. But in the sort of computers covered in this book — and indeed in the vast majority of all computers made today — the processor is a 'microprocessor', on a single silicon chip.

Actually, an increasing number of computers today have more than one central processor. Sometimes the multiple processors serve different purposes; sometimes the various processors share the work equally between them, one handling one program or process and one another; in some very expensive machines, there may be two or more processors working in parallel on the same data, so that in the rare event of one processor going wrong, the computing continues as if nothing has happened.

Special-purpose processors

Alongside the central processor, many microcomputers these days have additional processors for handling specialised functions, so as to relieve the load on the cpu. One example is the memory management unit used in the 6150. A very common type of co-processor, used on personal computers as well as multi-user machines, is the floating-point processor, which can dramatically speed up all kinds of mathematical processing, and floating-point arithmetic in particular.

In a multi-user computer, the bottleneck is often not the computation as such, but the control of the various terminals. An intelligent communications processor is very often provided to look after much of the low-level handling of terminal input/output, which the cpu would otherwise have to deal with.

Memory

Today's computers have memory of two kinds — RAM and ROM.

ROM (Read Only Memory) contains special programs and data put there in the process of manufacture, which cannot be altered. RAM (Random Access Memory) is used for holding your programs and data. With most kinds of RAM, when you turn the machine off, everything in memory is lost, so it should be regarded merely as a temporary store. In home computers, ROM is used for the operating system and other software. On UNIX machines, however (with a few exceptions such as the Hewlett Packard Integral), the software is held on disk and loaded into RAM as necessary. ROM is used only for specialised purposes, such as the 'bootstrap' program which runs when the machine is first switched on, and which loads the operating system from disk. So we can largely take the ROM for granted: the word 'memory', in this book and in talking about UNIX generally, nearly always means RAM.

RAM today comes in the form of chips (integrated circuits). The size of a memory chip is measured in bits; thus a memory of one megabyte could be assembled from eight chips of one megabit each, a single byte in memory being made up of one bit from each of the eight chips.

Storing information in memory, and fetching it out, is much faster than writing it to disk, and reading it back, but even so it may not be fast enough. Modern microprocessors running at, say, 16 MHz are so fast that memory may have difficulty keeping pace. The solution may be to introduce 'wait states' — that is, make the processor mark time until the memory can catch up — or perhaps to introduce a small amount of special high speed memory, known as 'cache memory', as an intermediate level between the main memory and the processor's own internal registers.

At one time, computer memories were built up out of magnetic cores, one per bit. This technology is long since obsolete, but has left its mark on the terminology. Thus if a program goes seriously wrong in UNIX, it may leave behind it some evidence in the form of a disk file called *core*, containing a 'core dump', that is an image of the contents of memory at the time of the failure.

The disks

The main storage medium today for computer data is magnetic disk. On microcomputers this takes two forms: 'floppy disks' or 'diskettes' which you can take out of the machine and put away for safe keeping, and a hard disk, nowadays using 'winchester' technology, which is permanently held inside the computer, and sealed to protect it from dust or damage. In the case of UNIX systems, references to 'disk' almost always mean the hard disk. All types of disk are of course direct access storage devices; in other words, the computer can access the data on any particular part of the disk almost immediately.

A disk drive usually contains several disk platters on a single spindle, and each platter may be double-sided. Each disk surface has its own read/write head, and all the heads move in and out together, to access the various tracks. The term 'cylinder' is used to mean the area that can be accessed with the heads in one position, comprising the corresponding track on each of the disk surfaces.

Before being used, a disk needs to be 'formatted', using a special utility which marks out various 'tracks' on the disk for the data to be fitted into. When comparing disk drives from various manufacturers, it is important to be certain whether they are quoting formatted or unformatted capacities – only the formatted sizes are of any relevance to the user.

On personal computers, hard disk capacities start at about 10 or 20 megabytes, but this would be barely sufficient to run UNIX: most UNIX machines have capacities in hundreds of megabytes. For comparison, however, the PDP-11 on which UNIX was largely developed had a disk with a maximum capacity of 512k (half a megabyte), and no file size could exceed 64k.

UNIX systems make very heavy use of the disks. As well as the various programs and data files, the disk contains a number of system files that the software refers to during the course of processing. For good performance it is essential to have enough disk; and the disks themselves, and the controllers which look after them, must be designed for high throughput.

Most UNIX machines come complete with disks, but extra disk storage can be added later. There are standard disk interfaces, such as SCSI (small computer standard interface), which mean that disks can be bought from third-party suppliers and added on.

Diskettes, otherwise called floppy disks, are not so important for UNIX systems as they are for personal computers. Nonetheless, most UNIX systems today have diskette drives, useful for instance for loading new software. The effective standard floppy disk for UNIX systems is the $5\frac{1}{4}$ inch disk; this may hold 360k, 720k, or 1.2 megabytes. Personal computers are now moving to the $3\frac{1}{2}$ inch disk, typically holding 720k or 1.4 megabytes, which is much more resistant to damage, as well as more compact; UNIX machines may follow this lead before long.

Optical disk

Optical disk appears to be the storage medium of the future. The principle is simple: the data is written onto the disk using a high powered laser, which causes a local change in the optical properties of the medium. Using a lower-powered laser, the information can be retrieved. The advantage of optical storage is that the data can be packed much more tightly onto the disk than with traditional magnetic technology; moreover, the data once recorded is much less prone to damage or accidental erasure.

Optical disk has already made a breakthrough in the world of audio equipment; compact disk (CD) has found a secure niche in the hi-fi market, providing very high quality sound at reasonable cost, but it is of course 'read-only': the information is recorded once when the disk is manufactured, and the user can access the recorded information, but not update it. Similarly, in the data processing area, there are read-only applications: 'CD-ROM' has been adopted as a medium of distributing large volume but basically static information.

The present generation of optical disk drives are no longer read-only, but 'WORM' – write once, read many times. In other words your computer can add information to the disk, but not change what is already there. Such a system has obvious benefits for security and audit trails, but of course it requires the ability in the application or the operating system to determine which is the most recent version of a file, as the disk may contain a number of versions, relating to different dates.

The next generation of optical disk storage will allow erasing and rewriting of information, and could therefore be a viable alternative to magnetic disk for general purpose storage where very large capacities are required. The access time for optical disk, however, is typically twice the time required for a Winchester.

Tapes and tape drives

Tapes are mainly used in UNIX systems for backing up or archiving files held on disk, so that if the disks or their files are damaged, the

UNIX Computers — the Hardware

data can still be recovered. The old half-inch reel-to-reel tapes familiar in films and television (being the most visibly moving part of a computer) are still used for this purpose, particularly on larger systems. On smaller UNIX systems a standard cartridge tape is much more common, being more compact and easier to handle; however, as disks get bigger, cartridge tape technology is not really keeping up. The half-inch tape is also useful for exchanging data with other organisations who have adopted this medium.

There are two different ways of using tapes. If a tape is being treated rather like a disk, and having records written to it one by one, the tape drive needs to keep starting and stopping, which takes an appreciable length of time. On the other hand, if the tape is being used for a bulk backup of a disk, it is much faster to use it as a 'streamer' tape; in other words, write the entire disk contents in one go, without stopping the tape.

Computer terminals

A terminal is the device which a person uses to communicate with the computer. By far the most common type is the visual display unit (vdu) comprising a keyboard and a display screen. One still sometimes sees terminals which have a printer rather than a display screen, and the original 'teletype' or 'tty' was such a terminal — it has left a number of traces in the design of UNIX, and in its terminology. There are also specialised terminals such as those used by workers 'clocking in', or the cash dispensers you use to draw money from the bank when it is closed. Even a till at a supermarket checkout these days can be a computer terminal, with its bar-code reader for input, and its printer for producing the receipt. But probably 99 per cent of terminals attached to UNIX machines are either straight vdus, or else personal computers pretending to be vdus.

Most vdus attached to UNIX systems are ASCII terminals; in other words they exchange data with the computer a character at a time, rather than in bursts, and use the ASCII code for representing letters and numbers (see Appendix A). But there are a bewildering variety of makes and models of ASCII terminals, differing in their keyboard layout, the size of the screen, and the way that special control characters are dealt with. The DEC VT100 is a very common standard, and has formed the basis of the ANSI standard (American National Standards Institute).

Many terminals have special setup keys, so that you can change the terminal characteristics, and maybe have it emulate a VT100 or some other model, while UNIX itself has the ability, via facilities such as *termcap* or *terminfo*, and support libraries such as *curses*, to allow the same application software to work correctly with many different types of terminal.

The keyboard

Terminal keyboards all include standard typewriter keys (in the familiar QWERTY layout), and a number of extra keys. The precise layout of the other keys varies considerably — the VT100 arrangement is quite common — but some standardisation is taking place. IBM, for instance, have just about standardised their keyboards, for personal computers as well as vdus, and the new IBM standard keyboard, like most IBM standards, will certainly be influential.

The keyboard also generally includes a number of 'function keys', often labelled F1, F2, and so on. These have no standard meaning, but different software uses them for different purposes. Often some of these keys (perhaps called PF1 and so on, for 'programmable function key') can be programmed within the terminal itself. Thus, to get a function key to work with particular software you may need to set up the terminal to send a particular code sequence when you press the key, and also set up the program running on the UNIX system to expect that code sequence and interpret it appropriately.

Some programs use the bottom line of the screen to show what each function key will do if you press it. Function keys are relatively new, and not altogether standardised, so most of the standard UNIX utilities do not use them.

At the right hand side of the keyboard there are normally a number of special keys, labelled with arrows, for moving the cursor around the screen, but again, not all the standard utilities recognise their existence.

One of the most important keys is the Return key, often a rather large key, sometimes called Enter, or perhaps marked with a crooked arrow symbol. It has two main functions — to advance to a new line, and to tell UNIX that you have completed the input of a particular command or data item. Other important keys include Esc (or Escape) and Del (Delete or Rubout).

As well as the shift key (to produce capital letters and some other symbols) there are control (Ctrl) and possibly alternate (Alt) keys. All of these are for you to hold down while pressing another key, to increase still further the number of key combinations available.

An increasingly popular adjunct to a keyboard is the 'mouse'. This is a little box on wheels or a rolling ball, with buttons on the top. You move it about on the desk and it makes the cursor on the screen move about in a similar way. You press the button on the mouse, and this is

UNIX Computers — the Hardware

the equivalent of pressing Return (or some other key) on the keyboard. A mouse is standard issue on many types of personal computer, and is also increasingly common on UNIX systems such as the IBM 6150, and systems designed with graphics in mind.

The console

In any UNIX system, one of the ports, and therefore the terminal attached to it, has a special status and is called the 'console'. When you first turn the machine on, UNIX uses the console to display the various messages that arise while it is sorting itself out. If you want to enter commands at this stage — while the machine is still in 'single-user' mode — it is the console you must use. Once the machine has gone into its normal 'multi-user' mode, however, the console is essentially no different to any other terminal, except that it is the one receiving occasional system error messages.

On certain classes of machine, however, the console is a 'memory-mapped' device, and can be used for high resolution graphics in a way that would not be possible with an ordinary terminal. Chapter 16 will cover this point in a little more detail.

Printers

The term 'peripherals' is commonly used to mean other devices connected to the computer. The most common of these are printers.

The simplest and cheapest sort of printers are dot matrix printers. The principle of these is that each character is built up out of a matrix of dots, which are clearly visible if you look closely at the output. The printing head contains a number of wires. As it moves across the page, the wires are used in various combinations to strike a ribbon against the paper, thus building up the character. This technique means that the printer is not restricted to its predefined characters, and so it can very easily be made to print in different alphabets, or indeed produce graphical output rather than text. The disadvantage is that when used for text, the quality of the printing is not really adequate for business correspondence. Also, matrix printers are slow and rather noisy.

Some matrix printers can take multi-colour ribbons, for colour printing, while most types can now produce 'near letter quality' (NLQ) although more slowly than in their normal 'draft mode'.

Typically, a matrix printer uses continuous stationery with sprocket holes. Unfortunately this means that the paper is not strictly A4 size: the sprocket holes are every half inch, so that the length of the paper must be a multiple of half an inch. A typical page length is eleven inches, which is slightly less than A4. Some matrix printers can use cut sheet paper, and those used for printing letters will generally be purchased with sheet feeders.

Daisywheel printers

Daisywheel printers employ a revolving wheel resembling a daisy, typically with between 96 and 130 petals. At the ends of the petals are the various letters of the alphabet, and the printer spins the wheel until it finds the one it wants, which is then struck against the ribbon. This method is slower than dot-matrix printing, but the quality is much better — equivalent to a good electric typewriter. Obviously the printing is limited to the selection of characters provided, but you can take the daisy off and substitute a different one if you want to use a different typeface for a particular document.

Daisywheel printers normally take either continuous stationery or separate sheets. Generally you can get a sheet feeder, which will take a stack of separate sheets and print them out, only screwing up the occasional page.

The main disadvantage of all impact printers — daisywheel or matrix — is that they tend to be very noisy. Even with an expensive acoustic hood to muffle the sound, they can make life in an open-plan office very uncomfortable. And the faster the machines are, the more noise they make.

Laser printers

The most important development in printing in recent years has been the laser printer, which combines the high quality of daisywheel printing with the flexibility of the dot matrix.

The principle is the same as the familiar office copier, except that the image on the drum is produced not by an optical image of the original, but by writing directly on the drum with a laser. Typical laser printers come with a number of inbuilt typefaces, and additional fonts are available, either as plug-in cartridges, or by downloading the font definition from the computer, so that you can switch, for example, between Courier, Prestige Elite, and Letter Gothic, and in any of these alternate between normal text, bold, and italics. Laser printers can provide printouts on A4 sheets in either landscape or portrait format (in other words with the longer edge of the paper either to the top or to the side).

More sophisticated laser printers can act as a very cheap but effective substitute for typesetting, with many different sizes of type, as well as graphics. The recent growth of 'desktop publishing' relies very much on such machines.

Laser printers are still not cheap compared to matrix printers. However, the price has fallen considerably since they were first introduced, and they are complete in themselves: they do not need separate acoustic hoods or paper feed devices (the printer is silent, and it takes cut sheet stationery as standard) so the total outlay can be cheaper than a daisywheel. The laser printer is also much easier to use, takes up less space on the desk, and is less likely to give trouble.

For most offices and word processing departments today, the laser printer is the ideal machine for quality output.

Line printers

Another type of printer, more often encountered on large mainframe computers, is the line printer — a very high speed impact printer, in which an entire line is printed at one stroke. Often, however, the character set is rather limited — perhaps even upper-case only.

Line printers in the strict sense are too inflexible and too expensive to have much of a place in microcomputer systems; however the term 'line printer' is often used loosely to mean the principal printer attached to a computer, and has led to the name *lp* for the main UNIX spooling utility.

Comparing the speeds of different types of printers is often difficult, because they are not expressed in the same terms. A matrix printer is often rated in characters per second (cps), a line printer in lines per minute (lpm), and a laser printer in pages per minute (ppm).

Printer connections

In all areas of computing, interfaces, the way in which one device links to another, are a factor to be contended with. In the case of printers, there are two main possibilities, serial and parallel.

The standard interface for matrix and daisywheel printers is parallel, like most connections within the computer itself. The cable connecting the computer and the printer contains eight wires, one for each bit of a byte (plus additional wires for control purposes). The computer can therefore send a whole byte or character at a time down the cable, generally using the 'Centronics' standard for the arrangement of the various data and control lines.

The alternative is serial transmission, whereby only one wire is allocated for the transmission of the data, so the eight bits of a byte are sent one after another. The normal standard for serial transmission is RS232 (or V.24), as used for vdu terminals and modems.

Clearly parallel transmission is theoretically eight times faster than serial. However, in the case of printers this is not significant – the potential speed of the cable in either mode is much faster than the capacity of the printer to accept data and do its printing.

A limitation with parallel interfaces is that the data on all eight lines must keep exactly in step. With very long cables the data may get slightly out of phase, and thus cause corruption. Consequently parallel interfaces are not normally used where the computer and the printer are more than a few yards apart. Moreover, a UNIX machine will normally have only one parallel port, but several serial ports, which can be set up either for terminals or for printers.

Today's printers are intelligent devices with their own microprocessor, and often with their own memory, both ROM (storing the combinations of dots that make up the standard character set) and RAM (storing any special characters that you or your software may have devised). The quality of the graphics output from a laser printer depends on the amount of data it can store in its memory, and varies from one make to another. Many laser printers have more processing power and memory than some complete computers.

A printer also has its own 'language' in which it must be addressed, with special control characters to turn underlining on or off, to start a new page, and so on. Unfortunately there is very little standardisation in the use of such control characters between one make of printer and another. Normally the software package you are using will take care of all this. For instance, when you buy a new word processing package you first of all need to 'install' it on the computer; part of this installation process involves informing the software what type of printer you will be using, so that when you come to print something out it will generate the correct control characters to achieve the effect intended.

Standard 'high level' languages for addressing printers are beginning to appear, with PostScript an emerging standard for 'desktop publishing' purposes (see Chapter 13).

Plotters bring colour to graphics

A printer is fine for text, and for certain limited graphical uses. However, if you are producing graphs, bar charts, and so on, you may need a plotter. Most plotters work on a co-ordinate principle – the plotter has a series of pens (each one a different colour) and moves them about the page under program control, thus drawing the various lines, and forming the characters of any text that may be required. Clearly special instructions need to be given to the plotter to make it do this, but most graphical software has the ability to generate commands in the appropriate language for the plotter in question. The language used to drive Hewlett Packard (HP) plotters in particular has become a common standard. For instance, the standard graphics package for UNIX System V includes the *hpd* command, which will output graphics to an HP 7221A. Clearly before investing in a plotter you should verify that the software you intend to use is capable of driving it.

Modems — an ear to the outside world

A modem (modulator/demodulator) allows you to communicate with the outside world using the telephone lines. It converts the signals inside your computer to the electronic equivalent of sounds, which can be transmitted over the telephone system.

Many modems have an auto-dial facility, so that they can automatically dial the appropriate number under computer control. Some have auto-answer, so that they can receive calls unattended. Modems generally come with a lead and plug, to plug into your telephone socket. Of course you should ensure that the modem you use is approved by the British Approvals Board for Telecommunications (BABT), or the equivalent in other countries, before connecting it.

When selecting a modem, the main variable to be considered is the speed. Typical speeds are 300, 1200, or 2400 bits per second, although much faster speeds can be provided by much more expensive modems. To connect to Prestel or similar viewdata services, the modem must run at 1200 bits per second in one direction, 75 in the other.

An older alternative to a modem is an acoustic coupler, which does not plug into a telephone socket, but is connected to the telephone handset, and makes actual noises into the mouthpiece. However these are unreliable and only work with certain types of telephone; they can be regarded as obsolete.

Chapter 5
Introducing the software

> *Note: in this chapter I describe various commands and suggest that you try them out. However, if for some reason you don't have access to a UNIX system at present, you should still read the descriptions of the commands, as the concepts involved are key to an understanding of UNIX.*

Getting started

Let us suppose that a UNIX-based system has been installed in your company. This installation of course involves more than just bringing the equipment in and turning it on: Chapter 24 covers some of what is involved.

Let us take all this for granted for the moment. The computer has been installed, and there is a terminal sitting on your desk, duly wired up and turned on. Beginning to use it is rather more formal than starting to use a personal computer. Before you can do anything else you have to identify yourself to the system. Probably, the terminal will already be inviting you to do this, by showing a message such as

unix login:

or something similar.

This is inviting you to type in your 'login name' (or user name), which you should have been given already: probably it will be your first name or initials, or some other word which can identify you as an individual. The first thing you have to do is to type it in, but make sure you use lower-case: if it appears on the screen in capitals you have probably pressed the 'Caps Lock' key. Put this right, otherwise your terminal may start doing strange things. End your name by pressing the Return (or Enter) key; you nearly always have to press Return when you have finished typing something in, so that UNIX knows that your input is complete, and can be passed on to the program waiting to use it.

Next the system will ask you for your password. I will be saying a lot more about passwords later; for the moment the main point is that your login name identifies you to the system, your password verifies that you are who you say you are. These two concepts, identification and verification, are keys to many of the security features that are part of UNIX.

When you type your password, you will not see anything appearing on the screen. This is for the obvious reason, to prevent anyone looking over your shoulder from knowing your password and later using it, pretending to be you. Obviously, you need to memorise your password very carefully, but without writing it down.

At the end of your password, hit the Return key as before. The system checks that your login name and password are correct. If all is well you will now be admitted to the system. On the screen you may see a welcome message of some sort (a 'message of the day') but the important thing to look for is a prompt at the beginning of a line, inviting you to make use of the system. The prompt may include your name, the time of day, or some other information. Most likely, however, it will be a single character, such as $ or %. Whatever form your prompt takes (and you can modify it to suit yourself, when you have learnt a little more) it is your open door to the manifold riches of the UNIX system.

Logging out

Having logged in successfully, the next thing you need to know is how to log out. Whenever you have finished a session at the computer, you should always be sure to log out, as otherwise someone else could come along, pretend to be you, and have access to all your files without needing to give a password.

Logging out is simple. Hold down the key marked Control or Ctrl. While holding it down, press the D key, and then release both keys. This combination is referred to as 'Ctrl-D' or sometimes as '⌃D'. The effect of the Ctrl-D is to tell the 'shell' — that is, the program that was waiting for your next command — that you have nothing more to say. Try it, and you will find that the computer logs you off, and the standard 'UNIX login' message reappears. At this point you can log back in again for the next lesson.

Finding your way around

Once you have got in, it is time to look around a little, and orient yourself. Unlike some of those adventure games, which tell you 'You are in a maze of little twisty passages, all alike', UNIX does not venture any information about your whereabouts unless you ask it. The next step, therefore is to be aware of some of the standard UNIX commands so that you can give the system instructions and ask it for information.

UNIX provides a large number of commands, and some of them can be very complicated in the way you use them. But we will start with one of the simplest: *logname*, which tells you who you are − that is, who UNIX thinks you are. Try it now. First of all type in

logname

just like that, in one word, in lower case (UNIX is very particular about that sort of thing). Follow it by pressing Return (you should do this after every command − I won't bother to keep repeating it any more). The system responds by displaying your login name on the next line, for instance:

fred

Another command that does something similar is *id*. The format for this command is again very simple − you just type:

id

The output from the *id* command, however, is rather different to that from *logname*. It will probably look something like:

uid=35 (fred) gid=6 (accounts)

In this case, *fred* is just your login name, as before; but note that *id* has also shown the numeric user identification (uid) by which you are actually known to the operating system; your login name is just a convenient alias, given that people unlike computers remember names more easily than numbers.

The other new piece of information (again shown as both a name and a number) is the group identity (gid). As well as having an individual identity, each user belongs to a group. Your group may, for instance, be the name of the department you belong to; on the other hand it may be something rather bland such as 'others' − different installations use the groups facility in different ways, and some do not bother much with groups at all.

The next command to try is *ls*. Type this in as one word:

ls

The system should respond by displaying on the screen a list of files (or documents) held on disk. If you are a very new user you may find that you do not have any files at all. You will very soon see how you can create some. Meanwhile note that the *ls* command is one of the most commonly used in UNIX, and can also be used in other ways to give more detailed information about files on the system. The name of the command is perhaps not very meaningful (short for 'list'), but then UNIX is naturally rather terse.

Directories

When you type *ls*, the number of files you see displayed is normally fairly small; certainly only a tiny proportion of all the files that are held on the computer's disk. If it tried to display all the files there would be far too many to get on the screen, and far too many for you to cope with.

So that you can see the wood for the trees, UNIX collects the various disk files into a number of directories. The *ls* command shows you only the contents of one particular directory, referred to as your current working directory. When you logged in, the system automatically put you into your 'home directory', and this remains your working directory until you move elsewhere.

Another UNIX command, *pwd*, tells you what your current working directory is (*pwd* stands for 'print working directory'). So if you type

pwd

UNIX will print the directory name on the screen. Probably it will be a name such as */usr/fred*. The word 'print' by the way is a reminder of the days when computer terminals had a keyboard and a printer, rather than a display screen.

Your home directory is a convenient place for you to create files and store information. But you are not restricted to it, as you might be in certain other operating systems. You can move around elsewhere within the system, and you can create files in other directories. For that matter, other people can create files in your home directory – unless you take steps to prevent them.

Now let's create a new file. Type in the following line:

cat > newfile

The > symbol here means that the output of the *cat* program is to be 'redirected' to a file on disk called *newfile*.

When you have typed this in (and hit Return of course) you will see the cursor waiting for you at the start of a new line. But notice this time that the normal prompt character has disappeared. This indicates that the program that is waiting for your input is no longer the shell, but a new program – actually the *cat* program, which is a general purpose utility for copying data from one place to another. *Cat* is waiting for you to type in some information, and whatever you type will now be stored in a new file called *newfile*. Type in some lines of text, hitting Return at the end of each line. When you have finished, type Ctrl-D at the start of a new line. This means, as before, that you have no more input. The *cat* program now terminates, and the shell prompt should reappear.

You can now verify that the *cat* program has worked. If you type *ls*, you should see that the name *newfile* has been added to the list on the screen. Moreover you can verify that it contains the text that you put in it. Type

    cat < newfile

(with a < instead of a > this time) and UNIX will show on the screen the contents of the file, which should be the text you typed in.

Notice what the *cat* command does. It takes its input from your keyboard, unless you redirect it using <, and it puts its output to the screen unless you redirect it using >. A great many UNIX commands work in this way. Of course you can redirect both input and output if you want. Type

    cat < newfile > newfile2

This creates a new file called *newfile2*, with the same contents as the original file *newfile*. Check that it does this.

Finally, of course, you can choose to redirect neither the input nor the output. If you type

    cat

just by itself, what will happen? The answer is quite logical – try it and see, but note that UNIX does not immediately pass each character you type to *cat*, but only a complete line, when you have hit Return.

Options

In UNIX you can often make commands work in different ways by means of options. For example, the *ls* command which we used before merely showed us the names of the files in the directory. To see other information as well as the names, type

    ls -l

Be careful not to leave a space between the '-' (a hyphen or minus sign) and the *l*. The *l* is short for 'long', and as you will see it gives you a long listing, showing the filenames down the right hand side, and several other columns of information. Many UNIX commands use a minus sign in this way (or occasionally a plus sign) to indicate that what follows is an option or series of options.

A typical output from *ls -l* would be something like this:

-rwxr-xr-x	1 fred	accounts	7636 Apr 16 13:45 aaa
-rwxr-xr-x	1 fred	accounts	7636 Apr 16 13:45 aprog
-rw-r--r--	1 fred	101	718 Mar 12 10:09 clientifile
-rw-r--r--	1 fred	accounts	6577 Apr 16 14:10 dec_test.c
-rw-r--r--	1 fred	accounts	5865 Apr 16 14:10 dec_test.ec
-rw-r--r--	1 fred	accounts	5968 Apr 16 13:50 dec_test.o
drwxr-xr-x	3 fred	accounts	256 Apr 16 09:36 letters
-rwxr-xr-x	1 fred	accounts	224540 Mar 31 13:33 newfile
-rwx------	1 fred	accounts	149717 Mar 27 15:46 news
-rwxr-xr-x	2 joe	other	476 Mar 30 09:40 notes
-rwxr-xr-x	1 fred	accounts	338521 Apr 10 14:50 oldData
-rwxr-xr-x	1 mike	accounts	205868 Mar 30 10:30 pm799.4ge
-rwxr-xr-x	1 fred	accounts	1036 Mar 30 09:12 ReadMe
-rw-rw-r--	1 fred	accounts	0 Mar 30 09:00 switch
-rw-------	1 fred	accounts	25 Mar 30 08:49 temp

Some of the columns in this listing will be explained later on. For the moment, however, look at the columns starting from the right hand side. Immediately before the filename is the date and time when the file was created, or when it was last modified, for instance 'Apr 16 13:45'. Look at the listing on your screen, and check the files you have just created: the date should be today and the time a few minutes ago.

To the left of the date is a number, which is in fact the size of the file, in bytes (characters). Check that the size of the files you have created is the same as the number of characters and spaces you typed in, including one byte for each Return or 'newline' character.

Arguments

The *-l* option is one kind of 'parameter' or 'argument' that can be passed to a command or program to modify its behaviour. Additionally you can specify other arguments, which are typically the names of files, and are not preceded by a hyphen. For instance:

ls -l newfile

This gives a long directory listing, but only for the single file *newfile*, rather than the whole directory. Note that if you use an option as well as other parameters, the option normally comes first, immediately after the name of the command. Of course you must leave a space between the various parameters, but if a command has more than one option, they can all be grouped into a single parameter. In other words they follow the hyphen, with no spaces between them — for instance:

ls -lrt

This gives a *l*ong listing, but in *r*everse *t*ime order — that is, oldest first, on the basis of the date and time of last modification.

Another command worth trying out is

who am i

This displays your login name, the name of your terminal, and the date and time when you logged in; something like:

fred   console   Apr 16 11.05

Now that you know about parameters, it should be clear that *who am i* is actually a command *who* with two parameters. In some versions of UNIX the system actually 'cheats' — it doesn't look at the parameters to the *who* command, but just counts them. So you could type in *who* followed by any two words on the same line, and the effect would be the same.

If you type in *who* by itself with no parameters, it shows you a list of all the users who are currently logged on to the system — often a useful thing to know.

The *cat* command that we looked at earlier can take filename arguments; they are taken as specifying the input to the program. So for instance

cat myfile > newfile

has exactly the same effect as

cat < myfile > newfile

It may seem a little superfluous to have two ways of expressing the same thing. The benefit of using arguments in this case is that you can have more than one of them. So, for instance, the command

cat file1 file2 file3 > newfile

will create a new file containing the contents of the three input files, one after the other. In technical jargon, it will 'concatenate' the three files — hence the name of the command.

Touching files

The date and time on the *ls -l* listing are updated every time you change the contents of a file. In addition, the *touch* command allows

Introducing the Software

you to change the date and time, without altering the data at all. Try this:

touch newfile

Then do an *ls -l*, and observe the date and time shown for this file. If you use the *touch* command but specify a file which does not yet exist, UNIX creates a file with that name for you. Try it out, and note that the length of the file is zero — not surprisingly, since you did not specify any data to be put in it.

More about the directory listing

We have still not covered all the columns on the *ls -l* listing. Starting from the left this time, there are four more columns (or 'fields' in computer jargon) to be dealt with. These are:
- the permissions — a string of ten characters something like *-rwxr-xr--*;
- the number of links — that is the number of different names by which the file is known in directories; usually 1, but sometimes 2 or more;
- the 'user' of the file, that is its individual owner;
- the group owner of the file.

For the files you have created so far, check that the entry in the 'user' column is your login name, and that the entry in the 'group' column is the name of the group you belong to. By the way, you may note that *ls* does not provide any headings to the various columns. This is quite usual in UNIX. It makes it easier to use the output of one command as the input to another, using the '*pipe*' facility discussed later in this chapter.

Permissions

The most complicated field in the *ls* listing is the permissions. This contains a series of ten characters each of which (except the first) is normally *r*, *w*, or *x*, meaning that read, write, or execute permission respectively is granted, or a minus sign, meaning that the permission in question is denied.

Read and write permission mean permission to find out what is in the file and to change it, respectively. Execute permission arises because in UNIX most commands are programs, and all programs are files, and can be executed by a user with the appropriate permission. Additionally, you can create a text file containing shell commands, and make it executable. Simply typing in the name of the file is then the equivalent of typing in the various commands one by one. You have thus created a new command. Such a file is called a 'shell script' and is a very powerful feature of UNIX.

For normal files the first character of the permissions field is always a minus sign. It contains a *d* if the file is a directory, and other characters for special types of files.

The rest of the field falls into three groups of three. Within each group the first character is *r* or a minus sign, the second is *w* or a minus sign, the third is *x* or a minus sign (or occasionally other characters). The first of the three groups relates to the individual user of the file, the next to the group owner, the third to all other users. When you create a file, UNIX decides how to allocate these permissions, according to rules that you can change if you wish using the *umask* command, but a typical setting might be

-rw-r-----

meaning that:
- you as user of the file can read it (for instance use *cat* to display its contents) or write to it (change its contents);
- other people in your group can read the file but not write to it;
- people not in your group can neither read not write;
- no one, including yourself, can execute it.

The most liberal setting of course would be

-rwxrwxrwx

meaning that anyone at all can read, write, or execute the file.

As a parenthesis, it may be worth pointing out that even a 'single-user' computer could usefully have similar facilities. In business, many personal computers are not totally assigned to one person, but several people use them from time to time. If the machine has a hard disk, different people may be creating and deleting files at different times, and it would be very useful to have the facilities which UNIX provides, of finding out who owns what, and controlling the access and updating of particular files.

Deleting files

Having created some files, it is as well to know how to delete them. In fact it is generally a good idea to delete files that are no longer used, so that the disk does not get too full up. To delete a file you use the *rm* command, short for 'remove':

rm myfile

Beware, however, that once having deleted a file, you cannot get it back again!

Displaying information

We have seen the use of the *cat* command to display the contents of a file on your screen. But *cat* is a very primitive command, and is not much use if your file is longer than the size of your screen, as the information will scroll away faster than you can read it. Actually, you can use the Ctrl-S combination to stop it in its flow, and Ctrl-Q to restart it, but this requires nimble fingers. A better method is to use a command specially designed for the purpose, namely *pg*. The syntax is as you might expect:

pg newfile

Unlike *cat*, *pg* displays the first page of the data, and then waits while you look at it. To see the next page, hit Return or the space bar. You can get the screen to scroll half a page forwards or backwards, and there are commands to search forwards or backwards for a particular string of characters.

On some UNIX systems, you may find the *more* command, which has a similar function, but is unable to search backwards.

Printed output

Very often, when you are using UNIX, it is sufficient to get your output displayed on the screen. But there comes a time when you need 'hard copy' in the form of a printed report, and certainly most commercial data processing systems produce large quantities of paper, including reports for internal use, and invoices, statements, letters, and other documents for sending to outside bodies.

If you use a word processing package, it will undoubtedly have its own printing facilities built in. If you are merely running standard UNIX commands, however, you can get output to the printer using the *lp* command.

Lp is a print spooler – that is, a program which allows several users to share the printer between them. Of course it would not be acceptable for everyone to send output to the printer at once, as all the reports would get jumbled up; on the other hand it would be inconvenient if you had to wait for the printer to become free before starting your print job. *Lp* overcomes this dilemma by providing queues: you can put your output into a queue at any time, and it will then be scheduled for printing when the printer is free. Each print file submitted to *lp* is assigned a unique id, which is displayed on your terminal when you issue the command. Subsequently you can use *lpstat* to find the status of files which have been sent for printing, and the *cancel* command is available to cancel a print request, even if it has started printing out.

If you use the *lp* command with no options, it will send the output to whatever printer is taken to be the default 'line printer'; the -*d* option allows you to specify a particular printer or class of printer by name.

A useful program to use with *lp* is *pr*, which allows you to format your output in a manner suitable for the printed page. You can get the output in multiple columns on the page (something that very many sophisticated word processors fail to provide), you can have headers and footers on each page, and you can even print several files side by side, each in its own column.

A typical command line might be:

pr −3 −d +5 −w75 myfile | lp

This will use *pr* to format the text of *myfile* into 3 columns, with *d*ouble spacing, starting from page 5, using a page *w*idth of 75 characters, and then send the formatted output to *lp* for printing.

Pipes and filters

In the example just quoted, you may have noticed the | or vertical bar symbol, used to make the output of one command become the input to another. This is termed in UNIX a 'pipe', and is one of the good ideas that make UNIX so flexible to work with, enabling you to combine the various commands in all sorts of ways. For instance:

who | wc

This will pass the output of the *who* command into the *wc* (word count) command, so that what you see on your screen is not the list of logged-on users, but a count of how many there are.

Staying with the plumbing analogy, UNIX lets you have T 'junctions' in your pipelines, by means of the *tee* command. For instance:

cat xyz abc | tee newfile1 | sort > newfile2

This will combine together the files *xyz* and *abc*, and sort the combined output to make *newfile2*. But on the way it will store a copy of the combined data, before sorting, in *newfile1*.

Programs and commands such as *pr* and *sort* are examples of 'filters' – that is they read a single input file, do some processing on it, and write the processed data to a single output file. There are many filters in UNIX.

Chapter 6
Concepts and Features

In the previous chapter I introduced quite a few of the main features of UNIX. At this point it may be useful to review some of the underlying features a little more thoroughly.

Tasks and users

UNIX is a multi-user system – that is, it allows a number of people to be logged in and working with the computer simultaneously, one at each terminal. If you are using the computer, you are running a program of some sort; as far as the operating system is concerned, this program is seen as a 'process'. At any one time, therefore, several different processes are loaded and active – at least one per user.

The concepts of a 'program' and a 'process' are closely linked, but quite distinct. A process (also called a 'task') is what actually runs in the computer; it has assigned to it several areas of memory. One of these areas contains the program, that is the code or set of instructions which tell the process what to do.

As soon as you log in, UNIX starts up a process for you. Normally this is running a program called the shell, or command processor, which waits for you to type in a command such as *ls* or *pwd*, and then tries to find the program corresponding to the command.

Every time you run a program from the shell prompt, you have got two processes active – the new program, and the shell itself. Of course the shell is not actively doing anything most of the time – while you run a program the shell normally (but not always) waits for it to finish before prompting you for the next input.

To see what processes are active at a particular time, you can use the *ps* command, standing for 'process status'. This command gives you a display on the screen of the various processes you've got running. The output from *ps* is available in several formats, but if you type just

ps

you will see a display which includes:
- the process id number (PID);
- the number of the terminal (TTY) from which you are running the process;
- the length of time for which it has been executing;
- the name of the command or program being run.

Whenever you run *ps*, it will mention at least two processes. One is the *ps* program itself, the other is the shell, usually called *sh* or *csh*.

Your manual will list the various options for the *ps* command, but notice one in particular:

ps -ef

This lists *every* process, and gives a *fuller* listing. If you use this option, you will see that there are quite a number of processes running, including at least one for every person logged on. Also note that if there are any terminals not in use, they still have a process running – probably the *getty* program, which issues the invitation to log in.

Programs and commands

The various commands so far described are all (or nearly all) programs. When you type in a command such as *ps*, the shell looks in certain predefined places on disk for a file of that name. On finding such a file it attempts to execute it.

Executing a file involves several steps. First of all, UNIX checks the permissions for the file to see whether you are allowed to execute it. It then checks the internal format of the file to see whether it is in fact a program. If the file is a program, the shell starts up a new process, and loads the program into memory; the new process continues by attempting to carry out the sequence of instructions contained in the program.

Some programs are not normally executed as commands from the shell, but run in the background, carrying out various system housekeeping tasks. This sort of program is often referred to as a 'daemon' – sometimes spelt 'demon', but this gives a diabolical flavour which is hardly appropriate. Actually, a daemon is regarded as a sort of spirit or tooth fairy, which does its business when no one is watching.

Another most important program is the kernel – a special program which is generally called simply *unix*. Unlike other programs, this does not run in a process of its own, but lies in wait ready to take over any user process, if the user program issues a 'system call', or receives an interrupt.

The directory structure

One of the key features enabling UNIX to cope with multiple users is the directory structure. Each user can use files and programs anywhere on the disk (subject to permissions) but the directory structure enables you to deal with manageable sets of files.

The directory structure is arranged as a tree, with a single root and many branches. The root directory (often shown at the top in diagrams!) is called simply /, and contains a number of second-level directories, some of which are always present, while others vary from one computer to another. The *usr* directory contains all the 'home directories' of the various users, each generally given a name corresponding to the user's login name. Users themselves can create further directories within their home directory (or elsewhere if they have the right permissions) and these directories can contain still further directories. The tree can thus grow downwards as far as you wish, within reason.

Any file in the system has a full name (or 'pathname') which enables UNIX to find it by starting from the root and working downwards through the various directories. The / or slash character is used to string directory names together for this purpose. For instance, a user called *fred* might have his own home directory, probably also called *fred*, within the main *usr* directory. Within his home directory he might open further directories, perhaps one called *letters* for storing correspondence. Within the *letters* directory he might have a file called *smith*, containing a letter to Mr Smith. The full pathname for this file is */usr/fred/letters/smith*. Note the additional / at the start of the pathname. This is the name of the root directory, not a separator.

Anyone who wants to read the letter can type

pg /usr/fred/letters/smith

However, this is rather long-winded. Fred, if he is in his home directory − or anyone else who happens to be there − can just type

pg letters/smith

Note that in this case the name does not start with /, indicating that UNIX should start looking not from the root, but from the current working directory.

Even this could seem a little long-winded. If you are going to make much use of this file (or others in the same directory) you can make life simpler by issuing the *cd* command, to move yourself temporarily to the *letters* directory:

cd letters

Concepts and Features

If you now use the *pwd* command, you will find that you have changed directory to */usr/fred/letters*. At this point you can read the letter by just typing:

pg smith

There are two special directory names which can be used wherever you are: . (a single dot) refers to the current directory itself, and .. (dot dot) to its parent. So if you are currently in */usr/fred*, the name . is equivalent to */usr/fred*, and .. is equivalent to */usr*. So if you want to look at a file called *memo* in */usr/joe*, you could type

pg ../joe/memo

Directories and security

The UNIX directory structure complements the system of read, write, and execute permissions on files. It is up to each user to determine what permissions to assign to his own files, but the system manager may need to be involved when it is a question of files containing company-wide information.

When files are initially created, the permissions they are given depend on a 'mask' for each user, which can be altered using the *umask* command. Subsequently, the permissions for a file can be changed using the *chmod* command. For instance:

chmod g=rw myfile

would set the permissions for members of the group owning the file to *r*ead and *w*rite (but not execute), while

chmod +x myfile

would *add e*xecute permissions for all classes of user. There are various other options to this command, which are best studied in the manual.

It is also possible for a user to sign away the ownership of his files, using the *chown* command, but not of course to reclaim them back again. Similarly *chgrp* will change a file's group ownership.

If permission bits on files are important, those on directories are even more so. If you allow other people to have write access to your directory, they may be able to delete your files, even without having write permission on the files themselves – a point to watch.

While on the subject of security, there is more to be said about passwords, which are after all the key to all UNIX security. It is most important to keep your password confidential; if for some reason you think it may have become known to other people, you can change it, by typing

passwd

The *passwd* program will first ask you for your existing password, for obvious reasons. It will then ask for the new password, which you have to key in twice to make sure you have got it correct; as usual, it is not echoed on the screen. If you succeed in entering the new password twice consistently, the password file is updated.

If you should forget your password, you are in some difficulty. The only thing to do now is to speak politely to your system manager, who will be able to change it for you.

The kernel

The most important program in a UNIX system is the kernel, which looks after the overall running of the system. One of its main functions is to look after time-sharing; it controls the birth and death of processes and also makes sure that each process receives a fair share of time on the central processor.

Another function of the kernel is to carry out input and output processing on behalf of other programs. For instance, when you are inputting data from the keyboard, it goes first of all to the kernel, which carries out some initial processing (and normally echoes each character back to your vdu screen) before passing it on to the program which is waiting for the data.

For obvious reasons, the kernel has special permission to do all sorts of things which are not permitted to ordinary programs.

The resources of the kernel are made available to user processes under very tightly controlled conditions. Generally speaking, a process needing to use kernel facilities (for instance to do input/output handling) will issue a 'system call', that is it will hand over control temporarily to the kernel, having first indicated what sort of service the kernel is to carry out. The kernel will then execute the appropriate routines within the user process, passing control back to the actual user program when it has finished.

Another function of the kernel is to deal with 'interrupts' — that is, with events which occur externally to the normal running of a program. An obvious example of an interrupt is when you hit the Del key to halt a program while it is running — but in fact any key depression by any user, or the completion of any input/output processing, is treated by UNIX as an interrupt, which it needs to deal with before resuming the ordinary flow of your program.

The shell

Another special type of program in UNIX is the shell, or command processor.

When you type a command at your terminal and hit Return, the kernel passes the complete line of input to the shell, which looks at the data, and tries to make sense of it. The main job of the shell is to receive your various commands and call up the appropriate programs, but there is a lot more to it than that.

Unlike the kernel, the shell has no special privileges. Moreover, if you don't like the standard shell, you can always use a different one. In fact several different shells are available on different UNIX systems, and you can use one or the other as you wish. For the moment, however, it will be simpler to concentrate on the main UNIX shell, supplied by AT&T with every UNIX system. This is a program called *sh*, and is often referred to as the 'Bourne Shell', after Steve Bourne of Bell Laboratories, who wrote the program.

Finding files and programs — paths and pathnames

When you use a filename as an argument to a shell command, you are specifying to the program in question where the file is to be found. Normally the program will start looking in the root directory if you have given a full pathname starting with /, or otherwise in your current working directory. This is a convenient way of dealing with ordinary files, but it may have occurred to you that it does not apply to the command name itself. After all, the commands that you type in are just programs, or in other words executable files (apart from a few 'built-in' commands within the shell itself). Obviously it would be wasteful to have all these files held in every directory so you could refer to them by name; on the other hand you do not need to prefix their names by */bin*, which is where they are mostly kept.

What actually happens is that when you type a command, UNIX looks for the program in several different places, one of them being normally the */bin* directory. The list of places to look is determined by one of the 'environment variables' which are given to the shell when it starts up, but which you can change if you wish. The variable in question is called PATH.

Finding files and programs — wild card expansion

If you have used a microcomputer with MS-DOS or CP/M you may be familiar with the idea of 'wild cards'. Just as a joker in a pack of cards can be taken as representing any card you fancy, so an asterisk in a shell command represents any combination of characters in an actual file name. For instance, if you have files called *temp1*, *temp2*, and so on, you could type

rm temp*

to delete them all. Similarly, a question mark represents any one character.

However, the concept is slightly different in UNIX compared to MS-DOS. A little knowledge of MS−DOS can sometimes be dangerous, as DOS has a number of features which have been copied from the UNIX equivalents, but implemented rather differently.

An additional feature of UNIX is that you can use ranges; for instance *file[a-z]* would match filenames *filea*, *fileb*, and so on, but not *fileA*, *fileB*.

Background processing

UNIX is by nature an interactive system: you key in a command, and wait (generally not very long) until the program has finished its work and hands you back the shell prompt. Alternatively, you may be using a program such as a data entry system or a word processor; in this case the program may well run for a long time, but only because you have a lot of data to input.

There are other types of program which take a long time to run, merely processing data already on disk, without needing new input. It is rather tedious to have to wait while they carry out their work, and you may wish you could meanwhile be doing something else. With UNIX, you can do just that. Say you had created a large text file, and wanted to check the spelling. The standard way to do this in UNIX (assuming you haven't got a word processor with its own spelling facilities) is to use the *spell* program, perhaps redirecting its output to collect any badly spelt or unknown words in a file:

spell myfile > errorlist

But if *myfile* is quite long, the spelling check will take quite a time to complete. Meanwhile you could be getting on with something else − perhaps typing the next document. So you should set off the spelling check in the background:

spell myfile > errorlist &

The & (ampersand) is all you need to set off the program in the background. UNIX responds by displaying a reference number (the process ID) for the background task, and then the normal shell prompt reappears. The process ID is a useful thing to know, so that you can check on the progress of the task, or kill it off if you wish.

Of course a program which requires input from the keyboard cannot realistically be run in the background. Similarly, a program which produces vdu output should have this redirected to a file, or piped into another program, as otherwise it will get mixed up on the screen with the output from other programs.

Background processing is a key feature of many data processing systems. A typical commercial system consists partly of interactive programs – for instance, allowing the users to key in invoice details – and partly of background programs such as posting a batch of invoices to the ledgers. Batch processes, which do not require any human intervention while they are doing their work, can very easily be run in the background without tying up a terminal; in some cases they may indeed be run overnight, when no one is actually logged in, and the load on the machine is therefore much lower. You will see later how one can set off tasks to run unattended at a specified time.

UNIX documentation

Most of the commands I have mentioned have a number of other options, which it would be too confusing to go into here; moreover, the actual details may differ slightly between one UNIX system and another. When you are in doubt, the best thing is first of all to ask your system manager or system administrator – the person within your organisation who is responsible for looking after the UNIX system. However, to find the precise form of any command, and all the options available, you may eventually have to follow the computer user's last resort: 'When all else fails, look in the manual!'

Actually consulting the manual may be a little more difficult than it seems; UNIX systems often come with a considerable amount of documentation, and it is difficult to know where to look for anything. Traditionally, the main documentation is collected in the UNIX Programmer's Manual. A copy of this manual will certainly be available somewhere or other, probably as a loose-leaf folder, and on some systems it may be held on disk and accessible using the *man* command, so that you would type

man ls

if you wanted more information about the *ls* command.

Be warned, however: the manual is not easy reading!

The first thing to understand is that the manual is organised in a number of sections, traditionally arranged somewhat as in Table 6.1.

Table 6.1 Sections of the UNIX manual.

Section	Title
1	User commands
2	System calls
3	Subroutines
4	File formats
5	Header files
6	Games
7	Special files

Further sections are sometimes used for system administration utilities.

Each page of the manual has at the top the name of the command, subroutine, or whatever, followed by the section number in brackets. Cross-references within the documentation make use of this convention, so, for instance, *chmod(1)* means see the entry for *chmod* in section 1. Actually, as well as the command *chmod*, which you can type in at the shell prompt to change the permissions for a file, there is also a system call with the same name, for use within a program. The documentation distinguishes between the two by referring to the command as *chmod(1)* and the system call as *chmod(2)*.

As a result of the increased 'seriousness' of UNIX these days, section 6 seems to have disappeared from certain issues of the documentation. The gap between sections 5 and 7 may be explained by saying that section 6 is 'reserved for future use'!

Actually in some recent versions of the documentation, the numeric references are being replaced by abbreviations, so that *chmod(1)* becomes *chmod(BU_CMD)* for 'base user commands', and *chmod(2)* becomes *chmod(BA_OS)* for 'base operating system calls'.

Chapter 7
Disks and Files

Computer systems over the years have used all sorts of media for storing data: punched cards, paper tape, magnetic tape, even magnetic 'bubbles'. Magnetic tape still has its place, but the predominant storage medium of the 1980s (and probably the 1990s) is magnetic disk. Every UNIX system uses magnetic disk, and the way the data on the disk is structured and used is central to the working of the operating system.

Most UNIX systems these days can read and write floppy disks (diskettes) but these are for ancillary functions only; it is the hard disk that is important. Personal computers, running operating systems such as CP/M or MS-DOS, can work with floppy disks only. UNIX on the other hand requires the continuity and the capacity of a hard disk, to store not only the users' data files, but also the programs and other files that make up the operating system itself and its environment. Today the operating system itself can require quite a few megabytes — depending, of course, on how many of the vast range of UNIX utilities you consider to be part of the operating system.

Actually there is at least one example of a UNIX computer with no hard disk. The Hewlett Packard Integral PC was designed first and foremost to be portable, and to be strong enough to withstand bumps (using the standard test that you can drop it one metre onto a hard surface without damage). No sufficiently rugged hard disk was available at the time, so the machine was designed without one. The UNIX kernel and some basic utilities are held in a 512-k ROM, other utilities being loaded in from floppy disk as required, or supplied in further ROM modules. Of course the Integral is purely a single-user machine.

The UNIX file structure

The basic data structure within a disk is the file. A file could, for instance, be a batch of invoices waiting to be posted to a sales ledger, a document produced by a word processor, or the word processing program itself. All these different types of files are treated in essentially the same way by the operating system.

UNIX systems tend to have large numbers of files. This is partly because a multi-user system has a lot of different users, each of whom may wish to create files for their own data — and UNIX makes it very easy to create new files. Additionally, UNIX itself uses a lot of files for its own internal workings.

It would be very inconvenient if all the files in a UNIX system were kept in one big heap, so that when you typed *ls* you got a list running into several hundred. Also, you would be hard put to it to find names for them all. UNIX therefore divides up the filestore into a number of directories. This not only makes things more manageable for the user, it also helps in keeping one user's files separate from another's, and forms an essential part of the UNIX security system.

Standard directories

The 'root' directory typically contains a few main directories, some of which are standard on all UNIX systems. For instance in UNIX System V you will always find at least the directories listed in Table 7.1.

Table 7.1 Standard System V directories

Name	Usual contents
/bin	the executable object or 'binary' versions of the UNIX commands and utilities
/etc	special system files, and a few special-purpose programs
/usr	files belonging to users of the system
/dev	files relating to physical devices
/tmp	temporary files created by the UNIX utilities
/usr/bin	user-written programs
/usr/tmp	temporary files created by users

Each of these main directories can contain both files and further directories, and the tree can be extended as far as necessary.

Because each file is held within a directory, you do not have to struggle to think of a unique name for every file on disk. All the files in one directory must, of course, have different names, but there is no danger of a file called *letter* in your directory being confused with a file called *letter* in someone else's directory. As far as UNIX is concerned, they can be referred to uniquely by specifying a full pathname, starting from the / marking the root. Thus if two users, *fred* and *joe*, each have home directories within the *usr* main directory, and each have a file called *letters*, the full pathname would be */usr/fred/letters* and */usr/joe/letters* respectively. Directories, like ordinary files, can have the same name, provided they are not in the same parent directory, as shown by the standard scheme having /usr/bin and /usr/tmp, as well as /bin and /tmp.

Note that directories and filenames merely give a convenient way of referring to a file — but the same file can be referred to if necessary by more than one name, perhaps in quite different directories. The move (*mv*) command in UNIX allows you to change the name of a file without affecting its contents, and the link (*ln*) command allows you to create a second name for an existing file. Another useful utility is *cp* (copy), which makes a new file with a copy of the data in an existing file.

Suppose, for instance, you have a file called *data* in your home directory, and want to let a user called *mary* have it in her directory, under the name of *info*. There are three ways you could do this:

mv data . ./mary/info

The file will now be in Mary's directory, but not in your own.

ln data . ./mary/info

The file will now be in each directory; if you subsequently change *data*, the change will also affect *info*, and vice versa.

cp data . ./mary/info

Again the file will be in each directory, but this time changes to one version will have no effect on the other.

Types of data

The simplest way of holding data in a file is as plain ASCII text. If you have typed a memo using a word processing program, the memo will be held on disk as a text file, each letter or character held as one byte (eight bits) of data. So a typical book of 70,000 words (at an average of seven characters per word) will take up nearly 500,000 bytes, or half a megabyte.

If you want to store numbers rather than text, this can still be done as one character per byte. So the number 1234.45 would take up six characters, including the decimal point. Some programs work in this way, but many others store numbers in binary form, which is both more compact, and also nearer to the way in which numbers must be fed to most microprocessors for the purpose of calculation. In binary form, all whole numbers between about +32000 and −32000 can be held in the 16 bits (two bytes) which is a common size for an 'integer', particularly on 16-bit micros.

Not all numbers are conveniently held as integers. An integer by definition excludes fractions, while some numbers are so large that no integer format would be suitable. Scientists dealing with the length of a light year, which is about 9,460,000,500,000,000 metres, generally refer to this astronomical number as '9.46×10^{15}'. Similarly computers often use a 'floating point' representation, comprising a 'mantissa' (for instance, 9.46) and an 'exponent' (for instance, 10^{15}, although generally expressed as a power of 2 rather than of 10).

There is little standardisation between versions of UNIX in the sizes and formats of different types of data item. The C programming language provides several standard data types, as shown in Table 7.2.

Table 7.2 Standard UNIX/C data types.

Data type	Meaning
char	character
short	short integer
int	integer
long	long integer
unsigned	unsigned integer
float	single-precision floating point
double	double-precision floating point

Because UNIX is mainly written in C, the above can be regarded as the standard UNIX data types. However, the way they are implemented varies from one machine to another. An *int* data item, for instance, is normally the most 'natural' size for a particular machine — that is, 32 bits on a 32-bit machine, 16 bits on a 16-bit machine, and so on.

Filesystems

Many microcomputers have a single hard disk — but many have two or more, and most probably have diskettes in addition. UNIX recognises this by allowing a computer to have multiple 'filesystems'. To take a simple example, say we have a machine with one hard disk and one floppy drive. Files on the hard disk are clearly available all the time, but files on a particular diskette are only available when that diskette is inserted into the drive. UNIX needs to know which floppy disk is loaded at any particular time, and therefore which files it can use.

In such a case, it is necessary to define two filesystems, one for the hard disk, one for the diskette. The root of the directory structure must obviously be in the 'root filesystem' on the hard disk, but this part of the tree has one of its branches free for visitors. Each floppy disk has its own self-contained sub-directory tree. When a diskette is inserted in the drive, the top of its tree is fitted into the vacant node in the main tree. Usually this has to be done explicitly, using the *mount* command, but some versions of UNIX, for instance IBM's AIX, can mount a diskette automatically without being given a special command.

After mounting, the files on the diskette become part of the overall directory structure, and can be referred to by pathnames. There is no equivalent to the 'A:' prefix in MS-DOS, since UNIX maintains a single unified directory structure, and files on the diskette are treated almost exactly like files on the hard disk. There are, however, one or two fairly obvious restrictions. For example, a file must reside entirely on one filesystem; moreover, the directory that the file is in must also be in the same filesystem, so it is not possible to link or rename a file to a directory on a different filesystem.

Even if a machine has only one hard disk, it will quite probably have more than one filesystem. In this case the different filesystems correspond to different physical 'partitions' of the disk. When you buy a version of UNIX for a particular machine, you will probably find that it requires specific named filesystems, although you may be able to alter their relative sizes if necessary.

Inodes and the inode table

Each filesystem contains an area called an 'inode table'. This contains one entry or 'inode' for every file in the filesystem. If you use *ls* with the special format *ls -il*, it will display the inode number for each file along with the other directory information.

One of the important points about UNIX is its flexibility. You can very easily create new files, delete files, make existing files longer. As far as the user, or an ordinary program, is concerned, a UNIX file is a continuous stream of bytes: you can start reading it at the beginning and go right on to the end. You might think that a file is held on disk in this way, as a continuous stream of bytes, but in fact this would not be practicable. If you create a new file UNIX will put it in the first empty space it finds, which may well be just after the end of the original file. What, then, if you want to extend the original file? Obviously there is no longer any room for it to just grow longer, so the additional data will have to be put in a separate place; the file is now physically in two separate pieces. However, the system must have a means of finding the various parts of a file and linking them together, so that as far as the user is concerned it still appears as if it were all in one piece.

The linking together of the different pieces of a file is done by the inode. The smallest chunk of physical storage that can be allocated to a file is a block, typically of 512 or 1024 bytes depending on the version of UNIX. If the block size is 1024, UNIX knows that byte number 1500 is in the second block, byte number 123456 is in the 121st block, and so on. The inode includes a table indicating where the various blocks making up the file are physically located, and the system can thus find any particular byte of the file.

File operations

When you are sitting at your terminal using the shell, you can issue commands to create files, copy one file to another, rename a file, delete a file, and so on. But programs themselves need access to files, and UNIX provides a number of system calls by which a program can use procedures in the kernel to access the data on a file.

A program can have a limited number of files in use at a time — typically a maximum of twenty in earlier versions of UNIX, a hundred in later versions.

Basic file handling functions available to a program include:
- Opening a file: finding the file that corresponds to a given filename in a given directory, and then associating this file with one of the twenty (or 100) 'file descriptors' which the program is permitted, so that from then on the file can be accessed directly without going through the directory structure.
- Seeking: advancing the 'read/write pointer' through the file so that it points at a particular byte, which will then be the starting point for reading and writing.
- Reading: inputting a given number of bytes from file into memory, starting at the byte number indicated by the read/write pointer.
- Writing: outputting a number of bytes to the file: either overwriting the existing contents of the file, or making the file longer if the writing takes place after the current end of the file.
- Closing: indicating to the operating system that the file is no longer in use, and releasing the file descriptor.
- Locking: marking a given number of bytes as locked, so that no other process can access this area until the lock is released.

The full list of system calls in Appendix C includes other file functions, such as creating a new file, deleting a file, reading or writing blocks or single characters. Note, however, that we have said nothing about 'records', and nothing about using indexes or other methods to find a particular piece of data in a file. A lot of software under UNIX uses such concepts, but they are not part of the operating system. Unlike many other operating systems, UNIX as such knows nothing about any record structure within a file, and merely treats it as a series of bytes, allowing you to access any particular byte by number, and to add bytes to a file more or less indefinitely.

Executable files

Amongst the files to be found on any UNIX system are a large number of executable files — that is, files for which you see an x somewhere in the permissions field when you do an *ls -l*. Any file can, of course, be made executable in the sense of having its permission bit set. That does not mean, however, that UNIX will be able to make any sense of executing it.

Real executable files fall into two main categories — shell scripts and programs. A shell script is a text file containing a sequence of commands which are meaningful to the shell — just as you would type them at the command line. An executable program on the other hand is a more complex kind of file, containing a series of machine language instructions in binary format, arranged in a special 'object file' format so that UNIX knows how to load it into memory, how much memory space to allocate, and so on.

Program files are created by special utilities including compilers, assemblers, and link editors, generally starting with a text format 'source program' that someone has written in a language such as C, COBOL, or Fortran. Included with your UNIX system (or perhaps available as an optional extra) will be a variety of compilers and other tools for writing programs, together with 'include files' containing standard coding to be incorporated into the source code of programs, and 'libraries' of predefined subroutines to be incorporated into object files as part of the compilation process.

Finding files

I said previously that UNIX does not recognise different types of files. This is largely true, but there are some utilities that do recognise different file types to some extent. It is obviously important for the shell when executing a file to know whether it is a shell script or a compiled program, as the method of executing it will be totally different. Program files, therefore, have a standard format, including a 'magic number' which gives information to the system as to what sort of program it is. The *file* utility makes use of this and other clues to guess at the type of data that a file contains.

Another useful utility is *find*, which enables you to search the filestore for files satisfying certain criteria; for instance, all those called *tmp*, or belonging to user *fred*.

Part II
Putting UNIX to Work

Chapter 8
Personal Computing

UNIX personal computing features

It may seem strange to start a discussion of UNIX at work with personal computing – surely UNIX is a multi-user system, and most people think of personal computing in terms of a single-user machine, running MS-DOS/PC-DOS or OS/2. A large proportion of personal computer users, moreover, use a few best-selling application programs such as the Lotus 1-2-3 spreadsheet which are not available for UNIX.

The fact is, however, that UNIX has many of the features that one could look for in a personal computing system. Moreover, an understanding of the personal computing aspects of UNIX is a very good introduction to some of the more advanced aspects such as database management. Part of the beauty of UNIX for personal computing is that you can do a lot of things with just the operating system itself, and the utilities that come bundled with it, without having to buy special packages.

In this chapter, then, I propose to look at UNIX for personal computing: UNIX for Personal Computers is another subject altogether, and is covered in Chapter 22.

Calculation

The first thing that computers were designed to do was to compute – to work out the results of mathematical calculations. Several of the utilities that come with UNIX provide calculation facilities.

The *bc* command invokes a simple calculator function. You just type in expressions such as 2+2 and it tells you the answer. Note by the way that computer keyboards have no multiplication and division signs – you use * (asterisk) for multiplication, and / (oblique or slash) for division. As well as the normal arithmetic functions, *bc* provides relational operators, 'if', 'while' and 'for' conditions, trigonometric and exponential functions (*sin*, *cos*, *tan*, *log* and so on) and higher mathematical constructs such as Bessel functions.

Another way of using the mathematical capabilities of UNIX is via the *stat* package of statistical and graphical commands, discussed in Chapter 13. Integrated packages such as Q-Office and Uniplex II Plus also provide calculators, while if you decide to write a program in C or FORTRAN there is a very wide range of mathematical functions available.

Lists and card indexes

One of the most common uses of a personal system is to keep lists of all kinds — simple databases if you like, but the word 'database' is best reserved for more complex systems, as covered in Chapters 11 and 12. UNIX is good at creating simple lists: you can regard them just as text files, and there are plenty of utilities that deal with text.

As a concrete example, let us take a list of people with their telephone numbers or extensions: a common requirement in business, or in the home for that matter. You could have a file on your computer (let's call it *namelist*) with the following contents:

    Jones Alan Accounts 231
    Wilson Mary Personnel 148
    Smith John Accounts 201
    Fortescue Jane Sales 153

This is just an ordinary text file that you might create with a text editor or a word processor. You could even create it using the *cat* command, but then you would need a different program to edit it subsequently.

Each line in the file has a common format: surname, first name, department, telephone extension, the various words separated by spaces, just as in normal English text. Note that the lines, and the words or fields within them, are variable in length. In UNIX as such there is no need to have fixed length fields padded out with blanks or zeros, although many packages do require this.

With some operating systems you would need to buy a package, or write a program, in order to be able to do anything at all with your list of names. In UNIX the standard utilities will do a lot of the work.

For a start, you might decide that you want the list in alphabetical order. This is easy to arrange:

    sort namelist

This command will sort the file according to the first word in each line (in this case the surname), and put the result on the standard output, in other words display it on the screen. Alternatively you might decide to keep the sorted version, perhaps putting it in a new file called *slist*:

sort namelist > slist

Perhaps you tend to think of people by their first name, so that this would be a better sequence for the file. So you would type:

sort +1 namelist > slist

This will ignore the first field in each line when doing the sort, and thus sort on the second field.

So far the commands have dealt with the file as a whole, but the point of a telephone list is to find the number for a particular person. The *grep* command (never mind its name for the moment) is useful here. You could type for instance:

grep Jane namelist

This will display on the screen any lines of the file which contain 'Jane'.

Like most other utilities, *grep* has various options. For instance:

grep -i jane namelist

will ignore distinctions between upper and lower case so, for example, it will find 'Jane', 'jane', 'JANE', and so on.

Another thing you might want to do with your file is to produce a version without the department name. To do this, you use the *cut* command:

cut -f1,2,4, -d " " namelist > newlist

This is getting more complicated, but it is reasonably straightforward once you analyse what is going in. It just means that you want to retain fields 1,2, and 4 of each line, and that the space character (" ") is what you use as the delimiter (*-d*) to mark where the various fields start and finish.

Regular expressions

The command *grep* that I described just now is actually much more powerful than the simple examples I gave might suggest. It owes its power to the UNIX concept of 'regular expressions' – in fact, the name *grep* stands for 'global regular expression print'. A 'regular expression' is one of those phrases that can totally confuse you until you realise that in UNIX it has a very specific meaning. Basically, a regular expression in UNIX is a way of specifying a pattern that you are looking for in a text file. An example of a regular expression would be

    ^.ow

which you would use if you were looking for lines of text whose first word was 'how', 'now', or any character followed by 'ow'.

Regular expressions crop up in a number of UNIX utilities, and there are special library routines, so that if you are writing your own programs they can follow the same rules.

Within a regular expression certain characters have special meanings. Some of them are rather like the 'wildcard' characters that you can use in specifying filenames to the shell, although the rules are somewhat different. The special characters are given in Table 8.1.

Table 8.1 Characters used in regular expressions.

Character	Meaning
.	The full stop matches any single character (except a newline).
*	The asterisk matches any number of occurrences of the preceding expression.
[]	If you put a string of characters in square brackets, this is equivalent to matching on any one of the characters. For instance, [abc] would give a match on any of the letters a b or c. You can also specify ranges, e.g. [a-z] would match on any of the lower case letters.
^	The circumflex means that the match should only occur at the start of a line. A circumflex as the first character inside square brackets has a special meaning – it reverses the matching against the other characters in the brackets. [^A-C], for example, matches any character *except* A to C.
$	A dollar sign means that the match should occur at the end of a line.
+	A plus sign means match at least one occurrence of the previous character.
?	A question mark means match zero or one occurrence.
|	The vertical bar is used to separate alternatives.
{ }	A pair of numbers in curly brackets indicate a match on the previous character occurring a specified maximum and minimum number of times. For instance, A{2,3} matches two or three letter As.

There are, in fact, some differences between the way different programs use regular expressions. In particular, the vertical bar (used when you want to search for one combination *or* another) and the + and ? symbols, are only used in 'extended regular expressions'. These are not recognised by *grep*, but they are by the related program *egrep*.

It seems likely that *grep* will be extended in due course to include the additional functions, since there is no real justification for the existence of two such closely related programs.

More on text manipulation

We have not by any means exhausted the facilities of UNIX when it comes to text manipulation. If you have a text document — perhaps a letter or a report — the following are just a few of the things that you can do with it, using commands that come as standard with UNIX.

wc textfile

This will do a word count on the file — very useful for authors. In fact it will tell you the number of lines, words, and characters.

head textfile

This command (not available on certain UNIX systems) will print out the first few lines of the file — useful if you're not sure whether it's the file you're looking for. Similarly

tail textfile

will print out the end of the file.
Another useful command is

spell textfile

This will check the spelling of the file, and display on the screen any words it doesn't recognise from its own dictionary.

Again, as with databases, there are special packages available for word processing and office automation, which go much further than the UNIX utilities, and are suitable for typists and others with no computer knowledge at all. But the UNIX utilities cost nothing (that is, they are normally included in the price of UNIX) and they are useful in very many cases, if you just take a little trouble to learn how to use them.

UNIX is thus useful because of the variety of standard commands and utilities. It is made still more useful by the ability to join these commands together in 'shell scripts', as discussed in Chapter 19.

Spreadsheeting

The spreadsheet is one of the most important applications which go to make up personal computing, although perhaps less so on UNIX than on true personal computer systems.

Like so many good ideas that have made fortunes for their inventors, the electronic spreadsheet is brilliantly simple in concept. Accountants and others have long used paper spreadsheets — large sheets of paper ruled into rows and columns — to give a rectangular array of cells. Each cell can contain a number, representing, say, the sales in a given area for a particular month. Certain cells are special, and contain totals; those along the right hand side might be the totals by month, those along the bottom totals by area, with a grand total in the bottom righthand corner.

Working on paper, you enter the various sales figures in the appropriate places. When they are all entered, you can calculate the various row and column totals. If one of the figures subsequently changes, you will have to change the totals for both the row and the column in which that cell is located.

The electronic spreadsheet similarly has rows, columns, and cells, in which you can put sales figures or indeed any other information. The spreadsheet as a whole is much bigger than could be shown on a vdu screen, so that at any one time you only see a portion of it.

The advantage of the electronic spreadsheet over the paper version is simple: as soon as you enter a value in a cell, or alter the value that was there previously, the row and column totals are automatically recalculated.

Advantages of the electronic spreadsheet

In fact, the spreadsheet is much more flexible and powerful than this example would suggest. In each cell you can enter a number, or alphabetic characters to be used as a label, or a formula, for instance to calculate a total. The totals do not need to be in any particular place, and as well as totals you can have percentages, averages, and indeed anything that can be calculated by arithmetic, based on the contents of cells elsewhere in the spreadsheet.

Spreadsheets are often used on an *ad hoc* basis, when you have a lot of figures that you want to manipulate. But a still more useful approach is to set up a standard matrix of cells, with headings and calculations related to your own requirements: for example, you might have standard column headings for each of the company's branch offices, and standard positions for inserting the current interest rate and so on. Such a matrix then comprises a 'model' of some aspect of the organisation's business, and you can use it again and again, entering new figures as they arise each month, but obtaining totals and percentages that are comparable with the month before.

Another very common use of spreadsheets is for 'what-if' modelling:

one or two values can be altered and the effect will ripple through the model. In this way you can explore the effects of price increases, interest rate changes, various possible levels of sales, and so on, and very quickly see what effect they would have on turnover or profits.

The best known spreadsheet at present is Lotus 1-2-3. It was specifically designed for the IBM PC, and is not yet available on UNIX, because it relies very heavily on specific features of the PC hardware. Nonetheless, it has become the 'industry standard' spreadsheet, and its influence has been considerable. A number of very similar products have appeared. In particular, the Santa Cruz Operation (SCO) have released a package called SCO Professional, which looks exactly like 1-2-3 but is a multi-user package running under XENIX.

Programming a spreadsheet

Some spreadsheets provide a programming facility so that you can set up command files − lists of instructions to perform a simple task such as generating invoices, calculating the total from unit prices and quantities, sub-totals, and VAT.

It is important, however, to remember that most spreadsheets do not segregate the data from the program. If you get your cell addresses wrong, you can easily end up overwriting the program by mistake. Care is needed as to where programs are positioned so as not to interfere with data.

All packages that are any good tend to provoke enthusiasm in those who use them. Unfortunately this sometimes leads to a package being used for a purpose for which it is not really suitable. With spreadsheets in particular there is a great danger of getting totally the wrong answers, not because the spreadsheet program itself has made a mistake, but because you have forgotten which cells contain formulae rather than data, which cells are used by which other cells, and so on. Spreadsheets are a *personal computing* application: it is a mistake to use a spreadsheet where a properly designed departmental or company system − say, an accounting system − is really required.

Spreadsheets for UNIX

For a long time, the only spreadsheets available for UNIX were versions of PC or CP/M products, of which Multiplan was perhaps the most widely used. More recently, however, a number of spreadsheets, such as Ultracalc, have been written specifically for UNIX and can, for example, make use of the larger memory that UNIX machines usually have available. Another example is the spreadsheet that comes with the Uniplex II+ integrated package.

In many spreadsheets, the columns are lettered and the rows are numbered, so that the cell in the second column from the left and the third row from the top would be called B3. In Uniplex on the other hand both the rows and the columns are numbered. The same cell in Uniplex would thus be referred to as R3C2. Additionally you can define ranges, blocks, and windows.

You can include graphics in the spreadsheet itself (character graphics that is, using the standard character set) and there is a menu to help you with this.

Formulae can be entered starting with the = sign. If you want to include specific cells within a formula, you can use the cursor control keys to point to the cell in question, and then the @ sign to identify it.

More spreadsheet packages will no doubt appear for UNIX, taking advantage of the larger memory and the processing power of UNIX-based computers. But a spreadsheet is still primarily an application most suited to single-user machines. A combination that should provide the best of both worlds is a database on the UNIX host linked to a spreadsheet on the PC. The Oracle database manager provides such a combination, allowing you to use a Lotus 1-2-3 compatible spreadsheet, in which additional commands can be used to emit SQL statements, so that the appropriate cells of the worksheet can be filled directly from the database.

UNIX as a home computer system

All the useful features of UNIX should make it very attractive for the home user, who wants something a bit more powerful than the standard home machines. There is one main factor that has been stopping UNIX catching on as a home computer system, and that is price. Domestic users have been limited to 8-bit computers, often with cassette tape, or floppy disk as a luxury item. A substantial memory (in the megabyte range) or a hard disk have been beyond most home users' aspirations. But times are changing. While this book was being written there were announcements for the first time of IBM-compatible personal computers under £500, and hard disk machines under £1,000.

UNIX itself is also not cheap, but again the price is dropping. Full UNIX systems (the software, that is) are now coming onto the market for under £300, and the price could drop still further. For a software supplier the marginal production cost of a UNIX system — what it actually costs him to produce — is now down to three elements: the licence to AT&T; the cost of the floppy disks and the effort of copying the software onto them; and the cost of the documentation.

Educational use of UNIX

UNIX has long had pride of place in university departments, either for teaching students the concepts of computer science, or for practical uses of one sort or another. AT&T have certainly encouraged the use of UNIX in this way, and have provided source licences on very favourable terms for educational establishments. UNIX itself has also been used as an object of study in computer science courses, although more recently AT&T have become more possessive about their source code, and prohibited its use in the classroom for undergraduate courses.

Why is UNIX regarded as a good vehicle for teaching people about computers? One answer is that the design of UNIX and the structure of the C programming language agree with a number of fundamental principles of good programming practice.

Many people try to teach themselves programming with BASIC, just because it happens to be the most common language on domestic micros. But BASIC, although specifically designed for beginners, is actually very unsuitable for this purpose; it tends to encourage a very poor programming style, so that the programs when written are difficult to debug and impossible to maintain. For educational use, UNIX scores because of the simplicity and elegance of its design, and the enormous range of commands it offers and the exceptional ease of combining them together. Most operating systems impose more or less arbitrary constraints on the user, but in UNIX it is nearly always possible to do what you want, provided you give it sufficient thought. So for the student interested in finding out what can be done with computers, rather than studying the limitations imposed by more primitive systems, UNIX is an excellent starting point.

Chapter 9
Text Processing and Word Processing

Text processing was one of the very first things that UNIX was designed to do — and today a very wide range of text processing aids is available. These vary a great deal in quality, and even more in ease of use.

There is a big gap between the utilities that come as standard with most versions of UNIX, and the packages that you need to buy separately. Perhaps the easiest way to summarise this is that the UNIX utilities provide text processing; they do not provide word processing. In a sense, of course, the two concepts are the same. The difference lies very much in the type of person who will use them: word processing is suitable for a typist; text processing is mainly suited for the programmer.

Text processors and word processors

One of the most widely used UNIX utilities today must be *vi*, the 'visual editor'. *Vi* was originated by the University of California at Berkeley, but it has found its way into practically every commercial version of UNIX, and is now part of official UNIX System V.

Vi is a full screen editor — that is, it uses the full area of the vdu screen to show as much of the file being edited as it can; your current position in the file is shown by a cursor, which you can move up and down and left and right.

Perhaps the biggest difference between an editor such as *vi* and a word processor is in its treatment of text files. *Vi* is typically used for special types of document, such as programs, shell scripts, and the various special-purpose text files that are so often used in a UNIX system (the password file is an example). Many of these files are structured in terms of lines. A new line in a shell script (generally speaking) means a new command; the newline character is very significant.

In a word processing document on the other hand, the important elements are the word and the paragraph. The end of a line is a mere accident imposed by the format of the page; you can normally reformat a document into new margins, and the line lengths will adjust themselves automatically. A word processing document in fact needs to cater for both 'hard' and 'soft' carriage returns. A 'hard' carriage return is one you deliberately insert at the end of a paragraph; a 'soft' carriage return is one that appears when the document is displayed or printed, but will move of its own accord if the page is reformatted.

A true word processor thus treats the text as a continuous stream of words rather than a series of lines. It is one of the basic principles of word processing that the division between one line and the next is fluid, and can change as you insert or delete words.

Editing with *vi*

An editor such as *vi* knows nothing of 'soft' carriage returns − all newlines are definitely hard. In fact when you are keying text in, you have the option of two different modes. The default mode is no word wrap: whatever you type will be treated as a single line until you actually hit the Return key, or until you exceed the maximum permitted number of characters in a line. On the screen it may look as if it is broken up into several lines, but this is purely a screen convention and takes no notice of spaces between words. If you use the cursor control keys to move up and down, you will soon see what *vi* thinks are the lines.

The other editing mode with *vi* uses word wrap. You specify a 'wrap margin', so many characters from the right hand end of the line. If a space between words falls within this area, *vi* converts it to a newline character. In this way you can ensure that your lines do not exceed a specified length, and that each line starts with a new word.

A word processor generally works the other way round: it waits until you have typed a word which would extend beyond the end of the line, and then moves it bodily to the next line.

Another way that *vi* differs from a word processor is that it operates in several different 'modes', and it is very necessary to be aware which mode you are in at a particular time. With most word processors, once you have got some text displayed on the screen, you can just start typing, and what you type will go into the file. In *vi*, on the other hand, when the program starts up you are in 'command mode', and need to issue a special command − such as *i* to insert, or *a* to add − before you can start typing in earnest. Similarly, when you want to move about the document, you need to go out of command mode, by pressing Escape, and you can then use one-letter commands such as *h* to go left, *j* to go down, *k* to go up, and *l* to go right. While in command mode you also have other options, such as *x* to delete a character, and combinations such as *2dw* to delete the next two words.

Vi offers yet another mode: if you are in command mode and type a colon, the cursor jumps to a special line at the bottom of the screen, and you can then use a large number of further commands.

Other editors

Vi is not the only editor with UNIX. In fact the most universal is a comparatively simple utility called *ed*. *Ed*, like UNIX itself, was originally designed for non-screen terminals, and is a line editor rather than a screen editor. In other words it assumes that your terminal has no means of moving a cursor up and down a screenful of text. You specify the line you want to edit (by line number or by contents) and then the change you want to make.

Ed became the basis of more sophisticated versions such as *ex*, and *ex* itself is part of *vi*; in fact the special colon commands in *vi* are all *ex* commands. If you want to understand *vi* thoroughly, it helps to have some familiarity with one or other of the line editors.

Sed is another type of editor — a 'stream editor'. *Ed*, *vi*, and *ex* all work on the basis of a complete file, which is loaded into memory, and written back to disk when you have finished editing. Clearly this will not be practicable if the file is very large (although this is less of a restriction on versions of UNIX supporting demand paging). The *sed* utility does not hold the file in memory, but reads it in a line at a time, edits each line according to the commands you have specified, and writes the edited version to its standard output.

Other text processing aids

I have already looked briefly at some other commands for manipulating text, including *wc* (word count), *sort*, *cut*, *head*, and *spell*, and the *grep* command, which scans a text file looking for particular combinations of characters, and tells you if it finds them. The *awk* program (named after the initials of its three authors) is a much more sophisticated version of the same thing. Whereas *grep* merely applies a single test to a file, *awk* provides you with an entire scanning and processing language, so that you can not only search the file, but produce reports detailing its characteristics.

Some other text processing commands, supplied in various UNIX systems, include:

- *col* (filter reverse linefeeds);
- *csplit* (split a file into chunks by context);
- *diction* (check for bad or wordy diction);
- *diffmk* (mark differences between files);
- *explain* (correct bad diction);
- *hyphen* (find hyphenated words);
- *paste* (merge lines of files);
- *split* (split a file into chunks of a given number of lines);
- *style* (analyse document for readability).

Word processing

Word processing is one of the commonest uses of computers today. UNIX itself was originally put to use in what we would now call a word processing application (producing patent applications for Bell Labs) although the facilities provided had much more in common with text editing than with word processing in the modern sense. Today word processing is most often done on single-user personal computers, which are really more suitable than a multi-user computer for this purpose. However, it is sometimes more convenient to do word processing on a UNIX system, particularly when the documents being produced are linked in some way to centralised applications and databases.

A word processing package — Uniplex

Uniplex, supplied by the British firm Redwood, is a full word processing package.

On loading the word processor, you are first of all presented with a menu containing various options. If you choose to create a new file it initially has no name — you are asked to give one when you come to save it later. If you decide to edit an existing file, Uniplex first of all makes a backup copy of the original, which you can recover if you make a mess of the editing session.

When you have selected the 'new file' option, you find a text area open on your screen, with a 'ruler' at the top (in other words a line showing the position of the left and right margins, and the tab settings) and a line at the bottom showing the use of various function keys. Uniplex, like many other packages, assumes that you have a terminal with a number of special keys marked F1 and so on — up to F8 in this case — but, if necessary, other combinations of keys can be used instead.

In all word processing systems, the use of the keyboard is an important aspect. UNIX-based systems, having to cope with a large number of different makes of terminal, present a particular problem in this respect; programs cannot assume that there is a 'PageUp' or 'Insert' key, as some keyboards may have them, others not.

There is probably no way of using the keyboard that will please all users. For instance, a typist will normally want to access the more common editing functions very quickly, with just one or two keystrokes, and preferably without taking her hands away from the standard typing position. For the causal user, however, speed is not so important as ease of use, and it has to be obvious how to use each function; failing that, the package should provide very good help facilities.

In Uniplex, you can get help by pressing Esc and then h, which takes you into a hierarchy of help menus, showing you the various combinations that you can use.

Commands in Uniplex

Uniplex provides two main ways of calling up special functions. One is by pressing Esc followed by one or sometimes two other keys; the other is by holding down Ctrl and pressing another key.

The combination Esc f allows you to search your text for a particular word or pattern. Esc F is the same thing but searches backwards. Similarly you have Esc g to search for a string and replace it − either globally (all occurrences) or interactively (prompting you wherever it occurs).

You can insert rulers at various points in the text where the format has to be changed − for instance, you might want a particular paragraph indented to show that it is a quotation. A ruler can be edited in the same way as actual text. Special symbols are used within a ruler, for example: I (indent setting), H (outdent), L (left margin) R (ragged right margin), J (justified right margin), T (tab stop), # (decimal tab stop), C ('centre' of line, for centred headings).

When you have finished typing, you normally want to save the file to disk. You do this using the standard Uniplex 'accept' command − that is, Esc E. Alternatively you may decide to abandon the file; in this case you hit Esc Q (for quit). To make sure you don't do this by mistake and lose all the work you have done, Uniplex asks you to confirm a quit command, by typing an asterisk. This in itself is a two-finger job (the asterisk is a shifted character on most keyboards) so there should be little danger of abandoning your work without meaning to.

Uniplex, like various other word processors, uses 'dot commands' to control the way the text gets printed out. A dot command is a special line of text starting with a full stop, which does not get printed out itself, but gives instructions to the program controlling the printing. The list of Uniplex dot commands in Table 9.1 will give a good idea of the facilities that the package offers.

Table 9.1 Uniplex dot commands.

Command	Meaning
.PA	start new page
.PMn	conditional page break
.PLn	set page length to n lines
.HEn	the next n lines are a header, to be printed at the top of every page
.HMn	the text should start n lines following the header
.FOn	the next n lines are a footer, to be printed at the bottom of every page
.FMn	the text should stop n lines before the footer
.PNn	start page numbering with this page as page n
.SPn	leave $n-1$ spaces between lines
.JN	do not reformat subsequent text
.JY	resume reformatting
.RE	remarks – in other words this line is just comments, not to be printed
.ME	merge in a specified file at this point
.SN	send a special code to the printer
.ST	send a code to the printer, at the top of the page
.SB	send a code to the printer, at the bottom of the page
.FS	start of footnote
.FE	end of footnote.

Uniplex also has a spelling checker. Unlike the standard UNIX *spell* utility, which merely reads through your file and lists the apparently misspelled words, Uniplex checks your file interactively – it stops on each misspelling and offers you a number of possible corrections; if none of these is the correct word, you can type in what it ought to be.

'Folios' are a distinctive feature of Uniplex files; they are a special area at the beginning of the document, separate from the text itself, and used to record information about the document, such as who wrote it, its subject matter, and so on. Uniplex lets you search for a particular document on the basis of its folio entries.

Mail merge in Uniplex

The mail merge feature of Uniplex is quite extensive, and enables you to send standard letters to large numbers of recipients, varying the name and address but keeping the text the same. A special record file needs to be set up using the word processor, with one page per person and one line per field, such as name, address, and so on.

You type your standard letter including a series of special dot commands, each defining the name of a field, for instance *.Vname*, *.Vaddress*. These must be in the same order as the corresponding fields on the record file. In the text of the letter you can include the fields as required, but begin each with an underscore character, for instance:

Dear _name,

When you come to print the letters, Uniplex will fill in the correct name and other details for each person from the record file. Various options are available. For example, the text can be moved up to accommodate names of different lengths without leaving gaps, and blank lines can be suppressed.

There is also an interactive mail merge facility. In this case the top half of the screen prompts you for the name and address, and you can see the letter being generated in the bottom half.

Nroff and troff

The *nroff* program was much used at one time for producing formatted output to printers. *Troff* is essentially the same as *nroff*, but designed for outputting to photo-typesetters. Both are part of the UNIX heritage, but are not included within standard versions of UNIX such as the SVID, and in any case have been overtaken by the advance of word processors on the one hand, and desktop publishing systems on the other.

To prepare a text file for *nroff*, you include dot commands within it, rather in the same way as in Uniplex. However, the actual dot commands available are quite different. Table 9.2 gives a selection.

Using *nroff*, you can reformat paragraphs, and adjust the length of lines, just as you could in a word processor. The difference is that in a word processor this happens interactively, before your very eyes — to use the jargon, a word processor is often WYSIWYG (what you see is what you get). With *nroff*, on the other hand, you include the formatting directives in the input file, and they take effect on the output file; only by running the file through the *nroff* program and examining the output can you see what effect it has had.

Table 9.2 Selected *nroff* dot commands.

Command	Meaning
.ll *n*	line length
.pl *n*	page length
.po *n*	page offset
.ad l	adjust left (left justification, ragged right)
.ad r	adjust right (right justification, ragged left)
.ad c	adjust centre (centre the text between margins)
.ad b	adjust both (full justification)
.sp *n*	leave *n* blank lines
.ce *n*	centre the next *n* lines
.ne *n*	keep the next *n* lines together on the same page
.ul	underline alphanumeric characters
.cu	underline all characters, including spaces
.bp	page break
.tl	title line (header)
.in *n*	indent text *n* characters from here on
.ti *n*	indent the next line only
.so *file*	incorporate the named file into the output at this point

Much of the usefulness of *nroff* lies in the ability it provides to define 'macros'. For instance, you could define a standard paragraph macro as follows:

.de PG
.sp
.ne 3
.in 0
.ti 5
..

The .*de* of course marks the start of the macro definition, and the .. marks its end. Having thus defined the *PG* macro, you now type

.PG

on a line by itself, wherever you want a new paragraph to start, and this will ensure that the paragraph spacing and indentation are consistent throughout the document.

A number of macro packages are available, including commonly used formatting definitions. The *mm* (memorandum macro) package is the most common of these, and covers far more types of text than just memoranda. *Mm* is easier to use than straight *troff* or *nroff*, but is still not exactly user-friendly. However, it does have the great advantage that you can use it to ensure that all reports and documents produced within your organisation are consistent in terms of typing and layout. It is particularly useful for documents with several levels of headings, for instance 1, 2 for chapters, 1.1, 1.2 for sections, and so on, as it will assign the numbers automatically and even generate a table of contents. Like much of UNIX, *mm* was originally developed for internal use within AT&T; if you fail to supply a value for the 'company name' variable, *mm* will often supply the default, and your document will be printed with 'Bell Laboratories' on the title page!

A more specialised use of macros is the *man* utility, which prints out the standard UNIX manual, either on a printer, or at your terminal.

A number of additional utility programs have been written to work with *nroff* and *troff*, including the following:

- *cw* (prepare constant width text)
- *deroff* (remove special characters and formatting instructions)
- *eqn* (format mathematical text)
- *mmcheck* (check usage of *mm* macros)
- *mmt* (typeset documents using the *mm* macros — equivalent to *troff -mm*)
- *prep* (prepare text for statistical formatting)
- *soelim* (copy included files within a text file, thus eliminating the *.so* directive)
- *tbl* (format tables).

Chapter 10
UNIX and Office Automation

Much has been said and written in recent years about office automation, and yet it seems at times that very little has really happened. Part of the reason is that there is a great deal of scepticism about office automation amongst those who might most benefit from it.

A number of the main elements of office automation — word processing, for example — are really most suited to personal computers or individual workstations. On the other hand, features such as electronic mail or centralised filing require the existence of a central computer or file server. The best type of system to support office automation in all its forms is therefore a combination of two elements: a central or departmental machine, running UNIX, and a workstation for each user.

Where a UNIX system has been installed, it is very easy to provide the basics of office automation. In fact, office automation on UNIX systems really encompasses two distinct classes of program — the standard UNIX facilities such as *mail* and *calendar*, and the packages such as Uniplex and Q-Office.

Mail

Electronic mail exists today in a variety of forms. Basically there is a distinction to be made between two ways of using electronic mail: as a replacement for the ordinary mail or telex, to communicate with other companies or private individuals; or as a substitute for internal memoranda within a company. UNIX, in different ways, can give you access to both of these, but the internal memorandum type is obviously the easiest to accomplish; this is the province of the *mail* program which has long been part of standard UNIX.

Mail often makes itself known as soon as you log in, by displaying the message

you have mail

If you see this message, all you need to do is to type

mail

The system will then show you the waiting message, also who it is from, and when it was sent. If you have been sent more than one message, it will show them one at a time, with a prompt (a question mark) asking you if you want to see the next one. When reading your mail you have various options, such as to go backwards and forwards through the stack of messages, to delete a message, to save it in a file of your own, or to forward it to another user. It is also possible to set up your mailbox in such a way that all your messages are automatically redirected to someone else.

Sending mail

Sending a message is easy provided you know the user name (login name) of the person you want to send to. If his login name is *fred*, for instance, you just type in

mail fred

Whatever you type from now until you hit Ctrl-D will become a message to *fred*, and will be stored in his mailbox for him to look at later. Of course you can also use *mail* to send a file that already exists; you do this by redirection in the usual way, for instance:

mail fred < message2

You can also use *mail* to send messages to yourself. This is more useful than it sounds: you can use it as a memo facility, which will remind you to do something the next time you log in.

The *mail* package thus provides all the basic facilities that you might want for sending and receiving mail. The only problem perhaps lies in the user interface. In common with quite a lot of UNIX facilities, *mail* assumes that you know how to use it — the prompt it displays is just '?', which does not give much guidance as to what you should do next. But given the structure of UNIX, it is not difficult to build a more user-friendly package around it, which is exactly what has been done in several of the commercial office automation systems.

Mail is also used by other UNIX facilities. For instance, the spooler can use *mail* to tell you that your printing is completed, and the *calendar* program sends you a message via *mail* to tell you that there are some appointments in your diary.

In more recent versions of UNIX there is a much enhanced version called *mailx*, with a large number of options.

Write

Mail, as we have seen, provides a non-interactive mode of communication: you send the message when you feel like it, and the recipient looks at it when he or she is ready. However, UNIX also provides a form of interactive communication: if the person you want to communicate with is currently logged on to the system, you can communicate with him or her immediately, using the *write* command. The syntax is simple:

write fred

followed by the message, a line at a time.

To receive a message in this way, you do not need to do anything at all: it will simply appear uninvited on your screen. However, if you are doing something important and do not wish to be disturbed, you can type

mesg n

which will stop anyone from sending messages to your screen. To allow messages again, type

mesg y

If you receive a message, you may well decide to use *write* to hold a two-way conversation. This can pose practical difficulties. In particular, nothing you type will appear on the other person's screen until you hit Return; so if you spend too long typing a line, he may think you have gone silent, and start typing in another message, which will then get mixed up with yours to him. AT&T recommend that you keep your message lines short, and use a convention such as 'o' for 'over' and 'oo' for 'over and out', to avoid the electronic equivalent of two people talking at once. Of course UNIX itself will not mind you both talking at once: it perfectly well knows what messages are being sent in which direction; it is the users who may get confused.

Cal and calendar

The *cal* program displays a calendar on your screen, for the month or year you specify, so that you can plan your schedule for the year, or work out how many Fridays there are in each month, or what day of the week Christmas falls on next year. When you invoke *cal* you must tell it the month and year to display, for instance

cal 12 1987

Notice that '1987' has to be in full — just '87' would of course give you the year 87 AD.

The calendar used is that appropriate to Great Britain and its colonies. At present, of course, Great Britain uses the same calendar as most other countries, but this was not always the case. If you know a little history you may recall the changeover from Julian to Gregorian, and the riots this provoked when people thought they had lost eleven days of their lives. If you type

cal 9 1752

you will see what the fuss was about.

Not to be confused with *cal* is the *calendar* program, used to look up your appointments diary. It makes use of a file (also called *calendar*) which it expects to find in the current directory. This should be a text file, containing one line for each appointment, each line to include a date in a recognisable format. Unfortunately for British users, the date formats recognised all use the illogical American arrangement, like several other UNIX utilities, so that 'June 29' is recognised, but '29 June' is not. The *calendar* program scans through the file, looks for lines with today's or tomorrow's date, and displays them on the screen. At weekends, 'tomorrow' extends through to Monday.

Building on a word processor — Uniplex II Plus

One starting point for office automation is the word processor. And one of the most popular integrated packages for UNIX systems is Uniplex II Plus, an extension of the Uniplex word processing system.

When you start Uniplex II Plus, you are presented with a much expanded set of options on the menu screen. In addition to the basic word processing functions, there are also two database options (Forms and Query) a spreadsheet, and some desktop utilities.

The various modules are largely self-contained — the database functions, for instance, are originally a separate package — in fact, a version of Informix SQL. But the component parts are made into a coherent whole by the consistent user interface — Esc H provides a help screen, Esc E marks the end of input, and Esc Q means quit, in all the modules. Moreover, you always have the 'desk utilities' available, one of which, called 'integration', allows you to move data between one application and another.

The essence of the 'integration' facility is that it allows you to deal easily with interruptions — you can break off in the middle of editing a document on the word processor, and start editing or viewing another document, or indeed using a spreadsheet or a database. Each new application that you run becomes a new window opened up on the screen. Moreover you can use the 'cut and paste' facilities to move data from one window into a scratchpad area, and from there into another window.

Other options from the 'desk utilities' menu allow you to call a simple desk calculator, or the calendar for the current month. Both of these appear in windows at the bottom of the screen, and remain active until you quit from them with Esc Q.

There is also a 'clipboard' which you can use for odd notes, and even a 'decision maker' which supplies at random answers such as yes, no, and maybe, while you think of a question.

Uniplex diary

The Uniplex diary facility gives you access to your own diary of appointments, and to other people's diaries if they permit you to see them.

To put events in your diary you key in the start time, end time, and a summary description of the event, using the standard Uniplex editing commands. The program will warn you if you schedule events which clash. If you wish, you can have two versions of the description of the event, one available to your colleagues, the other private, so that if you are having meetings with another company prior to a takeover bid, you can keep the details of who you are meeting with secret, and let your staff see just an innocuous description like 'progress meeting'.

To remind yourself of the meeting, you can get Uniplex to bleep at you using the loudspeaker on your terminal, or display a warning message, to be repeated if you log in shortly before the meeting is due to start.

The diary can be displayed in any of three display formats (weekly, fortnightly, and monthly), or you can get a printed list of forthcoming events.

If you use the diary program without telling the system otherwise, it will refer to your individual diary. But you can also create and maintain diaries for other people, or for inanimate resources such as conference rooms.

An extension of the diary facility is time scheduling, useful when you are trying to arrange a meeting with a number of people. You specify the earliest and latest dates when the meeting can take place, and the names of the people who need to attend. The program then searches each of their diaries, until it finds a time when they are all free, and at that point it schedules the meeting, and puts an entry in each person's diary.

Mail in Uniplex

The Uniplex II+ mail program starts from the same sort of functions as the standard UNIX version, but builds a set of menus on top, so that the whole thing is much easier for the casual user to understand. When you start writing a message, a heading is created, with spaces for you to insert the name of the recipient, the subject, and so on. It automatically provides a reference, and indicates who the message is from. You can send complimentary copies to other people, and you can 'attach' other documents.

The system bleeps you at your terminal whenever someone sends you mail (or the next time you log in). You then have various options as to what to do with the message, including PRINT (display on the screen), SAVE, REPLY, FORWARD, ARCHIVE, NEXT, and LAST.

Uniplex database functions

The two database options in Uniplex II Plus provide the same functions, but accessed in two very different ways. Database Forms uses a formatted screen display for the input of data into the database; you can use the same forms to enquire of the database, or use 'cut and paste' to transfer data to a spreadsheet or word processing document. Database Query on the other hand uses the language-type approach of SQL, as discussed in the next chapter. The two ways of accessing the data together constitute a tool that the non-specialist user can use effectively, while the professional user can manipulate it to create an entire system.

The real benefit of using Uniplex comes when you need close integration between database management and office automation facilities. For example, an import/export firm might need to maintain a database of contracts, and use this data for advanced word processing purposes, to create invoices, bills of lading, certificates of origin, and other specialised documents, with the wording adjusted to the particular circumstances.

Another office automation package — Q-Office

The Q-Office package, from Quadratron, is at the time of writing the main rival to Uniplex. Like Uniplex, it is essentially based round a word processor, in this case called Q-One.

When you enter Q-Office, you are shown an opening screen containing a calendar for the month, and also a menu with the following options:

Word processing
Notepad
Calendar
Phonebook
System utilities
Telex
Spreadsheet
Message
Mail
Forms management
Calculator
Menu processor
File retrieval

You can move around the menu using cursor control keys or by typing the initial letter of a command. When the cursor is on the required option, you select it by means of the Execute key.

Probably, by the way, your keyboard has not got an Execute key. Q-Office is one of that strange breed of software that refers on the screen to totally fictitious keys such as Execute, Cancel, Copy, Help, and Move. You are supposed to mentally convert Cancel to Del, Copy to 6 on the numeric pad, and so on, or else have a 'template' (probably a scruffy piece of paper) stuck to your keyboard to remind you. The origin of this practice is that the software has been modelled on defunct or obsolescent word processing machines which actually had such keys, but I am always amazed that software houses should think that this is a satisfactory solution.

Having said this, I must admit that Q-Office is an impressive set of programs. And for the skilled typist who has learnt what keys to press, it avoids the multiple key depressions of Uniplex.

Chapter 11
Database Management

One of the most important uses for UNIX systems is database management, that is, the storage of large volumes of data, with the ability to convert it into useful information.

Data and information

The simplest definition of information is 'useful data'. The difference between data, or inert facts, and information, or facts that satisfy a requirement, is not in the data itself; it is in the question that is asked.

For example, a telephone directory contains millions of items of data in the form of names, addresses and telephone numbers. This data does not become information until you ask a question, such as what is the telephone number of such and such a company. In providing the answer to the question, the inert data becomes information. But look what happens if you have a telephone number and want to find out the name and address it belongs to: the data certainly is contained in the telephone directory but it is almost impossible to obtain the information because of the way in which the data is arranged.

One of the benefits of today's computer systems, if properly organised, is that *databases* can be constructed, so as to allow the data to be accessed in many different ways, and turned into valuable information.

But the fact that data is stored in a computer does not mean that it is available when it is needed. In the past many computer systems were designed to collect large volumes of data, and to process them in a narrowly defined manner. To enquire on the data, and ask a question that the designers of the system had not envisaged, was well nigh impossible. Today, the ability to ask such unforeseen questions is a key requirement for many organisations, and modern 'relational' database systems, such as those available under UNIX, are specifically geared to supplying this need.

What is a database?

In the past, data processing systems often used large numbers of files, on disk or magnetic tape. For instance an invoicing program would read in a file containing details of sales and a file containing customer names and addresses and other details. It would produce a file of invoices, which might be sorted to produce a further file for printing purposes. Perhaps another file would be produced for input to the sales ledger, and other parts of the system might extract data from the ledger to a transient file, sort it to another sequence, thus producing yet another file for posting to an analysis suite. There were thus many files, containing the same data, or parts of the same data, in different sequences and combinations. Frequently discrepancies would arise, with multiple records of names and addresses, which might get out of step with one another. It was not at all uncommon for the same basic data — for instance, part numbers of the firm's inventory — to be held in different and incompatible ways on different systems.

Despite the many files of data, it was often very difficult to find specific information. Often a particular request from management for information could not be supplied at all, because the data was held on different files, in different systems, with no means of bringing them together.

A database represents the modern approach to system design. Rather than starting from the various processes and creating separate files to convey data from one to another, it is far better to start from the logical structure of the data, and build it into a unified database, with each item of information held only once, and related items grouped together in a logical fashion. A database, in this sense, can serve the various operational needs of the company for invoicing and so on; but it can also allow new information to be extracted from the raw data because it allows the data to be combined together in whatever way is required.

Databases and UNIX

Some operating systems — Pick and Mumps for example — have rudimentary database management features built in. UNIX is not like that. For database management, as for so many other aspects of computing, UNIX shows itself as a true general-purpose operating system. It includes some very basic facilities, but mainly it provides a sound basis on which full database management systems can be — and have been — written by independent software houses.

In some ways UNIX is well suited to database applications — for example, it is a multi-user system, and a corporate database is the most obvious example of a multi-user application, with many different users simultaneously enquiring on the same data, all wishing to see the most up to date version. In other ways, UNIX is not so suitable. In particular, the file system is not geared to high performance with large data files; fortunately UNIX itself offers the ability to escape from its own filing system in critical cases. Many database management packages take advantage of this.

What can a database package provide?

Computers have been storing and retrieving data for many years. They have used files on disk or tape, and innumerable application programs have been written, including routines to write data to files, to read data from the files, to find particular records based on a known key, to organise the structure of each record into fields. Why then do we need special software − a database management system (DBMS) − to help out?

The benefits of using a database system can be summarised under three headings:
- data independence;
- data security;
- faster software development.

Data independence

Data independence means that the programs written to use the data are independent of the format of the data.

The files of data that commercial systems deal with are typically very structured: a staff file will contain many records, one per employee, all identical in format, and each containing a field for the employee number, a field for the surname, a field for the salary and so on. In a traditional computer system, each program that accesses a file needs to include within it a definition of the file structure. Much of the DATA DIVISION of a typical COBOL program is made up of lists of the various fields on each type of record that the program may need to refer to, stating whether each field is alphabetic, numeric, etc., and how long it is. If seven programs access the same file, the same information about the structure of the records needs to be included in all seven. Of course you would only type in the data definition once, and use a library facility to copy it into each of the seven source programs; but if the file structure changes at a later date (perhaps because some extra field has been found to be necessary) then all seven source programs will need to be altered and recompiled.

One of the key points about a database management system is that it keeps the data definitions quite separate from the individual programs, in a special 'data dictionary' or 'schema', so that if the record structure needs to be altered, to add a new field, the programs and applications using the database can still run without any alteration — unless they are to use the new field, of course! Generally speaking, the programs should not even need to be recompiled.

Data security

Any computer system dealing with important commercial information needs to address three main security issues:
- access control, to protect the data, or parts of the data, from unauthorised access;
- concurrency control, to cope with multiple users attempting to alter the same record simultaneously;
- transaction control, to ensure that if the hardware or the software fails, the database is not corrupted, and can be restored to a consistent state.

Of course you could write programs specially to deal with all these aspects. But this would require a great deal of time and cost, and very careful investigation of the various problems likely to arise and appropriate ways of dealing with them. Any database product worthy of the name will look after all three issues, in a far more consistent and controlled fashion than you would otherwise be able to achieve without a great deal of effort.

Faster software development

Perhaps the most important benefit of databases is that you probably no longer need to write programs in the traditional way at all — at least not programs using languages such as C and COBOL. Many of the programs that make up traditional data processing systems are reports and enquiries — and these can generally be replaced by the standard utilities included within the database. For more complex programs, such as those which update the files, most database managers include 'fourth generation' facilities, intended to give substantial increases in productivity compared to 'third generation' languages such as C or COBOL.

Relational databases

Most database management systems that have been launched in recent years are described by their suppliers as 'relational databases'. What this means very approximately is that the database is modelled as a series of *tables* (corresponding to files), each consisting of a number of *rows* (records) and *columns* (fields). In strict relational theory the table is called a *relation* (hence the word 'relational') the rows are called *tuples* and the columns are called *attributes*.

Another concept you may come across is the *domain*. Sometimes this term is used as a synonym for a column, but it is more properly used to define a type of data item with a particular format or range of values, such as a date, a postcode, a vehicle registration number. The contents of a particular column must belong to the same domain in all records in a table. Certain packages use domains to provide validation checks on data being inserted into a particular column.

A complete database will contain many distinct tables — a staff table, a department table, a project table, and so on. In real life, there are clearly connections between one type of data and another — for instance, an employee is a member of a department — and some types of database include structures which explicitly recognise this, by having 'master records' with associated 'detail records', or 'pointers' from one record to another. All such structural elements are quite foreign to *relational* databases, which treat each table as if it were unrelated to any other. The values in the tables contain all the information in the database; there is no extra information implicit in the structure of the database itself.

Each table has a 'primary key' — that is, one of its fields (or a group of fields) which can be used to identify uniquely a record within the table. The primary key of a staff file, for example, is likely to be an employee number. It is this which allows the database to reflect the logical connections between data in one table and data in another: a table may include 'foreign keys' — that is, fields within a table which correspond to the primary key of another table. For instance, in a personnel database a staff table could contain a department number, corresponding to the primary key of the department table.

Some relational database systems recognise foreign keys explicitly, and can provide 'referential integrity'. They would not, for example, allow you to delete a department record as long as associated staff records still exist.

Relational facilities

True relational databases allow you to manipulate *sets* of records, rather than a record at a time. Using query languages such as SQL, you can define an update to be applied to a set of records matching specific criteria, without special programming. For instance, in SQL you can issue one command which will update by a certain percentage the salary of all the employees in a particular department.

There are three basic operations involved in obtaining data from a relational database. Using the relational terminology these are: *select*, to retrieve specified rows, *project* to extract specified columns, and *join*, to combine data from two or more different tables.

Relational theory may seem a little forbidding, and the terminology strange if not perverse. However, the ideas become a lot clearer when you look at a specific product, such as Informix.

A database management system — Informix-SQL

In an earlier chapter, I described a method of keeping a simple list of telephone numbers, using nothing but the basic utilities that come with UNIX. This is a rather primitive method, however, and most people need something a little more sophisticated — in other words a database package.

Informix is a well known database system, which offers a lot of features but is still very easy to start on. Actually there are several Informix products, but the one I will concentrate on is Informix-SQL, so called because you talk to it using SQL (short for Structured Query Language) which has become accepted as the standard language for this purpose.

Let us assume that you have got the Informix-SQL package loaded on your computer (not such a simple matter as it sounds — like most substantial software products it consists of a large number of files and programs which need to be put in certain directories) and have got it up and running. The first thing you need to do is to create the framework for your database.

Using the telephone list example from Chapter 8, you could set a database up as follows:

create database staff;
create table names
  (surname char(16), forename char(8), dept char(6), phone smallint);

Don't forget the semicolon at the end of each SQL statement.

Now you have created two structures — a database, and a table (or file) within a database. You have also specified the format of each of the fields in the table. In relational terms, each of these fields is regarded as one of the 'columns' of the database.

Each column has been defined as having a particular data type. Note that for each of the character-format fields you needed to specify its length — Informix, unlike certain other databases, works on fixed-length fields and records. When you subsequently come to put data in the table, Informix will validate it for you: in other words you will not be allowed to put alphabetic data in the telephone number column, or have a surname longer than 16 characters.

The next thing to do then is to put the data into the database – that is, insert some rows into the table. Again you can use SQL. For instance:

insert into names (surname, forename, dept, phone)
   values ("Jones", "Alan", "Accounts", 231);

and so on.

Actually, provided you list the values to be inserted in the correct order each time, you don't need to repeat the names of the fields. So your next entry might be:

insert into names
   values ("Snodgrass", "William", "Sales", 145);

When you have got all the names in, you can display the contents on the screen:

select * from names;

The asterisk in this statement is a wildcard, as in various other cases we have come across. It stands for 'all columns'.

If you want, you can be more selective, and just show the surname and number:

select surname, forename, phone from names;

Alternatively you might prefer the forename to come first:

select forename, surname, phone from names;

And you can get the output sorted to alphabetical order of surname:

select forename, surname, phone from names order by surname;

Moreover you can find the details for a particular person:

select forename, surname, phone from names
   where forename = "Jane";

So far so good. But a relational database starts to get more interesting when you have more than one table. Suppose you want to keep some more information about each department – say, the fact that each is housed on a separate floor of the building. Of course you could add a 'floor' column to the names table, but this would not be good practice: if a department subsequently moved floors, you would have to change all the individual records, which is not in accord with the spirit of relational databases. So it is better to create a new table for department-specific information:

> **create table depts (dept char(6), floor smallint);**
> **insert into depts values ("Accounts", 1);**
> **insert into depts values ("Sales", 2);**

You can now combine data from both your tables, in what relational theory calls a *join*. For instance, you might want to know what floor each person works on:

> **select forename, surname, floor from names, depts**
>   **where names.dept = depts.dept;**

Notice the format of this statement. To do the join you need to specify which columns in the two tables are to be used for matching. In fact, of course, it is the 'dept' column in each case. The two columns have the same name (they needn't have, by the way) so you prefix each with the name of its table, separated by a full stop.

Repeating the prefixes in full is a bit tedious. SQL gives us an abbreviated version:

> **select forename, surname, floor from names n, depts d**
>   **where n.dept = d.dept;**

Notice that in Informix, but not in all versions of SQL, you can omit the prefixes altogether if the column names occur in only one of the tables being selected from.

We have the beginnings of a personnel system here. To make it rather more comprehensive, let's add the people's salaries. First of all we need to set the database up to allow an additional column:

> **alter table names add (salary decimal (7,2));**

In Informix, unlike some other data managers, the ALTER TABLE statement does not require changes or recompilation to applications, and is carried out immediately. The actual data file itself is renamed and copied to produce a new version, with new fields set to a special 'not known' value called *null*. The length of time the alteration takes would of course depend on the length of the file.

Now you can add the actual salaries for each person:

> **update names set salary = 9500 where surname = "Jones";**

and so on.

So far, all the queries we have submitted to SQL have produced detailed outputs, one line per record. But much of the power of SQL is that it allows you to produce summaries. For instance, you might want to find the number of staff and average salary for each department:

**select dept, count (*), avg (salary) from names
group by dept;**

Alternative views of data

We have only skimmed the surface here of what SQL can do, and the examples given so far are of a very simple database. Clearly, in real life one would require many more fields and tables. Moreover, in real life some of the data might be considered confidential, such as employees' salaries, or their manager's last appraisal of their performance. You would obviously not want someone enquiring about a telephone extension to see this information as the result of a *select * from staff* query. Perhaps you might keep the sensitive information on a separate table or a separate database altogether, at the risk of duplication and possible inconsistency between the various versions. Another possibility is to define a 'view' or virtual table, containing a restricted number of fields selected from an existing table. The view can then be used for most purposes just like a normal table. Access to the full table could be restricted to the personnel department, while making access to the view much more widely available.

In Informix a view can include data from more than one table, to make it simple for users who often make the same type of enquiry. Additionally, if you use *with check option* when creating a view, it can be used (with some restrictions) for inputting data, and will check that the data you are inputting is valid according to the selection criteria used to create the view.

Data analysis

A system such as Informix-SQL will only be used to its full if considerable thought has been given to the structure of the database. There are well-tried methods for deciding how the data should be arranged in various tables to correspond to the real-life entities it refers to, and you may come across terms such as 'third normal form data analysis' which describe the established techniques in this area. If the data analysis is not done correctly, one may end up with a database that does not fit the circumstances — for instance, our example would not work if some departments spread over more than one floor: in this case the scheme of having the floor number as a column in the department table would really not do. Before embarking on the design of a database for a real life application, it is extremely important to do your data analysis — in other words, to study the real life systems, and ensure that your model of them is correct before you incorporate it into a computer system.

Other ways of using Informix

You could use SQL to create an entire business application, but this would not be very efficient or user-friendly. SQL is suitable for *ad hoc* enquiries, but routine inputting and reporting is best done using specialised tools, such as most database managers provide. The Informix-SQL software, for instance, includes the following modules:
- RDSQL — Informix's extended implementation of the SQL query language;
- FORMBUILD and PERFORM — for creating and using screen forms;
- ACEPREP and ACEGO — for creating and using printed reports;
- DBMENU — a front end menu system.

Additionally there is another product, Informix-4GL, which allows you to create programs in a 'fourth generation language' (see Chapter 20).

Speeding up access

Using SQL, and a package such as Informix, you can retrieve any record, and any combination of records, from the database. However, if the data files are large, retrieval could take a long time, unless special techniques such as indexing are used.

With very small files, such as the example I used earlier on, there is no problem. The program just looks at each record in turn until it finds the one that satisfies the criteria. But the bigger the files get, the longer this will take, and for most commercial databases the time taken could be unacceptable. For instance, if you're taking sales orders over the telephone, and want to find out if a particular product is in stock, your customer will not be happy to wait while the computer searches through hundreds of product lines for the one in question.

Now with UNIX it is not necessary to read through all the records in a file to find a particular one. Remember that a UNIX file is just a string of bytes, and the operating system in general does not know or care where one record ends and the next begins. But if the *program* happens to know, for instance, that the required record starts on byte number 2035, it can tell UNIX to go immediately to that byte, and start reading data.

But how does the program know where a particular record starts?

Fundamentally there are two methods, but neither will work unless the file has been set up to allow for it. One method is to calculate where a particular record should be put in a file, and then use the same calculation to find it afterwards; the other method is to make a note in a special index of where each record is put, so that this index can be consulted later.

Hashing

The calculation method (called 'hashing') can be very simple to implement. Say you wish to keep a personnel file with details of your staff. You have 60 staff, and need to keep 200 bytes of information about each of them. You can number the staff from 1 to 60, and assign 12,000 bytes to the file. The record for employee number 1 will start on byte 1; that for employee number 11 on byte 2001, and so on.

Note that the employee number has now been given a special status in the structure of the file — it is a 'key' field, used as the basis of distinguishing one record from another. For obvious reasons one needs to assign key fields carefully — it would be no good if two employees had the same employee number, for instance.

So far so good. But in practice life is not so simple as this. Employees will join and leave, and you will probably want to give new joiners totally new numbers: in time you may find you still have 60 or so employees, but with employee numbers going far beyond the 60 you started with. Or maybe for other reasons you have to use a numbering scheme with a lot of gaps in it.

To avoid having a file with a lot of gaps, and thus taking up much more room than necessary, you need to be slightly more subtle, and use a less direct method of calculating the disk address — a 'randomising algorithm', to use the jargon. However, this introduces the possibility that two or more employees would have their records put in the same place. With careful design you can stop this happening too often, but there will certainly need to be an 'overflow area' to hold records that can't be fitted into their 'proper' place. Further complications arise, as you might expect, if the records on the file are not all the same length. Fortunately, the database management system will sort out the various complications for you.

Indexing

An alternative approach, as I mentioned before, is an index, to record where each record was actually put. An index to a file is really rather like an index to a book: the index itself is organised in a way that makes it easy to find an entry, and the entry in turn points to the place in the file where the data is held.

Of course as a user of a UNIX system you will not need to know precisely how the indexing is organised — the database management software will handle it all for you. And doing enquiries or updates to the database is exactly the same whether there is an index or not — except that with an index it may run much faster.

Indexed sequential access methods

Commercial data processing on other operating systems often uses index sequential access methods (ISAM). As the name implies, an ISAM allows you to access the data file in two different ways; you can read all through the file in key sequence (that is, sequentially) or you can find a particular record very quickly, by means of the index.

UNIX as yet has no standard ISAM facility; however, there are moves in that direction. The C-ISAM product, which is part of Informix but also available separately, has become a sort of 'industry standard'. Moreover, the X/Open Group have included a subset of C-ISAM as part of their recommendations on data management. AT&T themselves have said they may include a version of C-ISAM in a future issue of the SVID.

The X/Open standard specifies the facilities that should be provided, but not how the indexing should work, which is very much up to the particular software package. In fact, C-ISAM itself, like a number of other UNIX products, uses a technique called 'b-tree' indexing. The records themselves are in no particular order, but you can access them by means of a tree of indexes: there is a top level index with pointers to second level indexes, and so on down to the lowest level — the 'leaves' of the tree — which contain pointers to the actual data records. The software keeps the tree 'balanced' as far as possible; in other words it avoids the possibility of certain leaves being much further from the root than others, which would make the access times uneven between different parts of the database. Using the b-tree, you can get to a specific record with just a few accesses to the indexes, or follow down the successive branches of the tree so as to retrieve each record of the file in sequential order of the key field.

Informix files are by nature unordered — records are added at the end irrespective of their contents, so the file is essentially in no particular order. C-ISAM is therefore provided as an optional indexing method, merely to speed up accessing; you can add an index to an existing file at any time, and drop the index again when it is no longer required. If appropriate, you can specify that the index is unique — in other words, Informix will not allow two records to be added to the file with the same value of the key field. In the staff file example, an index on employee number should normally be unique but an index on surname should definitely not be, as you may have several Smiths or Patels in the organisation.

AIX and data management

IBM's AIX implementation of UNIX includes a package called 'RT PC Data Management Services' (DMS). In DMS, each UNIX directory contains a additional file called *.SYSCATALOG*, giving further information supplementary to that in the UNIX directory and inode, such as the type of file, record size, and so on. A DMS file can be a 'record-level file', containing variable length records of undefined internal structure, or a 'field-level file', which is a table containing rows and columns. Indexes can optionally be defined for any data file, which is then implemented as a sub-directory, including two files: the data file itself and an index file.

DMS provides a number of special utilities, including *copy*, *delete*, *archive*, *condense*, *create*, *describe*, *list*, *move*, *recover*, *retrieve*. Several of these are parallel to UNIX commands such as *cp*, *rm*, and so on, but they are used to copy, delete, or move a 'file' comprising a data file and associated index, rather than a single UNIX file.

On top of DMS, IBM offer an optional data management package, based on the Oracle DBMS, which comes in two versions. SQL/RT is the SQL-based version. It uses SQL for all purposes — creating the database, adding and modifying the data definitions, entering and querying data, creating reports. Easy SQL/RT is a forms-based interface to the same database manager.

Chapter 12
More about SQL and Database Management

The previous chapter introduced SQL – Structured Query Language – as the data retrieval and manipulation language for Informix. Actually SQL is not specific to Informix – it was originally created by IBM, but is becoming accepted as an international standard, and is one of the standards supported by the X/Open Group.

As well as queries in the strict sense, SQL can also be used to change the contents of a table, and in some systems (including Informix) to change the actual data definitions.

Standard SQL statements

There is considerable variation among different implementations of SQL. The list in Table 12.1 is based on the X/Open Group Portability Guide, and may be considered typical. Informix, however, like various other packages, has quite a number of additional statements.

Table 12.1 Standard SQL statements.

Statement	Meaning
ALTER TABLE	change data dictionary
COMMIT WORK	confirm transaction as complete
CREATE INDEX	add an index to an existing table
CREATE TABLE	define a new table
CREATE VIEW	define an alternative view of data
DELETE	delete a record from a table
DROP	remove an index, table, or view
GRANT	assign permissions to a class of users
INSERT	insert a record into a table
LOCK TABLE	lock data temporarily
REVOKE	remove access permissions
ROLLBACK WORK	undo a partially completed transaction
SELECT	retrieve data from the database
UPDATE	change contents of an existing record

SQL is not just a language for interactive use − it can also be used embedded in traditional programming languages, so that programs can be written to take full advantage of the database package. Some additional SQL statements are required for this purpose (see Chapter 20).

The SELECT statement

The most complex SQL statement is SELECT, used to carry out a query on a database, and present the results to the user at the terminal.

Clauses within a SELECT statement include:
- FROM (specifying the table or tables from which the data is to be obtained);
- WHERE (specifying criteria for selecting particular records);
- GROUP BY (specifying that output is to be a summary − for instance count, total, average − with records grouped together on specified fields);
- HAVING (used within a GROUP BY clause to specify which groups are to be included in the output);
- ORDER BY (specifying the sequence of the output).

Joins and outer joins

In relational terminology, a *join* means a query on two or more related tables. For instance, given a staff table containing employee number and surname, and a project table containing employee number and project description, you might want a report containing just surname and project description, to show which employee is on which project. This would involve a join of the two tables on employee number, and would be specified in SQL as

**select s.surname, p.description from staff s, projects p
where s.empno = p.empno;**

This statement retrieves information for those projects which have a record in both the staff table *and* the project table.

Suppose, however, you want the report to cover all staff, including those not assigned to any project − quite a reasonable request, but one which standard SQL cannot cope with very easily. What you need is an 'outer join'; in other words the output should include not only records matching on employee number, but also those records on the staff table for which there is no matching projects record. Some implementations of SQL have this as an extension, for instance in Informix's SQL you can say:

select s.surname, p.description from staff s, *outer* **projects p where s.empno = p.empno;**

An advanced database system — Ingres

Informix is mainly used on small UNIX systems, and can cope very well where the size of the database is not too great. But it has (at the time of writing) some limitations such as the overall size of particular tables, or the number of columns that could be specified in a SELECT statement. For larger databases, a more powerful product may therefore be found to be necessary.

The Ingres database management system was originally written for UNIX, but its developers, Relational Technology Inc. (RTI), decided that VMS, the proprietary operating system for the DEC VAX range of computers, was more promising for a commercial product. Ingres was therefore developed mainly under VMS; but seeing the market moving more and more towards UNIX, RTI decided to port it back to UNIX. Ingres is now offered on many UNIX machines, as well as VMS and mainframe versions. There is also a personal computer version under MS-DOS. Another indication of the changing market conditions is that Ingres originally had its own query language, called QUEL. SQL is now offered in addition to QUEL, and most future purchasers are likely to choose the SQL version.

Ingres file structure

Ingres supports four data structures:
- hash;
- ISAM;
- b-tree;
- heap.

In the hash data structure, Ingres uses its own hashing algorithm to assign each record to a particular 2k page on disk. If a page is full, records go into overflow pages, and the file can be extended in this way as far as necessary. Hashing is efficient for finding individual records — it normally retrieves the record in a single access — but is not appropriate for retrieving ranges of records.

In many database systems, such as Informix, b-trees are the way in which an index sequential access method (ISAM) is implemented. Ingres is unusual in making a distinction between b-trees and ISAM as two distinct storage methods. In the Ingres ISAM, the data records are physically held in sequential order of the main key, which makes sequential access very efficient, but is not appropriate if new records are constantly being added to the file. Using b-trees, on the other hand, the records themselves are in no particular sequence, but there is an index entry for every record. New records can be added and their index entries will be incorporated in the correct place in the index tree structure.

A heap file is a plain serial (unordered) file, appropriate for small tables. Heap is the default organisation method, and it is usual to create tables as heap, and modify them to a different organisation when they have reached substantially their final size, or when performance is beginning to degrade.

There is a variant called 'heapsort'. If you modify a table to the heapsort organisation, the records are held in sequence on the field specified. However, there is no means of specifically finding an individual record, and new records from this point on are added at the end of the file, without regard to sequence.

The four structures relate to the organisation of the data file itself. Additionally, however, you can create supplementary indexes to any existing file. A supplementary index file itself can be any of the four structures.

Ingres forms editing — Vifred

The SQL approach to Ingres is fine for the relatively experienced user, who knows exactly what he wants, and needs the flexibility to formulate his own enquiries on the database. However, for everyday use, a forms-based approach, in which standard forms are displayed on the screen for you to fill in the boxes as necessary, is generally preferable.

Forms are the fundamental element in much of the Ingres processing. When you create a table, a default form is automatically set up, and can be used without more ado. However, you can edit the default form to produce tailored forms in different formats. This is a way of making the system more user-friendly, or of providing alternative views of the data suited to particular users. A form may alternatively be based on a 'joindef' — that is, a previously set up join between two or more tables.

Once a form has been generated, you can use it to enquire on the data, or to insert, update, or delete records from the table.

A 'frame' comprises everything shown on the screen at one time: that is, a form, and an 'operation menu' on the bottom line, showing the allocation of function keys and other menu options at a particular time. If, for instance, you are in the process of entering data, you can press the 'menu key' to access any of the menu line options. If there are more options than can be shown on one line, a > appears, and you can hit the menu key again to see more.

A special type of field is the 'table field', allowing several rows to be shown on the same screen.

Other Ingres facilities

Query by Forms (QBF) allows you to specify a query on the database using the standard screen forms. For instance, to find all employees called Jones, you would type 'Jones' in the surname box. Some quite sophisticated queries are possible, using AND and OR conditions.

If the form is not big enough to put in all the details you need to specify, you can scroll sideways or vertically. You can use * as a wild card, or a combination such as [A−K] to show a range. The same form can also be used to specify the sequence of the output.

The Ingres reporting facilities comprise reporting by forms (RBF) and a report writer, using embedded SQL. The recommended practice is to try RBF first, and resort to the report writer when you find that RBF can't cope with the specific requirement. (Actually the RBF effort is not wasted, since RBF generates report writer code which you can tailor.)

Ingres additionally has a simple graphics facility, using a form-based approach − 'graphs by forms' (GBF), also referred to as Vigraph.

Query optimisation

A complex database system can be very inefficient if it is not carefully tuned. For example, if a query involves a join of two tables, the speed of response can vary considerably depending on which of the tables is accessed first. Moreover, if a table has multiple indexes, so that it can be accessed in more than one way, the best method of accessing will depend on the nature of the query submitted, such as whether it involves most of the records on a table, or only a few.

Whenever Ingres executes an SQL statement, it generates a 'query execution plan' (QEP) using a query optimiser to work out the most efficient way of accessing the database. If the SQL statement is within a program, and the program uses the statement more than once (as it typically would in an order entry system with staff inputting many orders one after another) then the second and subsequent accesses will be appreciably faster, since the QEP is kept, and does not need to be recalculated.

Concurrency control

Any multi-user database system needs to provide concurrency control; in other words, the orderly management of multiple users of a single file. If two users updated the same record at once, the database could be left in an inconsistent state. All DBMSs, therefore, provide some form of locking: a record about to be updated is locked, so that no other user can access it for updating until the first update is complete. There are two main types of lock: shared locks, which allow any other user to access the data for reading but not writing; and exclusive locks, which allow only one user to access the data in any fashion. UNIX provides a basic locking facility, but a database manager will probably need something more sophisticated, for instance to avoid (or at least detect) the 'deadly embrace' situation of two processes each waiting for the other.

Different products such as Informix, Ingres, and Oracle, all organise their locking in slightly different ways.

Transaction control and rollback

Many commercial database applications require more than one record to be updated as part of a single transaction. As an example, entering a sales order might involve the creation of a sales order record and one or more order detail records, the updating of the customer account and the downdating of the available stock record. If the operator abandons the transaction halfway through, or if the machine goes down during the course of updating, the data on the various records could be left in an inconsistent state. Commercial systems therefore need to ensure that only complete transactions are applied to the database.

If a transaction is aborted or abandoned, the system ought to 'undo' its effect on the database. One way of doing this might be to hold the changes in working storage until the user issues a 'commit' statement, and then do all the updates at once. The user can then abandon at any time prior to the commit, and the files are unchanged. An alternative approach is actually to apply the updates as the transaction proceeds, and then physically reverse them if necessary.

In SQL, the COMMIT WORK statement can be used to mark the

end of a logical transaction, and causes the changes specified in a previous UPDATE, DELETE, or INSERT statement to be permanently applied to the files. You can abandon a change to the database by using the ROLLBACK WORK command, and a hardware or software error has the same effect. The precise details of how this is implemented in different database managers vary, but most keep a special file of 'before images' of the database, showing the state of the records before the update.

Of course the definition of what constitutes a 'transaction' cannot be left to the DBMS, which has no way of working out which updates necessarily belong together, unless the program tells it. The program must therefore be written with the COMMIT statements in the appropriate place to ensure that the transaction is correctly processed.

The alternative to rolling back partly completed transactions is to restore the files to the last backup state — for instance by reloading them from a dump tape — and then to use a transaction log file kept by the DBMS to roll forward from there on, omitting of course any transactions that were incomplete at the time of the crash.

An extension of the commit procedures described above is the 'two-phase commit', which is now becoming an international (OSI) standard under the name 'CCR' — commitment, concurrency, and recovery. The idea is that the transaction first of all checks each of the records to be updated to make sure that they are available, and then locks them. When all are checked, the program proceeds to the actual update, and then does a commit, to confirm the updates. This procedure is essential for reliable updating of distributed databases, where the various records may reside on different machines many miles apart, and multiple users could be attempting to update them at once. RTI are providing two-phase commit in conjunction with their new distributed Ingres system.

Some other database managers

Besides Ingres and Informix, there are a number of other database managers available for UNIX.

Oracle is often regarded as the main competitor to Ingres. Like Ingres, it is available on several other operating systems as well as UNIX. Its most distinctive feature is that all fields and records are variable in length, which has obvious advantages for use with data such as names and addresses, which are variable by their nature.

Unify is a database manager designed for high performance. It has been developed into a 'Fourth Generation Environment' under the name of Accell.

An interesting development is uniVerse, which provides under UNIX the facilities of the Pick operating system and data manager. Pick is often seen as a competitor to UNIX, with particular advantages in certain types of application, but it is by no means as flexible as UNIX. Using uniVerse, one could have many of the benefits of Pick, including the substantial range of software packages written for that environment, without being locked into a closed operating system.

Chapter 13
Graphics

Today's personal computers and home micros use a lot of graphics, both on the screen and to a lesser extent as printed output. UNIX systems by comparison have tended to lack any visual excitement, and are often thought of as producing nothing but text and tables of figures. Actually UNIX systems can cope with extremely sophisticated graphics; the limitations are more likely to be in the hardware than the software, and UNIX itself includes several programs of a graphical nature.

Business graphics — pies and bars

The most common form of graphics today is the graphical presentation of figures, in the form of bar charts, histograms, pie charts, and line graphs. On personal computers, this is often provided by a spreadsheet program. In the UNIX environment, graphics are appearing as part of certain database managers such as Ingres and Oracle, while there are a variety of specialised packages.

The simplest form of graph is the scatter diagram, showing one variable (say sales) plotted against another (say monthly rainfall) with dots, crosses, or circles, to indicate the various values.

If the graph has only one data point for each position on the x-axis, it is often helpful to draw lines between the various values, to indicate more clearly which way the trend is going. The graph has then become a line graph.

Sometimes it is not realistic to regard the various data items as forming a series, so there is no point in drawing lines from one data point to the next. For instance, if you have a set of sales figures for different regions, there is no sense in trying to draw a line graph, since the slope of the line would not mean anything. A better presentation in this sort of case is a histogram — a series of bars (normally vertical bars) so that the reader can take in at a glance which is taller and by how much. A variant on the histogram is a 'stacked bar' in which each of the columns is made up of a number of elements — such as sales revenue broken down by type of product.

Chapter 13

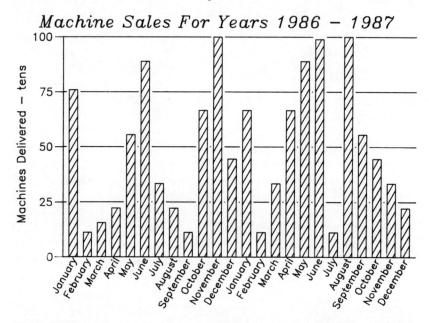

Fig. 2. UNIX graphics — a simple histogram. (Produced on a plotter, using software from Pacific Basin Graphics on an AT&T 3B2 microcomputer.)

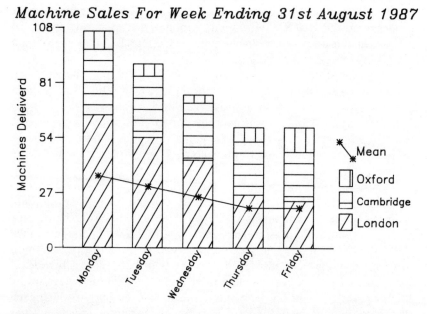

Fig. 3. A combined line graph and stacked bar. (Produced on a plotter, using software from Pacific Basin Graphics on an AT&T 3B2 microcomputer.)

Graphics

A pie chart is the standard presentation to show how some variable (such as sales, or national income) is divided up amongst a number of subdivisions.

Other types of graph may be used for particular purposes – a map of a geographical area, for example, with the different regions coloured according to their population, sales, rainfall, and so on.

Yet another type of graphical presentation is the organisation chart or 'organogram', showing how the various departments in a company are related to one another. This is very similar to a 'visual table of contents', for which there is a special UNIX utility.

A considerable number of UNIX utilities and packages are in fact available, for producing all the standard types of graph and diagram, and also 'presentation graphics' – the use of pictures and diagrams to illustrate a talk or lecture.

Standard UNIX graphical utilities

To begin with, UNIX provides some standard commands for graphical purposes. The *graph* command is an example. You feed it with a series of pairs of numbers, which the program interprets as co-ordinates of successive data points, and it uses them to produce a simple line graph.

A rather more sophisticated facility is provided by the *graphics* command. This starts up a special graphical subshell. The ordinary shell prompt disappears and is replaced by a ⁀ symbol, and you have access to *stat*, a collection of statistical and graphical commands, in addition to the normal UNIX commands.

Some of the new commands, such as *hist* (generate a histogram) or *spline* (generate a smooth curve) are obviously graphical in nature; others are more mathematical or statistical, such as *cor* (calculate correlation coefficient) or *root* (calculate square roots – or other roots).

All the *stat* commands are concerned with manipulating a 'vector' – that is, a series of numbers. More precisely, a vector is a text file, which the graphics shell scans to find strings of characters which it can interpret as numbers. Some of the commands generate vectors, such as *prime* (generate prime numbers) or *rand* (generate random numbers); other commands transform the numbers; others again use them to create a GPS (graphical primitive string – a set of instructions for creating a picture); others turn a GPS into a picture on the screen or a plotter. The full list of commands is given in Table B4 in Appendix B.

Just as in the ordinary UNIX shell, pipes can be used to convey the output of one command to the input of another.

UNIX also provides a graphics editor, *ged*. This is normally used to edit a GPS created by one of the *stat* commands. Editing functions are called up by single letter instructions such as A (arc), B (box), C (circle), e (erase) and so on, but if you have the right sort of terminal you can use a mouse or other device to manipulate pointers on the screen itself.

The UNIX graphics library

UNIX also provides a library of graphics routines for use within C programs, as shown in Table 13.1.

Table 13.1 The standard graphics library.

Name	Function
openpl	prepares the target device for writing
erase	erases the screen, or starts a new page
label	prints a label
line	draws a line between two given points
circle	draws a circle with a specified radius and centre
arc	draws an arc of a circle
move	moves to a point
cont	draws a line from the current point to a new point
point	puts a point at the specified location
linemod	specifies the kind of line: dotted, solid, longdashed, short-dashed, or dotdashed
space	defines the plotting area
closepl	flushes the graphic output

Between them, these routines provide most of the low level commands needed to construct normal business graphics out of straight lines, circles, arcs, points, and text. They all work on the basis of co-ordinates — each location within the plotting area is specified by a pair of numbers, denoting its horizontal and vertical co-ordinates respectively. The point '0.0' is always the bottom left hand corner.

The routines in the standard library are 'device-independent'. That is, they work just as well with any type of graphical output device, which is another way of saying that they do not work directly with any device. What you actually do is to write and compile your C program, using the standard graphics library. When you run the program, the output does not go directly to a printer or plotter, but should be piped into the *tplot* utility, which will need to be told the actual device to be used. *Tplot* is a filter — it takes a stream of data in at its standard input (in this case a stream of device-independent graphics commands) and produces a modified version at its standard output (in this case commands suitable for the particular device you have specified). Provided the device is one that *tplot* can cope with, the output should then come out correctly. For example, if you had just compiled your graphical program, the C compiler would have produced an executable file called *a.out*. You could then test the program as follows:

a.out | tplot -T4014

The *-T4014* option in this case means that the output will be suitable for the Tektronix 4014 terminal (a special kind of graphical vdu).

A standard for graphics — GKS

The Graphics Kernel System (GKS) has attained recognition as an international standard, and seems likely to be used more and more in the future. GKS is not a graphics package as such, it is a standard for defining the way a computer program will call for graphical effects. GKS contains four main functions or 'primitives':
- polyline (for drawing lines);
- polymarker (for marking points);
- fill area (for shading in an area defined by lines);
- text (for including text in the picture).

The four primitives between them cover most aspects of graphics — after all, every picture consists essentially of some combination of lines, points, and shading, with or without text — but they need some additional functions known as attributes, to specify the type of shading, the alignment of the text, and so on. The attributes are as follows:
- set polyline index;
- set polymarker index;
- set fill area index;
- set character height;
- set character up vector;
- set text path;
- set text alignment;
- set text index.

A number of software packages are now becoming available under UNIX which allow programs to be written including GKS graphics.

Desktop publishing

'Desktop publishing' is a new computer application that has appeared in recent years. At the simplest level, it involves the use of computers to create the artwork for producing leaflets, magazines, and other printed material. The techniques involved include typography (producing text in a variety of fonts and sizes) and the integration of the text with visual images from various sources.

The hard copy device for producing the output is nearly always a high resolution laser printer. There are a number of standard 'languages' in which such printers can be given their instructions and one of the most powerful of these is PostScript.

PostScript has the advantage of being independent of the resolution of the output device, so that it can be used in the same way whether the output will be to a plotter, a vdu screen, or a high resolution graphical display. Of course the quality of the picture will differ considerably depending on the device used.

A typical command in PostScript would be

50 700 moveto

This would move the cursor to a position 50 points from the left hand side of the picture area and 700 from the top, a 'point' in this case being the standard printer's measurement of 1/72 of an inch.

Other commands in Postscript include *lineto* (draw a line) and *showpage* (send the image to the hard copy device and eject).

Desktop publishing was initially associated with the Apple Macintosh computer, and later spread to other types of personal computer. However, a number of programs are beginning to appear on UNIX machines, of which Interleaf is a good example.

Computer-aided design

The most advanced form of graphics that UNIX-based machines regularly have to cope with is computer-aided design (CAD). The computer here is being used as a tool for the designer or draftsman, to help in both the design process itself, and in keeping all the various drawings up to date when there are changes to the product.

Companies such as Sun and Apollo produce high performance computers for this purpose. Such a machine is generally termed a 'workstation', and is normally a single-user computer, with high resolution colour display, and a graphical hard copy output device such as a plotter. This specification is quite different to the usual UNIX machine; however, UNIX has become established as the standard operating system for CAD workstations. This is partly because UNIX makes it so easy for a new manufacturer to enter this relatively young and very specialised market, without having to design a new operating system from scratch.

Using a CAD workstation, you can call up the design on the screen, rotate it so as to look at it from a different angle, zoom in to look at an element of the design in close-up. You can define a repertoire of commonly used elements, so that the drawing can be built up from its constituent parts, and these can be reassembled or moved around as necessary. Colour is a useful enhancement to the picture for various purposes; it is essential in certain cases such as integrated circuit design, in which different colours can be used to highlight the various layers and substances to be built up on the silicon chip.

Graphical hardware

The best graphical programs in the world are no good without the hardware which can show off the output.

Ultimately most graphics will need to produce 'hard copy' on paper. If the image is in black and white only, a laser printer is normally the best method, although a crude version can be obtained on a matrix printer. If you need colour, there is probably no real alternative today to a plotter, the main drawback here being the slowness of the output.

For display on the vdu screen, the main restrictions are the size of the screen, and the way it is addressed. Many vdu screens are text-only. This does not rule graphics out absolutely, since the text character set often includes a number of special graphical characters, suitable for drawing lines and boxes, or simple histograms and bar charts. However, the character set on one display may be different to another, and programs written for full graphical displays will certainly not work. Full graphics require a 'bit-mapped' or 'all points addressable' (APA) screen, in which each dot or pixel making up the picture can be separately addressed, rather than as part of a preformed character.

Some vdus can alternate between text and graphics modes. For instance, the Cifer T4 terminal has both a text plane, emulating VT100 and other terminals, and a graphics plane emulating the Tektronix 4014. Using a special key on the keyboard you can switch between the two planes, or have one superimposed on the other.

Chapter 14
Communications

The terminals linked to a UNIX computer may be in the same room, or elsewhere in the same building. They can just as easily be in a different town or a different continent. By means of a modem you can connect your terminal through the international telephone network to a similar modem connected to the computer, and the computer will have no idea whether the terminal is local or remote — it will respond in exactly the same way.

Aspects of data communications

Whether the terminal is local or remote, it must obviously be set to use the same speed and general method of communications as the computer is expecting, and the modem will partly determine this. For communicating over the ordinary telephone lines, modems can be set to run at speeds such as 300 baud or 1200 baud, whereas a local connection would be typically at 9600 baud or even more. By the way the baud rate is a measure of the speed of the transmission. For the sort of communication we are talking about, a speed of 1200 baud is equivalent to 1200 bits per second.

There are two quite distinct ways of parcelling up data to send it over a communications line — synchronous and asynchronous. UNIX terminals almost always communicate asynchronously — each byte is sent down the line individually, as a seven or eight bit ASCII character, preceded by a start bit, followed by a stop bit, and often accompanied by a parity bit to help detect errors in transmission. The start and stop bits tell the receiving device where each character starts and finishes, so that it can cope with delays of varying lengths between characters. With asynchronous communications, a speed of 1200 bits per second equates to 120 characters per second or perhaps less.

Synchronous communications on the other hand involves a number of bytes being assembled into a 'frame' or 'packet', with special flag bytes added, and often a more sophisticated form of error checking, rather than a parity bit on each byte. The point of synchronous transmission is that the two ends synchronise their clocks — or indeed use the same clock — so that data can be transmitted reliably at much higher speeds than could be possible with the asynchronous method.

If you think of the communication that goes on between a terminal and a UNIX computer, the asynchronous method is obviously quite appropriate. Each character you type is immediately sent to the computer, and examined by the UNIX kernel (or perhaps a special communications processor) and echoed back to your screen before being passed on to the applications program. On the input side at least there is no scope for bundling several characters into a frame.

Other types of computer — particularly the IBM mainframes — use synchronous communications, with 'block mode' terminals, such as the IBM 3270 or equivalent. In this type of terminal, the echoing on the screen, and the handling of backspace characters and so on, are all done locally in the terminal itself, or in the controller to which one or more terminals are attached. When you press Return, the complete block of data is sent down the line, at high speed, so that synchronous communication is appropriate.

In the UNIX world, communication with terminals is almost always asynchronous, but synchronous communication arises when one computer talks to another (see Chapter 21).

Packet switching

Normally, when you make an ordinary telephone call, or dial up a remote computer to communicate using your modem, you are connected via the Public Switched Telephone Network (PSTN). If your company has a branch somewhere else with which it often needs to communicate by voice or data link, there may be a leased line, in which case you are connected automatically without the need to dial. A third alternative is to use a packet switched service (suitable for data only, not voice). In this case there is no switching in the normal sense: the various 'packets' making up your transmission contain an 'address' within them, and are routed from point to point by intelligent digital exchanges, which examine every packet to see where it should be sent next. The principle is very similar to a letter in the postal system being examined in the various sorting offices along the way.

You can use the packet switched services in two ways: either by connecting directly to a packet switched line provided for you by British Telecom, in which case your terminal must be a 'PAD' (Packet Assembler/Disassembler) and follow the X.25 protocol, or by using an ordinary terminal, and dialling through to a PAD or your local packet switched exchange. In either case you need to subscribe to the packet switched service (PSS in the UK) unless you are merely using one of the databases such as Dialog, in which case your subscription to the database service will include PSS charges (right through to the USA if necessary) on a 'reversed charges' basis.

Accessing other hosts

As well as the obvious type of communication, linking a remote terminal to a UNIX computer, it is quite often convenient for the UNIX machine itself to pretend to be a terminal, accessing a remote host computer (typically a mainframe).

Accessing a host computer in this way requires the UNIX machine to emulate the communications protocols that the host expects its terminals to use. The 3270 standard is fairly commonly supported on UNIX machines for emulating IBM block mode terminals; another class of IBM standards are 2780 and 3780 for 'remote job entry' (RJE), i.e. submitting a complete batch of data to a job to be run on the host.

Other types of host have different protocols — for instance, CO3 for ICL mainframes. There are also some industry standard protocols such as Kermit, used to transmit files of data and detect transmission errors, while for interactive use the networking protocols such as TCP/IP (discussed in Chapter 21) may be the answer.

Public communications services

The most obvious use of data communications is to link together the various parts of one's own company; but today there are an increasing number of external services which one can link to, given a computer, a terminal, and a modem.

Some communications facilities are specifically related to UNIX. In particular a number of UNIX machines in Europe and North America, particularly in the academic world, have linked themselves together using the *uucp* utility, and it is not uncommon to see published electronic mail addresses including the telltale exclamation mark, which *uucp* uses in its network addresses, for example:

ubvax!cae780!hplabs!decwrl!pyramid!amdahl!twg-ap!styx

The American network USENET (with the corresponding EUnet in Europe) uses *uucp* to provide a 'news' service, with items being broadcast across the network, rather than delivered to a specific individual. There are also various 'bulletin boards' which users can access to leave messages of general interest.

External electronic mail

Just as you can use the UNIX *mail* command to send electronic mail to other users in the same office, public electronic mail networks enable you to communicate with people in other organisations, in this country or throughout the world.

In the UK there are several such services, of which Telecom Gold, operated by British Telecom, is the best known example. Each Telecom Gold user has a mailbox, held in the central Telecom Gold computer. Other users in other parts of the world have access to the same facilities and can exchange messages with London and with each other. The DialCom company, which originated the service in the USA, and runs it in several other countries, has now been taken over by British Telecom.

Having signed on to Telecom Gold and given your password, you have a choice of three main options: Send, Read, or Scan.

The Send command allows you to send mail to another user. You specify the person to send it to, and any complimentary copies (CC). You can specify acknowledgement requested (AR) if you wish to check that the recipient actually reads the message. You next enter the subject, and the text of the message. There are a number of options, which are specified (just as in Uniplex and other packages) by a full stop at the start of a line, followed by a special code.

The Read command enables you to have your messages displayed to you one by one, the most recent first, except that express messages get priority. Having read a message you can reply to it, send it on to a third party, or file it under a subject heading.

The Scan command allows you to see quickly what messages are waiting for you. You are given the sender's name, the date and time, the length of the message, and the subject.

Other features of Telecom Gold include a bulletin board and lonely hearts column, and various facilities designed for internal use by companies who have adopted Telecom Gold as their own company messaging and information service. There are also links to telex, telemessages (the equivalent of the old telegram service) and even radio paging, so that the person you are sending the message to can be warned by his bleeper going off.

There are a number of other messaging services, such as Comet and One-to-One, while a primitive electronic mail system is available as part of Prestel.

An international standard, X.400, has been devised (although not yet finalised) to provide a common means of linking different electronic mail services together, and X.400 facilities are beginning to be available on certain computers running UNIX.

External databases

Various organisations now offer information services which your computer can access by means of a modem. The classic example is the giant US databases such as Dialog, which can provide references and information about an enormous variety of subjects. Using packet switching facilities provided by the information sources, it is today relatively cheap in terms of telephone charges to access American networks, although the information itself may be expensive. The Knowledge-Index service provides a subset of the main Dialog database at much reduced prices, available outside working hours. Other services are provided by UK organisations such as the British Library, whose BLAISE gives details of both current and older British books, while Euronet Diane provides a similar service on a Europe-wide basis.

On a more specialised level, organisations such as Reuters offer information concerned with the stock market, money movements, commodity prices, and so on. In the past these were generally offered as a completely bundled package, running on special terminals which could not be used for any other purpose. Today, such is the proliferation of different services that users are becoming resistant to the idea of having multiple terminals on their desk, and looking to their own computer to bring together the various different sources of data and present them on a single vdu screen.

Value added networks

A number of organisations are now providing 'value added networks' (VANs) – special networks for a specific purpose, often with special hardware and software which the subscriber is offered to enable him to link to the service. Indeed a service such as Telecom Gold probably falls into this category.

Electronic data interchange (EDI) allows you to exchange business documents over the telephone network. Just as electronic mail could one day replace the sending of letters through the mail, so EDI could one day replace the printing and posting of invoices, orders, and so on.

The potential benefits of EDI are obvious. Most big organisations today have purchase order processing systems on their computers. These generate orders which are sent to their suppliers. Staff at the suppliers' offices key these into their own sales order processing systems on their own computers. The transaction works its way through the computer systems till it reaches the invoicing and sales ledger programs. These print an invoice, which is sent by post to the other firm and then entered into their purchase ledger system. Clearly there would be substantial savings of effort and cost, and less likelihood of error, if the computers at either end could talk directly to each other.

Today, this is happening, but as yet only in particular industries. Obviously, EDI will only work if both parties agree to it, and if there are standards for the format and content of the various types of document. Such standards now exist, and trade associations in different industries are promoting the further growth of EDI.

Viewdata and Prestel

Viewdata is a public communications service designed originally for the home market. Consequently it uses slow speed data transmission, simple 40-character screen displays suitable for domestic televisions, and a very simple user interface, reflecting the original assumption that users would have numeric-only keyboards. The UK implementation of Viewdata is called 'Prestel'. It offers information of all sorts such as weather forecasts and train timetables, services such as lonely hearts columns (both gay and straight) and a variety of special interest groups for micro enthusiasts and others. It has also been used as the vehicle for an experiment in home banking.

Viewdata is somewhat apart from other communications services, because of its unusual screen format and its need for split-speed modems (1200 bits per second in one direction, 75 in the other). However, a number of suppliers now offer viewdata emulation under UNIX.

Telex

Telex is still one of the most widely used forms of office communication, despite the more fashionable media such as electronic mail that have grown up in recent years. Many people probably still associate telex with a clanking machine in the basement, which you feed with punched paper tape, and which outputs ungrammatical messages on rather nasty paper, but this need no longer be the case. If you have a UNIX-based computer you can attach special hardware and software such as the S-Telex product, and let it take over the job of producing telexes, saving you a lot of bother. For instance, it can automatically re-try engaged lines, send the same message to multiple destinations, or do automatic dialling at a later time of day.

Another approach is via one of the many gateways that now exist. For instance, Prestel (in the UK) has a telex facility. If your computer has a viewdata modem and the appropriate software necessary to access Prestel, you can send and receive telexes via the Prestel mailbox facility. A number of other publicly available services also provide telex gateways, for instance Telecom Gold. A common feature of all of these, however, particularly where the recipient uses a similar service, is that the message is not transmitted end to end in real time — it may be held in a mailbox awaiting onward transmission.

Which method you choose for telex will depend mainly on how much telex traffic you have or expect. If telex is just an occasional requirement, it will be much cheaper to use one of the gateway facilities. On the other hand, if telex is the lifeblood of the organisation, as it is in many companies with substantial overseas trading, then a telex line into the office, and the appropriate hardware to link to it, will be faster, more convenient, and cheaper in the long run.

A new service called Teletex has been introduced in several European countries, as a high-speed, high-quality replacement to telex. However, it has had remarkably little success so far in the market.

Chapter 15
Accounting and Business Systems

The most common use of computers today is probably still for business and accounting purposes. UNIX is an excellent system for tackling this sort of application.

With languages such as COBOL available, UNIX is a very suitable operating system if a company needs to have an accounting system specially written. However, it is much more common to use packaged software, since packages are not only enormously less expensive, but also increasingly sophisticated and flexible, so that most organisations would find at least one of the available systems able to fit their needs.

What does an accounting system do?

Accounting systems vary considerably in detail, but they all of necessity follow the basic accounting conventions that have been unchanged for centuries. The most important of these is the 'double entry' system of book-keeping. Double entry means that every transaction has two aspects — a debit and a credit. For example, if a driver working for a company buys petrol, paying for it immediately by a company cheque, this one transaction is both a credit to the cash book and a debit to (perhaps) the transport expenses account.

In business, purchases are typically not paid for immediately; if a company sell some goods for £100 to a customer, they will raise an invoice — perhaps for £115, including VAT (at the UK standard rate for 1987). Within the company's accounting system, the invoice represents a debit of £115 to the customer's account and credits of £100 to the sales account and £15 to the VAT account. Some time later the customer will pay the invoice. This is then a credit of £115 to the customer's account and a debit of £115 to the cash book.

Traditionally, all the various accounts were kept in a big book called a 'ledger'. It should be fairly obvious that if the 'double entry' principle is adhered to, the grand total of all the accounts on the ledger must come to zero, although many of the individual accounts will have debit or credit balances.

The ledger often became a very big book indeed, and was divided up. Three common divisions are the Sales Ledger, the Purchase Ledger, and the General Ledger.

The Sales Ledger contains an account for every customer – or at least regular customers – and is sometimes referred to as a 'Debtors Ledger' or 'Accounts Receivable', since it contains people or companies from whom you expect to receive money. The Purchase Ledger contains an account for every supplier from whom you regularly purchase goods or services, and is alternatively called the 'Creditors Ledger' or 'Accounts Payable'. The General Ledger, often called the 'Nominal Ledger', contains other types of account, representing aspects of the company's business, such as sales, VAT, wages, rent, and so on.

All computer accounting systems have computer files representing the ledgers. Sometimes the Sales, Purchase, and Nominal Ledgers are kept quite separate and have entirely different parts of the system looking after them; sometimes the system follows the original arrangement of just one ledger file containing all types of account.

Benefits of computerised accounts

A computer accounting system is helpful for several reasons. First of all it can make sure that the ledger really does balance; in a manual system it is only too easy to have a transaction debiting one account with £123 and crediting the other account with £132. The mistake will be detected eventually, but it may take a lot of searching for; with most computer systems, the discrepancy could not arise in the first place.

A computerised accounting system will also look after the management of sales and purchase ledger accounts. On the sales side the aim is to keep track of how much the customer owes you, and how long it has been outstanding. Most systems will print statements that can be sent to the customer, to remind him what he owes, and summarise it so that he can send one cheque to cover all his outstanding debts. Frequently you can get an 'aged debtors' printout, showing those customers who have invoices outstanding more than 30, 60, or 90 days. Many systems will automatically send reminder letters of increasing severity, from 'May we draw this overdue amount to your attention?' to 'Unless you pay immediately we shall take legal action to recover the debt.'

In order to send out the letters and statements, the system must keep a name and address record for every customer, usually with other information such as maximum credit limit, or permitted discount level.

On the purchase side the aim is again to keep the accounts under control. This normally means ensuring that you pay the invoices soon

Fig. 4. The Victor V286 – an inexpensive multi-user sytem.

enough to keep on good terms with the supplier, or perhaps to qualify for a prompt payment discount, while not paying any sooner than necessary. A computer system is very good at doing this. Most accounting systems are able to print cheques (itself quite a complicated procedure, as you may need to keep track of cheque numbers and so on) and also remittance advices, detailing exactly which invoices are being paid, and so how the amount of payment is arrived at.

As far as the nominal or general ledger is concerned, the main outputs from the system will be the company financial statements for each month or accounting period or for the year as a whole. Typical statements include the balance sheet and the profit and loss account. A less formal, but very useful, statement is the trial balance, which summarises all the accounts on the ledger, giving for each the opening and closing balances, and the movements during the period. Clearly the trial balance should always add up to zero.

As well as accounting information in the strict sense, the invoices and other transactions that constitute the input to an accounting system also carry a variety of other information which is crucial to understanding how the business is doing. Using a computer system, much of this can be captured by means of 'analysis codes', and used to generate various analyses for management information purposes. For instance, on a sales invoice you might code the type of product, the department, the geographical area, the name of the salesman responsible for the sale, and so on. The ability to generate analyses in a variety of different formats is an important feature of a good accounting system.

An accounting system — SunAccount

SunAccount, supplied by Systems Union, is a widely-used package running on MS-DOS (single-user or networked) as well as UNIX. It is written in COBOL.

Rather unusually, SunAccount uses the concept of a single ledger, containing all types of accounts. A key stage in setting up a SunAccount system is to define the Chart of Accounts for your organisation. Of course when setting up an account you have to state whether it is a debtor, a creditor, or nominal account — (actually there are two types of nominal account: balance sheet, and profit and loss). It is usual although not obligatory to differentiate the different types of account by ranges of account numbers.

SunAccount has no predefined transaction types. All transactions are input to the system via 'journals'. In some accounting systems a journal is a particular type of transaction, used, for instance, to correct posting errors. In SunAccount, however, the word is used more in its original sense of a 'day book' into which all transactions are entered prior to posting to the ledger. A single journal is a batch of transactions, normally of the same type, consisting of a number of pages, each of up to eight lines. Each line represents one posting to a particular ledger account.

When you set the system up, you define what the transaction types are to be, and what codes and other information must be input. You can set the transactions up in such a way that they are self-balancing. Thus when you have entered, say, the invoice amount and the debtor account it is to be posted to, the system will automatically generate a matching line to credit the general ledger account for 'sales' or whatever. Thus this transaction — that is, this page of the journal — will balance.

It is not obligatory for a page to balance, but the journal as a whole — that is, the batch of invoices, for example — must balance: you are forced to make it balance or else abandon the input. Once the journal is balancing correctly, and you are satisfied that it is complete, you type P and the transactions are immediately posted to the ledger.

Open item and balance forward

In SunAccount, each debtor or creditor account is either an 'open item' account or a 'balance forward' account. A balance forward account is very much like your credit card account; every month you get a statement showing an opening balance, a number of transactions, and a closing balance. The following month, this month's closing balance has become the new opening balance, and the various transactions which went to make it up are no longer shown on the account.

In certain types of business it is usual to keep open item accounts. These have no opening balances as such, but the individual transactions remain on the account until they have been specifically cleared off. Running an open item account means you have to do a bit more work. If a customer has been invoiced for £1,000 and has paid you £1,000, the net balance on his account is zero, but both the invoice and the payment will continue to appear on the statement month by month, which is not what you normally want. So you use SunAccount's Account Revision feature to 'allocate' the cash against the invoice, by entering a Y against both transactions. A cash payment can relate to more than one invoice — you merely put a Y against each of the transactions. The only restriction is that the items you mark as allocated must all total to zero. Sometimes a cash payment may be for part of an invoice only. In this case you can 'split' the invoice, and the system replaces it by two lines, one of them allocated, the other not. Items which have been allocated will be shown on statements at the end of the month, but will thereafter disappear from the printouts.

SunAccount allows you to define up to ten analysis codes. Five of these are transaction analysis codes, and are input on individual transactions — they might include the department, the type of goods, and so on. The other five are account analysis codes, and are associated with each account, so that you do not have to input them for each transaction. These might include the type of customer, the region, and so on. Obviously the use of these codes is very much up to an organisation. For instance, if each customer is assigned to a particular salesperson or representative, then the rep code might be an account analysis code; in another organisation, several salespeople might sell to one customer, so the rep code would be a transaction analysis code. A company in a different line of business might have no need to analyse by salesperson at all. Sun is particularly flexible in the analyses that are possible.

The ledger, with all its associated data files, is referred to in SunAccount as a 'database'. You may need to have several databases — for instance, if you operate several subsidiary companies. However, for certain reports the system can consolidate information from more than one database.

Associated with each database are three passwords, representing three levels of privilege. These passwords are quite distinct from the standard UNIX passwords: they are the same for all users of a given level for a given database, whereas the UNIX passwords are normally allocated one per person.

Other business systems

Accounting is in some ways the easiest of all business systems to automate, as it does not vary too much from one type of business to another. Virtually all business organisations issue invoices and receive payments, while even non-trading organisations have to buy things and therefore have some sort of purchase ledger.

But the invoice, although it is the starting point for accounting systems, is often the final outcome of a long and complex process, which differs quite considerably from one business to another. There are, however, some common elements. Often a starting point is the receiving and processing of an order.

Sales order processing

A sales order processing system will generally allow orders from customers to be entered to the computer system as soon as they are received. If the orders are taken by telephone, then the person receiving the call can type them into the system while the customer is still on the line, and the system can be checking the stock situation, so that the customers can be told straight away how long they may have to wait for delivery.

Once the order is captured in the system, the processing that follows varies considerably from one industry to another. Perhaps the items need to be bought in, or made to order. If they are standard stock items, part of the current stock may have to be allocated to the order; if there is insufficient stock, orders may need to be placed on suppliers.

Eventually, the order will result in the goods being ready for dispatch. At this point, various printouts are likely to be required, such as picking lists to tell the storeman what to issue, dispatch notes to go with the goods, and most important of all an invoice which will be sent to the customer and also entered into the sales ledger system.

Invoicing

The production of the invoice itself is often quite a complicated business. A typical invoice may contain a variable number of detail lines, representing different items that the customer has ordered. The price of each item will need to be obtained from the price lists, and multiplied by the quantity to give the amount for each item line. Perhaps there are different prices for the same item depending on the customer or other factors. A variety of discounts may need to be applied, and in most types of business Value Added Tax will have to be calculated at the appropriate rate for each type of goods.

Stock control

Stock control is closely linked with sales order processing. The system will need to record the quantity of each kind of stock item in each warehouse, updating the records whenever it is notified of receipts or issues. Records must be kept of stock allocated to particular projects or sales orders, and stock which has been ordered from suppliers but not yet arrived. Stock may need to be valued, and for this purpose it may be necessary to keep records of how much was obtained from what source, and at what price. Most stock control systems assist with the decision of when to order new stocks, taking into account the likelihood of running out, set against the cost of buying and holding stocks, and the possibility of obtaining discounts by ordering less often and in larger quantities.

Manufacturing systems

In an increasing number of organisations, order processing and stock control are being integrated with systems that control and schedule the manufacturing process, working out how many nuts and bolts and pieces of metal are required for a particular part which has been ordered, and when it can best be made taking into account the capacity of the production departments. In certain industries such automated scheduling is beginning to join up with the automation of the actual production process, using robots or process control automation.

UNIX at present is not suitable for the actual control of machinery, which needs special real time computers; however, UNIX can be very suitable for undertaking the remainder of the manufacturing systems, and one of the biggest manufacturers of all, General Motors, is standardising on UNIX in this area.

Payroll

The final business application for which computers are often used is payroll. Payroll is particularly suitable for computers, because the rules relating to income tax and National Insurance contributions are complicated, tedious to administer and essential to get right, but at the same time very clearly defined. Many organisations, however, find it better for security and other reasons to have their payroll run for them by an outside computer bureau, rather than on their own machine.

Most organisations have both weekly and monthly payrolls. The monthly payrolls are generally much easier to program, since the basic pay is a twelfth of the annual salary, whereas weekly pay may be on the basis of hours actually worked, with overtime and bonuses to be calculated. At one time, weekly wages were generally paid in cash, and employees could insist on this. With more recent changes in the law, one can expect that the vast majority of employees will be paid either by cheque or by credit transfer. If a cheque is the method, the computer system will have to deal with cheque stationery, and incorporate security procedures to ensure that the cheques are not printed twice. If credit transfers are used, the system will probably produce output to the Bankers' Automated Clearing Service (BACS) on magnetic tape or other means.

Of all the usual business applications, payroll is particularly suitable for a standard package, rather than writing your own programs: many of the complications in terms of income tax and so on are common to all employers; moreover, when the Government change the rules, they may do so at fairly short notice, and you must not fail to comply. A reputable software house, which has produced a payroll package, will be poised ready to adapt the system to such changes when they occur.

Chapter 16
UNIX with a Friendly Face

The need for user-friendly systems

As hardware and software become more powerful, they can also become more difficult to use. There has been much research into the theory of user interfaces, but the theory has not always been well put into practice.

UNIX in particular is sometimes criticised for being 'not user-friendly'. This is a rather strange criticism, and it would be difficult to think of an operating system that really is user-friendly.

Some of the criticism of UNIX is really trivial and misses the point. It may be odd to have to type in *cp* to copy a file, but if it really annoys you you can use the *alias* command in the C shell or Korn shell to rename *cp* as COPY if that would suit you better − or even PIP if you're nostalgic for CP/M! In fact people who use the shells regularly soon get quite familiar with the odd names of the commands, and are often grateful that the commands to be typed are generally (and intentionally) short.

A more fundamental point is that ordinary end users can quite easily be shielded from ever seeing the shell prompt at all. For instance, if you are a manager or secretary, and use the computer only for typing, sending messages, using the spreadsheet, and general office automation tasks, then an integrated package such as Uniplex will cater for virtually everything you ever need to do − you can stay in the package and use its menu system for going from one function to another, without ever having to come out to the shell. In this case it is the user-friendliness or otherwise of the application software that is important.

Similarly with the major database management systems such as Ingres, you can use the menu system to do enquiries, run applications, enter transactions into the database, and produce printed reports, all from within the one package.

So for many people, the friendliness or otherwise of UNIX is beside the point − all they need to do is to log in and then type the name of the application they want. It may be possible to avoid even that stage, by having the application set up as a login program, so that the user remains in the application all the time, and is automatically logged off when choosing the 'quit' option from the application's master menu.

Having said all that, I must admit that it would be nice if UNIX as such had a menu-driven interface as an alternative to the shell — one that would be applicable whatever application you were running. Those who have ever used an Apple Macintosh will know what can be done to make a computer user-friendly, and to make diverse applications behave in the same way, so that you don't have to keep remembering different command sequences.

The Macintosh had the great advantage that its designers were starting with a clean sheet, and did not have to take account of existing application software. With UNIX, the history of nearly twenty years of software development means that you can't just start from scratch. Moreover the Macintosh is a closed system, and its software is all designed for very specific screen and keyboard specifications, whereas a UNIX system may need to cope with all manner of terminals attached to the same computer, and even, at different times, to the same communications port.

Menus and commands

There are two main ways in which programs allow you to converse with them and give them instructions: by typing commands (the standard approach taken by the UNIX shell and utilities) and by selection from a menu.

The choice between a command interface and a menu interface is a fairly fundamental one in the design of any computer software, but one that should not be made too hastily. The best answer may be to have not one or the other exclusively, but a mixture of both, or perhaps allow users themselves to choose depending on their familiarity with the system. It is usually the case that new or occasional users will be happier with a menu (provided that the menu items are unambiguous and easy to understand) while more experienced users may prefer a command approach, which can be quicker to use.

The traditional menu on older computer systems comprised a full screen, one line per item, often with numbers. You were instructed to type the number corresponding to the selection required, and possibly then hit the Return key. More modern user interfaces feature different types of menu, which do not take up the full screen, and are easier to use.

These days it is common to provide several methods of selecting items from menus. The most straightforward is by 'pick and point' — in other words there is a menu cursor, often taking the form of the entire menu item being highlighted on the screen; you can move the cursor up and down till you reach the item you want, and then hit the Return key to confirm the selection. Most menus also have another means of selection, by keying in a number corresponding to the menu item, or the first letter of the option in question. The various menus in the Q-Office software are an example of this approach. Occasionally one comes across software which has *only* pick and point, or *only* selection by initial letter, but this can generally be put down to poor system design.

The Lotus 1-2-3 spreadsheet package has made the so-called 'ring menus' popular. By hitting a special 'menu' key (the '/' key in the case of Lotus) a single line menu can be displayed at the top of the screen showing the various options as one word items. One of the items is highlighted, and this item is explained in more detail on the line below. You can move the highlighting from one item to the next, and hit Return when satisfied, or you can type in the initial letter of the command word. Ring menus based on this approach are now beginning to appear in UNIX software packages such as Ingres.

The experienced user may find menus tiresome and prefer a quicker route. Some software therefore allows you, depending perhaps on your 'skill level', to bypass the menus, and enter commands directly instead.

Mode independence

One generally accepted rule is that at least for the unskilled user, interaction with the computer should be 'mode-independent'. Some programs break this rule quite extensively. For instance *vi*, perhaps the most widely used text editor for UNIX systems, uses the ordinary alphabetic keys of the keyboard as control keys when it is in 'command mode'. Thus if you hit the *x* key, this will sometimes put an x in your text in the normal way, and sometimes delete the character that the cursor is positioned on, depending whether you are in command mode or insertion mode. Still worse, there is no display on the screen to remind you which mode you are currently in. Not surprisingly, new users find they are constantly doing the wrong thing by mistake. Indeed a new user getting to grips with *vi* can be recognised by the sound of muffled cursing, mixed with repeated bleeps from the terminal as the system rejects erroneous commands.

The *vi* type of user interface is no doubt good for programmers and hackers, who can become very proficient in making the product sing and dance, and often take a pride in their mastery of such a recalcitrant package. But it should not, for instance, be given to a manager wanting to compose an internal memo, as it will confirm all his worse beliefs about computers in general and UNIX in particular.

It is actually one of the more annoying facts about UNIX that its standard screen-based editor is so difficult to get to grips with, and so non-intuitive in its command structure for the casual user. When people are learning various aspects of UNIX, such as programming in C or a 4GL, or just using SQL, it is often convenient to use an editor to prepare source files. Unfortunately this either means a non-standard editor, or the need to expend some effort getting to know *vi* and its peculiarities.

Text input is actually a key part of the user interface to computers. Nearly every computer function needs some amount of inputting of text by the user, whether it be the name of a command to the operating system, or customer name and address details in an order entry program.

The standard terminal handling routines in the UNIX kernel are available to deal with a few of the most basic editing functions, such as the use of the backspace key to delete the character you have just typed in. However, when it comes to more sophisticated functions, such as going back to the start of the line or the previous word, there are no real standards, and different programs work in quite different ways.

Help facilities

Quite a lot of software these days incorporates 'help' facilities, which you invoke by pressing a special key (perhaps the question mark, or function key F1). The best help facilities are context sensitive − in other words, wherever you are in the program, you get help messages specific to that part of the application, advising you what you could do next. Like many other aspects of a good user interface, a help facility has a cost in terms of the disk space that must be provided for the help text, and the logic that must be included in the program to retrieve the appropriate piece of text and take you through it from one page to another.

Recent versions of UNIX offer the *assist* package, which gives much better help to users working at the shell level as to the format of the various UNIX commands.

Response times

The speed of response of a computer system can be an important factor in determining how user-friendly it appears to be. It is irritating if you type in a command and then have to wait a long time for the computer to respond. It is still worse if the response time is very variable. This can easily happen with multi-user systems, particularly those, such as UNIX, which aim to be 'fair' to all their users, and respond to increased load on the system by reducing the time allocated to each task, and thus causing the service to all the users to slow down. In certain applications the variability of the response can be so distracting that it is better to put in artificial delays, and slow down the response when the system is lightly loaded, so that the difference when the system is more heavily loaded does not seem too great.

An inappropriate response time may actually confuse the user as to what is going on. In particular, if a command is going to take an appreciable time to execute, it should respond immediately with some message to the effect of 'processing your request — please wait', as otherwise the user may think the program expects some more input, and may start pressing additional keys, or repeatedly hitting Return, which in its turn may cause problems. The 'please wait' message should be prominently displayed, and perhaps flashing, which at least gives the impression that something is happening, although too much flashing can be tiring on the eyes.

The WIMP approach

Many of today's ideas on the user interface come from the work of Xerox's Palo Alto Research Centre (PARC) who developed what has been called WIMP (window/icon/mouse/pointer). The WIMP approach, although devised by Xerox, owes its popularity to Apple, whose Macintosh personal computer has made this type of presentation very popular.

The WIMP type of presentation takes the pick and point technique one stage further. The idea is that rather than moving a text cursor about with the arrow key, you have a special input device such as a mouse. A pointer moves about on the screen in time with the movements of the mouse on the desk. Rather than having to type commands, or select an option from a menu, you are shown a number of little pictures ('icons') on the screen. You can select items to be actioned by moving the pointer over the icon in question and pressing one of the buttons on the mouse. Other features of this type of presentation include 'pop-up' or 'pull-down' menus, which appear only when requested.

The key to the WIMP approach is that the display screen becomes a graphical display, divided up up into a number of windows. Some systems have the windows side by side, others have them partly overlapping, in analogy to papers lying around on a desk; each window represents a program or task in progress, or a document being processed. The mouse allows you to move around easily from one window to another, and to manipulate objects via their icons.

The use of windows is particularly useful where there are several entirely different contexts which the user may need to switch between.

The WIMP approach lends itself particularly to high resolution graphical screens, but it is possible to approximate it using a text-only screen (providing it has at least line drawing facilities). The Accell 4GL package, and recent versions of Informix, use windows in this way. However, the essence of windowing is that the windows themselves should be clearly distinguished from their surroundings — if the normal screen display uses lines and boxes, a window may not stand out very well.

Coping with interruptions

UNIX, as should be clear by now, is a multi-tasking operating system. One way this feature can be put to use is to cope with the interruptions that naturally occur. For instance, you may be writing a report, when suddenly the telephone rings and you need to drop what you're doing, answer the phone, maybe look up some facts, calculate a price, make an appointment in your diary, and finally pick up the original task where you left off. All of these tasks could be automated, but they would involve a number of different programs: programs take time to load in from disk; the time could just be too long to be tolerated. With traditional single-tasking systems it would be as if, when the phone rang, you not only had to put your pen down, but also close the book (having finished the sentence you were writing) and put it away on the shelf, before picking the telephone up. By this time, the caller might well have rung off.

Ideally, you need to have several programs loaded, and switch quickly from one to the other. UNIX as such does not help very much here. With the conventional UNIX system you can certainly set off several tasks at once (using the '&' option in the shell, for instance) but it is difficult to see what more than one task is doing. In fact you are generally advised to use the '&' option only with tasks that do not use the screen, otherwise the output from the foreground and background tasks will get jumbled up.

A number of UNIX systems allow you to have multiple foreground tasks on a single terminal. Some systems use multiple windows on the screen, each representing a different program; others, such as the SCO version of Xenix, have 'multiple virtual terminals' — in other words, the entire screen is given up to one program, but at the press of a button the display will be instantly replaced by one for a different program. Specific implementations of UNIX have tended to support one or the other version — UNIX as such merely provides the underlying mechanism for either to be implemented by a specially written 'shell'. However, System V Release 2 onwards additionally has 'job control', providing a virtual terminal facility.

Job control (rather a confusing use of the term for those familiar with other computer systems) allows a single user to have more than one shell active at a time, and switch from one to another using a special key combination. Each copy of the shell is described as a 'layer', and a new command, *shl*, allows the user to control the various layers. Layers not currently in use continue running, but do not receive any input from the keyboard until you switch back to them.

Problems with windowing systems

To implement the WIMP approach on a UNIX machine, you ideally need a graphics terminal with a mouse. You also need to be able to exchange data very quickly between the computer and the terminal. Personal computers have 'memory-mapped' display screens — part of main memory is reserved for the image of the screen. Each dot or pixel on the screen corresponds to one or more bits in the computer's main memory, so that the screen can be changed very quickly — the program just needs to change the contents of the appropriate memory location, and the screen changes immediately.

A UNIX system does not generally work in this way; communication with a terminal normally takes the form of a stream of data and commands sent down a communication line, which the terminal receives and interprets. This is a very slow method compared to a memory-mapped display.

A memory-mapped display requires quite a lot of memory, particularly if it is in colour, and therefore needs several bits per pixel, and it would not be practicable to provide this facility for every terminal. Moreover, the displays in question need to be fed with video signals rather than standard serial data.

A standard vdu terminal connected to a serial port will find it difficult to keep up with the processor in heavy graphical applications, or for a full-scale WIMP user interface. Most terminals (at least those in the same building as the computer) operate at a speed of 9600 baud, or say 1000 characters a second. This may sound fast, and it certainly is for the teletype style of program — if you are using the shell, the letters you type seem to come up instantly on the screen, even though they have actually been up to the computer and back, and processed by the kernel on the way. But for full-screen working, 9600 is slow; remember, a screen of 25 lines by 80 columns contains 2000 characters, so changing a full screen would take about two seconds, rather than being virtually instantaneous as on a personal computer. The position is even worse for a high resolution graphics screen, which can have the equivalent of many more than 2000 bytes-worth of data: a Sun colour workstation display requires two megabytes.

Of course most applications try to avoid changing a complete screenful of data at a time, but if you have an interactive graphics program, using the mouse to move the cursor and modifying the picture in real time to follow it, data needs to flow back and forth between computer and terminal very quickly, as otherwise the movement of the cursor on the screen can get disturbingly out of synchronisation with the movement of the hand and mouse.

Despite the speed problems, the WIMP approach is beginning to catch on in UNIX, at least for certain types of computer and certain applications. For a start some UNIX machines do in fact have memory-mapped displays; a personal computer running Xenix, an IBM 6150 running AIX, or a graphics workstation, all have memory-mapping on the console although the other terminals, if any, have to be treated as ordinary vdus. This is why applications which demand high resolution graphics are generally done on a single-user basis, even though the computer may be physically capable of having other terminals connected to run more conventional applications.

In fact, some very high-performance UNIX computers – for instance, some of the Sun Microsystems range – now allow you (at a price) to add extra terminal controller boards with their own memory, so that you can have multiple memory-mapped displays.

Another complication with windowing systems under UNIX, as opposed to single-tasking systems such as the Macintosh or MS-DOS, is that each window may logically represent a separate process, and so the operating system or the windowing software needs to ensure that the various processes do not encroach on each other's screen space. This is often achieved by means of a separate Window Manager process, which controls the screen display as a whole, and arbitrates between the various application processes, interacting with them via inter-process communication.

Opentop

Opentop was produced by the British company, Torch, initially to run on their TripleX range of UNIX-based micros, but they are also making it available on Xenix and other versions of UNIX. The Torch approach whereby each terminal is a UNIX computer in its own right makes it very suitable for a graphical user interface.

Torch decided that the business world of the 1990s would come to demand windowing, and Opentop supports up to seven simultaneous windows per terminal. Each window can be up to 24 lines of 80 characters, and you can easily change the size of a window, move it around the screen, use it to scroll up and down or sideways within a large document, or close it altogether.

The screen supports colour in up to 256 shades. It displays icons representing various programs and types of file; a picture of a folder, for instance, represents a subdirectory. There is a special utility allowing you to design your own icons.

The two-button mouse supplied allows you to select an item such as a file or program, and 'drag' it to another location on the screen (for instance, another directory). You can run a program by selecting it and hitting the mouse button, or you can drag another icon on top of the program icon, to tell it which file it is to work on.

Opentop is designed so that you can customise the system for your own use. For instance, you can define a 'desktop' on the screen, containing various files that you use frequently, collected from various directories.

Multiview

Multiview (previously IOS – Integrated Office System) is a product from JSB Computer Systems, available on a number of UNIX computers. It aims to provide a user-friendly interface to integrate various office automation applications. You can have up to six windows on the screen at once, and their sizes and positions can be individually controlled. Multiple windows on the same terminal can be used to cope with concurrent active processes, and the system also provides a means of transferring data between one application and another, using cut and paste. Pull-down menus are available, and the 'system manager' can be used to tailor the features of the operating system to individual users.

Unlike most other products in its class, Multiview will run on any vdu terminal, since it uses character graphics, and therefore does not require bit-mapped graphics screens. Additionally, however, a bit-mapped version is being developed.

Like some of the equivalent products for the personal computer market (GEM, Microsoft Windows) Multiview is supplied complete with some application software – the basic functions of address book and telephone directory, card index filing, and a scratchpad for making notes.

Curses

UNIX has its own windowing facility, in the shape of the *curses* library of routines for inclusion in C programs. *Curses* has been adopted as part of the X/Open Group standard, and offers basic facilities for defining windows of various sizes on the screen, and for manipulating the cursor within them. Multiple windows on the screen can be 'tiled' (side by side) or overlapping. Where windows overlap, the window which was refreshed most recently will appear on top.

Curses is very closely linked with the *terminfo* database of terminal characteristics, and allows UNIX programs to use features such as pop-up menus and help windows. However, it is somewhat primitive compared to more recent products such as NeWS and X/Windows.

NeWS

The NeWS product, from Sun Microsystems, is intended to be independent of both the hardware and the operating system. NeWS (short for Network Extensible Windowing System) works on a 'client/server' basis. In other words an application does not send its output directly to the screen, but to a separate process which handles the screen windows. Communication between the client and server is by means of the PostScript language, described in Chapter 13. The great benefit of the PostScript-based approach is that the application program produces its output in a high level language, which the server process can interpret according to what type of hardware is in use. The same application program can thus run without change on different types of display screen.

X/Windows

The main competitor to NeWS is X/Windows, which is a public domain standard embodied in a variety of commercial products.

At the time of writing, X/Windows is at Version 10. The various versions have not been entirely compatible with one another. Version 11, currently in beta test, is expected to become a standard. Sun have announced that the next version of NeWS will emulate X/Windows, as a result of user pressure. In fact it will apparently be possible for X and NeWS applications to run side by side on the same terminal.

Support for X/Windows has also come from IBM, who now support it under AIX, implying that their own standard, called Andrew, will not be promoted as a commercial product.

Using colour

Colour is useful on vdu screens, not only for graphical purposes, but also for emphasis.

Colour vdu terminals are widely available, and a colour display is particularly popular on personal computers. Colour allows the software designer to achieve a much greater degree of emphasis and distinction between different parts of the display, but of course it should not be over-used, for practical as well as aesthetic reasons. Moreover, it is dangerous to rely totally on colour: you need to remember not only the sizeable minority of the male population with defective colour vision, but also the much larger proportion of the vdu population with monochrome only (some of them representing colours by differing grey-scales, others not).

Part III
Behind the Scenes

Chapter 17
How UNIX Works

The title of this chapter may seem a little ambitious. To explain the full workings of UNIX — even those parts that AT&T allow to be made public — would take an entire book considerably larger than this one. However, in order to appreciate what UNIX can do for you, it may be helpful to understand a little of how some of the main features are implemented.

For a start, let us look rather more deeply at what happens before — and after — you log in to the system.

The login process

Of course you can't log in at all unless UNIX invites you to. The program that issues the invitation is called *getty*. Normally, for each terminal which is waiting for someone to log in, there is a process running *getty*. The word 'tty' that occurs in the name of this and other programs is short for 'Teletype', a common way in UNIX of referring to a terminal.

Let's go one step further back. When you first switch on a UNIX computer, one of the things that happens is that a program called *init* is set running. Whenever you do a *ps -e* you will see the *init* program working away, and note that it has process ID number 1, to confirm that it started when UNIX itself was started up. What *init* actually does is governed by a table called */etc/inittab*. This table has (roughly speaking) an entry for each line to which a terminal can be connected. The entry states whether the line is to be considered a 'login' port, and gives details of the program (normally *getty*) to be started up. *Inittab* is just a text file — one of several with special uses in UNIX.

To be more precise, *inittab* is actually at least two tables in one. One table relates to the normal multi-user situation, the other to the single-user stage which each UNIX system goes through while it is starting up. In single-user mode, only the console is designated as a login port.

So for every terminal on which users are allowed to log in, *init* sets off a process running *getty*, which displays a message such as

UNIX login:

and then waits until someone takes up the invitation. When someone does type something in reply, *getty* takes this as being a login name, and also decides what sort of terminal is connected to the port. For instance, if you log in with a name all in upper case, it will assume that you have a very old-fashioned terminal that works in upper case only.

Next, *getty* calls a program called *login*. It looks up your login name in the password file (another standard text file, called */etc/passwd*); if it finds an encrypted password against your login name it asks you for your password, encrypts it, and checks the encrypted version against the password file. If the passwords fail to match, or if it cannot find the user name at all in the password file, the login is rejected.

The password file also contains other information used during logging in: your initial group and home directory, and the name of the login shell or program which UNIX starts running for you if your login is successful. This program is usually one of the standard UNIX shells, enabling you to access the various features of UNIX, but another program could be specified instead. In either case, as soon as this program terminates (for instance if you type Ctrl-D to signify the end of input to the shell) you will be immediately logged off.

The kernel

The essence of UNIX to a user often appears to be the shell and the various commands and utilities. However, these are only the superficial façade of the operating system. The real UNIX is the kernel, which the user never sees.

The kernel as such does not have a process of its own, but is available as a resource that any process can use. The interface to the kernel is within each program: whenever a program needs to do input or output, or use the resources of UNIX, it communicates its needs to the kernel, using a variety of standard mechanisms known as system calls. There are about 70 different UNIX system calls (I have given a list in Appendix C) but the exact number depends on the particular version of the operating system.

The UNIX kernel occupies an area of memory to itself, separate from the various user processes. This area includes, for instance, a table with entries for each process currently active, showing its status and other information.

When a process executes a system call, or responds to an interrupt, it changes from user mode to kernel mode, or supervisor mode. Many makes of microprocessor recognise this change specifically in hardware – a process in supervisor mode has access to particular instructions which are not available otherwise. In software terms, the UNIX kernel can certainly do many things that the same process running in user mode could not do. The kernel, because of its special status, is thus able to exercise overall control over the running of the system, and keep the various user programs from running amok.

Dealing with terminals

I have already mentioned that anything you type at the keyboard is normally scrutinised by the kernel before being passed on to the shell or to the application program. In fact the kernel includes a 'line discipline' for this purpose, and can operate either in 'raw mode' or in 'canonical mode'. The word 'canonical' implies that the kernel translates what the user typed into what he really meant. For instance, when you are typing a command to the shell, you may realise that you have hit the wrong key by mistake, and use the backspace key to rub it out. The kernel, if it is acting in canonical mode, will recognise this, and omit the erroneous character (and the backspace character itself) from the line of text it is building up. Similarly, if you hit the 'line kill' key (often Ctrl-X) the kernel will abandon the entire line and start again. Only when you hit Return does the kernel pass the line it has been assembling on to the shell or application program.

You can control what the kernel does by means of the *stty* command. Used with no arguments, the command will tell you the terminal settings currently being used for your particular terminal, but you can alter them, for instance to change the speed of transmission, or to assign a different character to act as erase, line kill, and so on.

The following are some examples of *stty* commands.

stty -echo

This tells the kernel to stop echoing input back to the screen – appropriate if the terminal itself does its own echoing, for instance with half duplex data communications. Normally, all input is echoed except for passwords.

stty 9600

This sets the kernel to expect input and output at 9600 baud.

stty oddp

This sets transmission at 7 bits per character with odd parity.

stty raw

This turns off canonical processing, and lets the kernel pass the input straight through, a character at a time.

stty sane

This sets all modes to some reasonable values.

Hardware help for terminal handling

Dealing with terminal input obviously places quite a heavy load on the processor. Each time you press a key, an interrupt is caused, the current program is suspended, and the system has to switch into kernel mode, process the character, and then switch back to user mode. Not surprisingly, many UNIX-based computers have been designed to relieve the central processor of this task. One method is to do more of the processing locally within the terminal, but this implies the use of intelligent terminals, or perhaps personal computers running suitable software. The other method is to build extra hardware into the UNIX host in the form of 'front end processors', or 'intelligent communications processors', which handle the screen echoing, the canonical processing, and the assembling of the input into complete lines.

Of course this will not help very much in the case of programs which require raw terminal input, which many programs do. A program designed to respond instantly as you hit each key, rather than waiting for a complete line of input, will effectively be doing its own canonical processing, rather than relying on the kernel or on any communications processors. Such programs are the norm for personal computer applications such as word processing and spreadsheeting — one reason why such programs impose a particularly heavy load on a UNIX-based computer.

One difference between the two word processing packages that I discussed earlier is in their terminal handling. Q-Office uses raw input, and is therefore able to treat many of the keys on the keyboard as special control keys, at the expense of generally slower performance. Uniplex on the other hand has 'cooked' terminal handling, which can achieve better performance, but restricts the repertoire of control sequences (the Escape key is used extensively, since this, like the Return key, is processed specially by the standard tty handlers).

Handling the vdu screen

The basic terminal handling as controlled by *stty* is sufficient for the shell, and for utilities which are line-based rather than screen-based in their use of the vdu. But for *vi*, and for the various UNIX-based packages which use full screen displays, something more sophisticated is required. For instance the system needs to know how many lines and columns there are on the screen, whether it can support colour, blinking, or inverse video, and if so what control characters need to be sent to achieve these effects.

UNIX handles these and many other terminal characteristics by means of a database called *terminfo* (terminal information) − or *termcap* (terminal capabilities) on older systems. The database contains details of virtually every type of terminal likely to be encountered, and new terminal descriptions can be added if necessary.

Of course to make use of *terminfo*, UNIX needs to know what type of terminal is attached to each port. It uses an environment variable called TERM, which defines the terminal type in use by a particular user. The TERM variable is set up when the user logs in: sometimes it is supplied in a startup file in the user's home directory, and sometimes UNIX can obtain it directly from the terminal, as many terminals can be programmed to identify themselves to the computer on request, by sending an 'answerback' message.

Controlling processes

An important aspect of the UNIX kernel is the control of processes. Each process is a program being executed, and each is represented by at least three regions or segments in memory:
- the code segment, also sometimes confusingly called the 'text region', containing the actual machine language instructions to be carried out;
- the data segment, containing the various constant and variable data items that the program is working on;
- the stack, used to keep track of the calling of subroutines.

UNIX allows segments to be shared between processes. The code segment in particular is often shared, since UNIX programs are typically 're-entrant'. In other words, the program code cannot be modified while the program is running, and there is no reason for two or more processes running the same program to have their own individual copies of it.

In recent versions of UNIX, data segments can also be shared: if two processes are co-operating closely and need to exchange data, they can do so much more efficiently using shared memory than by means of pipes, which was the traditional method. Of course the two programs will each have their own non-shared data areas.

When the process looks at its own memory space, it sees the various regions as occupying memory addresses starting from zero up to some maximum. But these cannot be real addresses in memory, since there are many processes loaded at a time, and only one of them could actually start at address zero. In fact the program cannot have any idea where its segments will actually be put. The program therefore refers to the various parts of its address space by means of 'virtual addresses', and hardware or software in the kernel translate these as required to real addresses without the program needing to do anything about it.

The start of a process

When a new process starts, it always begins as a child of an existing process (except of course when the system is first starting up). To give birth to a new process, a program can use the *fork* system call. Following the *fork*, there are two processes where before there was only one. Both processes (for the moment) are running the same program, and the contents of their data segments start off identical. However, each can tell whether it is the parent or the child: when the *fork* system call is complete and hands control back to the program, it returns a value. The value given to the child process is zero, while that given to the parent process is a number equal to the child's process ID.

Normally the program will include instructions to examine the result of the *fork* call to see which it is. Thus from this point onwards, the parent and the child will diverge.

A program could thus include some logic of the general form:

issue the *fork* system call;
if this is now the child process, issue the *exec* system call to execute a new program;
otherwise, this is still the parent, so issue the *wait* system call, to suspend processing until the child has done its work and terminated, then continue;

The *wait* system call in due course returns a value to the parent process, containing the exit status of the child process. This status is zero if the child completed its run normally.

The *fork*, *exec*, and *wait* system calls are nicely packaged together in the *system* subroutine, which is the normal way of firing off a new process from within a program.

To take a specific example, suppose you are at the shell prompt and type

cat myfile > newfile

The shell first of all *forks*, so there are two processes, each of them initially running the shell. Both return from the *fork*, one as the parent, the other as the child. The child process immediately issues an *exec* call to run the *cat* program. The parent puts itself to sleep, waiting till the child process has terminated (at the end of the *cat*) and then wakes up again.

If on the other hand you type

cat myfile > newfile &

the parent process does not sleep, but continues by prompting you for your next command, while the *cat* is still doing its work.

Time-sharing in UNIX

Once a process has been created, and *exec*ed a new program if required, it starts running under the control of the new program. But clearly it cannot be just left to run indefinitely, as none of the other users on the system would get a look in. So from time to time the process needs to be interrupted to let other processes have a chance. In other words a 'context switch' takes place, and another process is set running instead.

All time-sharing operating systems have a scheduling scheme which allocates time between the various processes, interrupting user processes when they have used up their time allocation, and scheduling the next one to run. In UNIX the scheduling is done by the kernel. Whenever a program makes a system call, or is interrupted in what it is doing, it stops running the user program, and starts running the program routines contained in the kernel; this is an opportunity for the kernel to schedule a context switch if appropriate. Such opportunities occur very frequently, since i/o processing is nearly always going on, and giving rise to interrupts. If, however, the process goes for some time without receiving any interrupts or making any system calls, it will eventually use up its time slice (typically a second) and the kernel will force a context switch; there is a special interrupt called a clock tick which occurs at regular intervals − perhaps 100 times a second − and calls in the kernel scheduling routines.

Sleeping processes

Often, a process would be unable to continue even if the scheduler permitted it, and therefore puts itself to sleep − usually because it is waiting for some external event to be completed. A process is always executing in kernel mode at the time when it goes to sleep, which is just as well, since there is some tidying up to do, to ensure that all will be in order when it wakes up again.

As an example, let's look at what happens when a process wants to read data from a disk file. Some operating systems provide for asynchronous input/output — in other words the program can set off some i/o processing, and carry on with something else while the i/o is happening. UNIX, on the other hand, provides only for synchronous i/o: a UNIX program which has requested an i/o transfer cannot do anything else until the transfer is complete. In other words, as soon as it has asked for data to be read from disk, it has to wait.

Compared to other types of processing, input/output activity such as reading from the disk will take a long time — more if UNIX actually has to fetch the data physically from disk, less if it happens to be already in a buffer in memory — so it is only fair now to hand over to another process, which will be able to make better use of the processor. The process therefore puts itself to sleep; but before doing so it leaves a memo in a special kernel table, specifying what will cause it to wake up — in this case, completion of a disk transfer.

As soon as the process has gone to sleep, the kernel does a 'context switch' — that is it selects another process and sets it running.

Eventually, the disk transfer is complete, and the hardware indicates this to the processor by means of an interrupt. Let us assume that some other process is running in user mode at this time. The interrupt causes the process to break off from what it is doing, switch into kernel mode, service the interrupt, and then resume. 'Servicing the interrupt' in this particular case means waking up the original process, and indeed any others which were asleep waiting for a disk transfer.

'Waking up' does not mean that the process starts running immediately; in fact the process goes into a 'ready to run' state, so that it will be one of those that the scheduler considers, the next time a context switch occurs or a running process has used up its time slice. The decision as to which of several processes should run next is based on the priority of each process, which is partly determined by how long each has been waiting.

All of this has taken some time to describe. But the essence of scheduling in a time-sharing system such as UNIX is that it must happen extremely quickly; if several people are typing at their keyboards, UNIX is switching between one and another so quickly that each can often be unaware that anyone else is using the computer.

Memory and swapping

If there is enough RAM, many processes can run concurrently in this way, each with its own allocation of memory. But there is nothing to stop additional processes being *fork*ed, to the point where not all of them will fit in memory at once. When this happens, the swapper comes into action.

The swapper is a special process that runs all the time in the background. The process in question actually started when the machine was turned on, even before *init*, and has process ID zero. As necessary, it swaps sleeping or ready-to-run processes out of memory, and later swaps them back in.

Swapping a process out means that its entire image in memory (text, data, and stack regions) is copied to a special area of disk. This area does not contain files in the usual sense, and swapping does not use the usual file handling mechanism, which would be too slow.

A table in the kernel is maintained showing what processes have been swapped out, and for how long.

If a process needs to expand in size, it is automatically swapped out, so that it can later be swapped back into a larger area of memory. But swapping also occurs to make room for processes to be swapped in, in which case the kernel selects the process to be swapped out — generally one that is sleeping, or a 'ready to run' process with a low priority. When there is room in memory, the swapper swaps processes back in from disk, depending on how long they have been swapped out. A swapped in process cannot be swapped out again until it has been in memory for two seconds.

To be strictly correct, one should not quote actual figures such as 'two seconds' when speaking about UNIX in general. As part of the general process of standardising and generalising UNIX, more and more specific figures such as this are being replaced by tunable parameters, so that they can be modified to suit a particular machine or a particular installation.

UNIX provides a special system call — *plock* — which can lock a process in memory, to stop it being swapped out at all.

Demand paging

Swapping whole processes in and out is rather a crude mechanism. System V Release 3 uses the more sophisticated method of 'demand paging', which recognises that some parts of a process are used more than others. For instance, many programs include special initialisation routines that are executed once only when the program starts up and then not used again, or error routines, which are only called when some obscure error condition arises. These parts of the program do not need to be kept in memory all the time the program is running, but they do need to be available if the condition in question should arise.

In a demand paging system, each region of a process is divided into pages of a fixed size (2k, in Release 3) and each page is capable of being swapped in or out individually. Thus a program may be running but only partly resident in memory. In fact you can load a process that is bigger than the entire physical memory.

If the program needs to access a part of its 'virtual memory' which is not actually present, a 'page fault' occurs. A page fault is a type of interrupt and calls a kernel routine which looks for the page in question. If the page has been swapped out previously, it will now need to be swapped back in; if it has never been loaded, it may need to be loaded now from the executable program file. In either case, a disk access may be necessary to obtain the page, in which case the process goes to sleep in the usual way.

Whenever a process accesses a page in memory it marks it as 'used'. The kernel regularly surveys all the active pages to see when they were last used; when it needs to swap pages out it chooses those that have not been used recently, on the assumption that these are less likely to be used again in the near future.

More about files and filesystems

A filesystem, as you may remember, is the collection of files stored on a particular disk volume, or sometimes a partition within a disk. A filesystem is divided physically into blocks of a fixed size — generally 1024 or 512 bytes on System V.

The first two blocks in a filesystem are the boot block and the superblock. The boot block is used when the computer is turned on: the machine looks there to see what operating system it is to load, and how to find the kernel and load it into memory. From then on, UNIX itself takes over. All filesystems have a boot block, but only one of them is actually used. The computer will probably be programmed in ROM to treat a particular physical device as the 'boot disk', to be consulted at startup time.

The superblock is the starting point for information about the various files on the disk. It includes basic information such as the size of the inode table, the address of the free list, and so on. When a filesystem has been mounted, a copy of its superblock is kept permanently in memory, as the system needs to refer to it very frequently.

Following the superblock is the inode table, containing an inode for every file in the filesystem. Each inode occupies 64 bytes. The size of the table as a whole, like that of the filesystem itself, cannot be changed without unloading the data, so that there is a limit to the number of files which a filesystem can contain.

Actually not all the inodes on a UNIX system refer to disk files. Certain inodes for 'special files' refer to devices, that is printers, terminals, and so on. By giving them inodes, UNIX enables them to be treated for certain purposes as if they were files. For instance, they have directory entries, normally within the /dev directory, so that output from a program can easily be directed to either a file or to a device as necessary.

Each inode contains the following data:
- file type: regular, directory, device (character special or block special), or FIFO (pipe);
- access permissions: read, write, and execute permission for the individual owner, the group owner, and others, respectively;
- number of links (number of names the file has in the directory hierarchy);
- individual owner − user identification (uid);
- group owner identification (gid);
- file size;
- table of disk addresses for data blocks;
- time of last access (last change to file, last access to file, last change to inode).

The inode does not of course contain the name of the file; names are a matter for the directory structure, not the inode, and of course a file has only one inode, but may have several directory entries and hence several names. An ordinary pipe, on the other hand, has an inode, but has no name or directory entry.

The size of a UNIX file is measured in bytes. Unlike certain other operating systems, UNIX does not make you define this length in advance − a UNIX file may grow in length as required. Disk space is allocated in blocks (each comprising 512 or 1024 bytes), and the inode contains the disk addresses of individual data blocks. However an inode, having a fixed length, could not hold the address of every block in the file. In fact it has individual entries for only the first ten.

The inode contains a table of thirteen 24-bit disk addresses. The first ten of these hold the addresses of the first ten blocks of the file, thus giving 'direct addressing' for the first 10k of a file (assuming 1k blocks). The eleventh entry in the contents table is the address of a block which contains 128 further block addresses (32-bit addresses this time) thus providing 'indirect addressing'. The twelfth entry uses 'double indirect' addressing (that is, it contains the address of a block containing addresses of further blocks of addresses) and the thirteenth uses 'triple indirect' addressing.

This method can accommodate very large files − in fact the maximum file size is usually determined not by the addressing method but by the 'file size' field in the inode, which is typically a 32-bit field, limiting a file to 2^{32} bytes, or 4 gigabytes. More realistically, a practical limit to the size of a file is set by the size of a physical volume or partition and hence the size of the filesystem.

If files get anywhere near their theoretical maximum size, a proportion of the data is accessible only by triple indirect addressing, so that in order to reach a particular area of data the system needs to access three separate address tables from disk (not counting the inode itself, which is held in a table in memory). In practice, however, the address tables themselves will probably also be in memory, if the relevant portion of the file has been accessed recently.

The filestore is thus optimised for small files, which agrees with the original purpose for which UNIX was first devised, namely program development and text processing, but could be considered less suitable for very large databases.

Locking

Locking of files or parts of files, to prevent simultaneous access or update by more than one user, is generally considered an important feature of a commercial data processing system. For a long time it was not provided in standard UNIX, and was one of the 'enhancements' included in commercial UNIX implementations such as Xenix. Locking is implemented in System V from Release 2 onwards.

Actually, Release 2 provided only advisory locking: each process should issue a lock or test lock statement before accessing the data, and UNIX will report an error if the data is already locked. Advisory locking is fine if all programs obey the rules, but has obvious weaknesses as a program can just ignore the locks. System V Release 3 additionally provides mandatory (enforcement mode) locking: locking a file in enforcement mode prevents any read or write access by another process, even if that process does not test for locks.

In other operating systems locking may be applied at record level, or at physical block level. UNIX does not recognise records, and does its locking at byte level. It is up to the database manager or the application program to determine what area is to be locked – for instance, a record, or perhaps a field within a record, or a group of fields or records – and to translate this to actual byte addresses.

Locking in UNIX uses a table in the kernel. This is fast and very secure. The drawback is that the size of the table is limited – typically 100 entries – and this may well not be sufficient in a commercial multi-user environment. The operating system itself can do something to help – for instance, if two adjacent areas are locked this can be turned into a single lock covering both areas – but this probably does not help very much in a typical commercial application.

Data in files

UNIX knows nothing about the contents of a file. Of course UNIX, and various UNIX utilities, do require certain files to be in particular formats — for instance, the common object file format (COFF), or the standard layout of the password file. Appendix D lists some of the main file formats which are special as far as UNIX is concerned. But as far as the operating system is concerned generally, a file is nothing more or less than a stream of bytes. A file may contain text or binary information, but the application which accesses it must take care of the format of the data.

If a file is divided into 'records' or other structures, this again is the concern of the database manager or the application, not the operating system.

Unlike CP/M files and some types of MS-DOS files, UNIX does not have end-of-file markers: the end of a file is determined solely by the file size field in the inode.

Some database managers and other packages use the convention of filename suffixes or 'extensions' following the user-assigned name. For instance, in Informix, a table called 'staff' would give rise to a data file called *staff.dat* and an index file called *staff.idx*. UNIX, unlike MS-DOS, does not handle such extensions explicitly.

Using files

Each file can be identified uniquely by its inode number. But neither users nor programs refer to files by inode number as a rule. Each process includes a table listing all the files that it currently has open. This table has a fixed length — typically 20 or 100 — so the number of files a process can have open at once is necessarily limited. If a process creates a new file, an entry is made in the table, pointing to the new inode. If a process opens an existing file however, it needs to identify it, using the filename and the directory structure.

There is a further way a process can get a file: by inheriting the file descriptor from a parent process. This is how UNIX copes with pipes (a pipe is essentially a special type of file with no name and therefore no directory entry). No program can open an existing pipe, since it does not know where to find it; but it can inherit a pipe from the parent process, and in this way the parent and child can communicate with one another using a channel that is invisible to all other processes. By the way, UNIX can also have 'named pipes', allowing unrelated processes to communicate.

Reading from disk is generally handled by a standard library routine. In C it could be the *fread* routine, which is part of the standard i/o library. The library routine in turn calls the *read* system call, which hands over control of the process to the appropriate part of the kernel. The kernel looks up its copy of the inode to find where the data is located on disk, and issues instructions to the disk controller to supply the data.

In practice, it would be very inefficient if each read or write by a program had to be serviced by a physical disk access. Remember that when UNIX accesses disks it does so a block at a time − in other words a physical unit of 512 or 1024 bytes. The logical record that a program writes to a file on the other hand can be of any length; it may be a small part of a block, or may span two blocks or more. UNIX maintains a 'buffer cache' in kernel memory, containing the contents of recently used disk blocks. If the *read* system call refers to a disk block which is currently in the buffer cache, UNIX can satisfy it immediately, without actually needing to read the data from disk.

The basic i/o system calls such as *read* and *write* are actually not very efficient or convenient for use in programs. Instead, a library of standard i/o routines is provided. These routines use system calls, but provide an additional level of buffering within the user process rather than the kernel. The standard routines also allow for formatted input and output, consisting of integers, character strings, and so on, whereas *read* and *write* merely treat the data as an unformatted series of bytes.

The standard i/o routines are not always appropriate, however; since they buffer data within the user space they are unable to detect any locks which were put on the data since it was transferred from the kernel's buffers.

Chapter 18
Controlling a UNIX System

The role of the system manager

If you have a single-user micro on your desk, you can very well look after it yourself, just seeking specialist help when things go wrong. Of course there are good practices that you ought to follow, such as taking regular backup copies of your files, but if you don't do this, you will perhaps be the only one to suffer.

A multi-user system, such as a UNIX system, needs much more in the way of management. Partly this is a matter of hygiene; if several different people are using a facility, be it a computer system or a kitchen, you begin to need rules or controls, to make sure that particular users don't behave badly (through malice, selfishness, or just carelessness) and make life difficult for everyone else. With a complex system such as UNIX, the necessary rules and disciplines need someone responsible for co-ordinating them.

Another important point is that a UNIX system is generally an expensive and powerful machine, supplied for a business purpose. The information held on it may be crucial to this purpose. Loss of the information could often be far more costly than the machine it is held on, and even put a company out of business.

The system manager is the person responsible for managing the machine itself, its users, and their files and programs. In addition, the system manager will inevitably become a source of practical information and help to the users, whom they will call on when things go wrong — or when they appear to go wrong!

The super user

Any UNIX system has a special user, with special privileges; the superuser, given the uid number zero, and normally the login name of *root*, can look at any file on the disk, run any program, and change the password of any user. This ability is esssential for system housekeeping purposes, as it allows an authorised person (one who knows the password) to take special steps to get users out of difficulties, or to make changes to the way the system is set up.

The system manager will thus need to become super-user at times — there are certain system management functions that cannot be done without it — but it should not become a habit to log in as super-user. For one thing super-user privileges are very dangerous — it is quite possible to delete all the files on disk by mistake.

Working as super-user also does not reflect the normal user situation. If you are system manager, you may need to change the permissions on files and programs related to some software package. Once you have done this, you should run a system test to make sure that all is well. If you test the system with your super-user hat on, you may well find that it appears to work correctly, whereas in real life it does not. It is most important therefore to change back to the status of an ordinary user before testing any changes you may have made.

Managing files and disks

A common problem with most computers, but with UNIX systems in particular, is that the available space on disk gets filled up. The system manager needs to take action when this happens, to free some space for the system to continue working. Better still, he should regularly monitor the situation, to make sure that action is taken well before it gets to the point of running out of disk space.

There are several reasons why disks get full up. One, of course, is that the disk originally purchased is not big enough for the organisation's needs. If a proper job of systems analysis has been done, the analyst should have worked out roughly how much space the system will need to begin with, how much after a year's running, and so on. But these calculations can never be precise, since they rely on predictions of the volume of the company's business and are therefore subject to the universal uncertainties that arise in trying to predict the future. Moreover, just as a new motorway, if it is successful, will encourage people to make additional journeys, so a computer, if it is really serving the needs of an organisation, may end up being used far more than those who installed it ever expected. So it is not at all unusual to find, after a computer has been in use a short time, that you really need more disk, more memory, and perhaps a faster processor, to cope with the extra demand that has materialised.

But before rushing out to buy additional disks, it is as well to consider exactly why and how the disk space is filling up. The reason can vary considerably depending on the sort of application that is being run.

If the main application of the computer is word processing and office automation, or personal computing by individuals, then disk space is likely to be eaten up by large numbers of small files, which users create for some temporary purpose, and fail to remove when they are finished with them. Probably they use file names which bear no relation to the contents. When the computer first arrives, the disk available seems so vast that no-one bothers to keep track of what files are created. After a time, the users themselves may forget what the files contain, why they were created, and whether they have been superseded by a later version of the same data.

UNIX itself helps to a certain extent. On a UNIX system, unlike, say, a DOS-based personal computer, you can always tell who created the file (or at least who is its current owner — files like those we are talking about are unlikely to have changed ownership). You can also tell when the file was last modified, which should give some idea of how out of date it is likely to be. Certain packages give you more information about files than the meagre amount included in the UNIX directory and inode. For instance, the 'folios' in Uniplex can be used to record background information about a file, which may be of use later in deciding how important it is to keep it. If the file is a program developed within the organisation, or some document relating to software development, the programming staff may have kept track of its successive versions using *sccs* (see Chapter 20) and so it should be clear what is the up-to-date version and how it was arrived at.

The important thing really is discipline. A typist should have some clear policy about how long to keep letters on file: perhaps they should be kept for a month, and then archived to tape or diskette and removed from the system — or else kept only as a 'hard copy' on paper (unless space for paper files is even more scarce than disk space). Similarly, the freedom that UNIX gives its users to create temporary files can easily turn into licence — if you create a file that you know is required only for the duration of this session, then you should give it a name like *temp*, or a name ending in *.tmp*, to indicate clearly that it can be removed afterwards — a shell script could be run overnight to search for all such files and remove them. There is actually a library subroutine specifically designed for creating temporary files: *mktemp* will assign a unique name, including the current process id, to be used as part of a filename for a file within the */tmp* directory.

When a UNIX system is started up again following a power down, it may well clear out the contents of */tmp* and */usr/tmp*.

There is another reason why you may run out of space — not because of the proliferation of small files, but because the main database files get bigger and bigger. Several factors can affect the growth of files in this way, some less obvious than others. An increase in the volume of business, or a miscalculation as to what the volume really is, can obviously affect disk sizes. Most companies know pretty accurately how many invoices they issue during a year, but how many know accurately the average number of detail lines per invoice? If you do the sizings on the basis that the average is four, and it really turns out to be six (perhaps including some special item such as freight which you had forgotten about) then your invoice detail file will be half as big again as you thought.

Databases and disk space

The use of a database manager can have quite an effect on the efficient use of disk space. This has both a static and a dynamic aspect. The static aspect is important where there is a great deal of variability between one record and another in the amount of space required. Name and address records are the classic example where allowing enough room for the worst case means a lot of wasted space in most of the records. The dynamic aspect relates to the reuse of space when records are deleted. In applications with large numbers of insertions and deletions, this can become very critical.

The Oracle database manager is a case in point. Records in Oracle are variable in length, and Oracle is thus very good as regards the static aspects of disk utilisation (although there is an overhead for the free space in every page). On the other hand it does not reuse space freed by deleted records, so the dynamic disk utilisation is poor. Obviously it is important when selecting a database manager to bear in mind the likely pattern of the data files, and the expected change over time.

Indexes are also an important factor in determining the disk required. Often the space required for the indexes to files can be nearly as large as that needed for the files themselves.

Whatever database package you use, there will be from time to time a need to reorganise the database, to tune it, and generally to review its performance in the light of the demands being made on it by its users. One of the main benefits of a modern database system is that it should allow the data to be used in ways which could not be predicted in advance. But this suggests that the database structure which was worked out in advance may not be the most efficient for coping with the use that is actually made of it once it has been installed. Database suppliers often provide documentation and training courses specifically covering ways of tuning the database to make it run faster.

Managing terminals

Terminals pose quite a different sort of problem for system managers. The problem is usually that the users are using them wrongly, or do not understand them. Even if a user is used to personal computers, the change to a vdu may bring unexpected problems. For instance, most terminals have a special setup key to allow the characteristics of the terminal itself to be modified — the line speed, whether local echo is on, and so on. If the user hits the setup key by mistake, he or she will find the terminal displaying a special setup menu, and acting in a totally different fashion from its normal behaviour under the control of UNIX. The natural tendency at this point is to panic and hit every key in sight, thus actually changing the characteristics of the terminal, so that when in due course it goes back into its normal mode it will no longer work correctly.

Some problems with terminals are soon overcome. For instance, many terminals turn off the display if they are unused for a certain time, so as to increase the life of the vdu screen. A user who does not know this might think his terminal had been turned off or broken, when all he needs to do is to hit any key to bring the picture back.

The ideal, of course, is for all users to be properly instructed in the use of the terminal, as well as the computer, but this sort of training is often bypassed, so that complaints like 'my terminal's broken', or even 'the computer's broken', are far too commonplace. Usually, of course, the problem can be put right very easily, but the system manager does need to have a good understanding of all the types of terminals used in the organisation, and the way that UNIX interacts with them.

Passwords and security

Passwords are the key to security in any UNIX system.

As I mentioned in the previous chapter, the passwords are held on the password file in an encrypted form, and encrypted when you type them in. The password as you type it in never appears on the screen and is never held on file in the system. Even if several different users have the same password, the encrypted forms will be different.

If you forget your password, all is not lost, as the super-user can change it for you. One thing he cannot do, on the other hand, is to find out what it was before he changed it. The encryption means that it is effectively impossible for anyone to find out a password from the system, other than by making likely guesses and seeing if they work.

All the security that UNIX applies to passwords is, of course, wasted if the passwords become known by human error. There are two dangers. One arises when users choose (or are given) passwords which they find difficult to remember. They are then likely to write them down in easily discovered places — perhaps on pieces of paper left in the desk drawer, or even stuck to the terminal. The other danger is

that people choose a password that is easy to remember because it is obvious — obvious enough, in fact, that other people can guess what it might be. In either case, the password is not doing its job, which can be summarised as two main objectives:
- to allow access to authorised users and keep others out;
- to enforce the proper use of login names to distinguish one user from another, so that any changes to a database can be traced back to the person who keyed them in.

Obviously if passwords in general need to be kept secret, the secrecy of the super-user password is absolutely critical. As few people as possible should be given access to it, and it should be changed from time to time. On the other hand there must always be at least two people who know the password — otherwise if the sole super-user is taken ill, or becomes unavailable for any reason, administration of the system will grind to a halt.

Using the password file

One of the system manager's most important duties is to add and remove users from the system. A serious multi-user system requires a certain amount of security. The basic point is that everyone who will use the system should be identified as an individual, and should be an authorised person. Some systems have 'guest' accounts, perhaps for demonstration purposes, but these should be kept very strictly under control.

The key to managing users is the password file, which determines who are considered to be users of the system, and what they can do. If you examine the password file (normally called /etc/passwd, you will find that it is a plain text file, one line per user, each line divided up into fields by colons, and looking something like:

ross:k8xOELtQsk6jc:37:5:Ross Burgess:/usr/ross:/bin/csh

The fields are as follows:
- login name;
- encrypted password;
- user ID number;
- group ID number;
- comments;
- home directory;
- login shell or program.

The encrypted password will, of course, give no clue as to the password in its unencrypted form. However, it may include a subfield, separated off by a comma (UNIX conveniently ensures that commas and colons do not occur as the result of encryption). The subfield is used to control password ageing, and the system manager can set it up to ensure that all users change their own passwords at regular intervals. There is a particular option to force the user to change the password the next time he or she logs in, which is a good thing to do when users are first admitted to the system.

The comments field on the password file is optional, but can be used to give the person's full name or perhaps telephone number, as a source of reference to the system manager and others. The only danger which arises is if users have foolishly adopted their surname or some other obvious word as a password, in which case the comments field could help a hacker to guess what the password might be.

Groups

Every user can belong to one or more groups. The group concept is a way of extending the permission structure of UNIX, and gives you a great deal of flexibility in organising the security arrangements; however, the setting up of groups does need some careful thought.

Every user has a default group: on logging on you become a member of your default (login) group, as determined by the password file, and can enjoy the privileges (that is, the various file permissions) attached to that group.

If at any time you want to work 'with a different hat on', you can change your group temporarily using the *newgrp* command, and use a different set of files. Of course there are restrictions on changing groups in this way. The group file, */etc/group*, contains for each group a list of the users who are permitted to change into it.

Theoretically, you can change to another group without being listed in its group file entry, by using the group password. In practice, however, this never happens, as UNIX does not give you any means of entering group passwords.

In fact the entire group facility is rather under-used in UNIX. This is perhaps due to the way it is implemented. It is obviously convenient to have a group called *accounts*, comprising all the members of the accounts department, who are allowed access to certain financial files and programs. Similarly one can imagine a group called *board*, comprising all the company directors, with access to secret board minutes. But what about the company treasurer, who is both a director and a member of the accounts department? The obvious answer, as UNIX permits, is to make him a member of both groups. But he can't be actively a member of both simultaneously: you can give him the ability to switch from one to the other, by means of *newgrp*, but this is a bit tedious for him to remember (he is not too familiar with UNIX commands) and he may tend to forget which group he is in at any time.

It seems likely that new versions of UNIX will allow you to be a member of several groups at once: this is proposed in the POSIX standard, and has already been implemented in AIX.

Users and groups in practice

There is no right or wrong way to use a UNIX system. This is particularly true when it comes to the use of usernames, groups, and home directories. For instance in some cases it may be convenient for several individuals to have the same username and therefore the same password. Generally speaking, however, it is best to give each user his or her own username and associated password.

Introducing a user to the system thus becomes a matter requiring some thought and a certain formality, but this is just as it should be. Those who are given access to a UNIX system could as well be given the keys, if not to the safe, then at least to the office door, and the privilege should not be bestowed too lightly. Having said this, however, in today's office environment there are likely to be more and more people with a genuine need to access the system; the cost of workstations is coming down, and the problem for the system administrator is to decide what each person should be permitted to see and do.

The best arrangement of groups and directories will depend a great deal on the application. If, for instance, a number of data entry clerks are all working on the same accounting files, it is probably best for them to have the same home directory, and the same login group.

A word processing department demands a different approach. Each typist will normally be creating and editing her own files, and can probably best be left to decide what she calls each document. To avoid possible conflicts with what her colleagues are doing, she should therefore have her own home directory. As far as groups are concerned, the arrangement will depend on the organisation of the company. If the typists are organised as a pool, with work parcelled out between them, and can stand in for one another, it is best to put them in a single word processing group. On the other hand, if each typist works specifically for a single manager or department, the group ID should be that for the department in question, so that documents created in that department can more easily be kept confidential from the rest of the company.

Adding users

In order to allow a new user onto the system there are quite a number of things that need to be done.

The first thing is to choose a login name. UNIX systems are traditionally informal, and most people will want to be known by their first name. But if there are six Johns in the department, some arbitration may be necessary.

Next, you need to choose a user identification number (uid) — one that is not already in use. Probably there will be a system administration utility to help you with the process from here on, and it will choose an unused uid — that is, one not currently used in the password file. It may be advisable, however, to check that the uid really is unused — maybe it belonged previously to a user who has been removed from the password file, but whose files have never been reassigned. If there are any files belonging to the uid in question, the new user will inherit access rights to them.

Other things to be done when creating a new user are to choose a default group ID (and other groups if required), and to decide on the shell or other program the new user is to use. You can then implement these decisions, using the administration utility (if there is one), otherwise by creating a home directory, editing the password file and group file, creating startup files if necessary, and using the *passwd* command to set up an initial password.

When you have done all this, you could try the new user out by sending test mail, and trying to log in to the new account. If all goes well, you can hand over the account, and instruct the user in how to use the system. In particular, of course, you should tell the new user to change his or her password immediately, and you can give some advice on password selection.

Removing a user

Removing a user, like adding one, is often catered for by standard utilities, but again it is as well to have an idea of what the necessary steps are.

The first thing to do is to change the user's password. If the person in question had super-user privileges, you had better change the super-user password as well.

The next thing to do is to remove or redistribute the user's files. This does not just mean files in his home directory (although this is the most likely place to find them). In principle, files belonging to a single user may be scattered throughout the directory hierarchy. The *find* command is useful here. If the user was called *fred*, you could type:

find / -user fred -print > fred.files

This will create a text file called *fred.files* containing a list of all the user's files wherever they may be.

Having found all his files, what do you then do with them? Obviously some of them will be temporary files that can now be removed; equally obviously, perhaps, some will represent useful work that the user had been doing (otherwise why was he allowed on the system at all?) and these need to be given to other users, and perhaps moved to different directories.

When all the user's files have been disposed of, you can remove his home directory and mailbox. Note, by the way, that his home directory may have files in it belonging to someone else, which will have to be moved elsewhere.

Finally, you can remove the user from the password file, and any entries in the groups file. At this point, he is well and truly removed.

Running processes at predefined times

A very useful technique for system management is to be able to schedule processes to run at a particular time, either just once, or regularly every day, every week, and so on.

One of the 'daemons' that lurk unobserved in the background of a UNIX system is called *cron*. *Cron* comes to life once a minute, and examines a text file called the *cron* table, or *crontab*. Entries in *crontab* are instructions to carry out a particular function every minute, every so many minutes, every day, every week, and so on. In many installations, one of the things to be done, in the middle of every night, is to delete from the system all temporary files — for example, those in the */tmp* directory. Another thing to be done, perhaps every five minutes or so, is to run the program *atrun*, which looks for tasks to be executed once only. *Cron* is reserved for use by the super user; however, a feature of recent versions of System V is that ordinary users can have private *crontab* files, to run their own commands on a regular basis.

To take advantage of the *atrun* facility, the command to be used is called *at* (as in 'at 5 pm'). Clearly, there is no point in making the time specified for *atrun* more precise than to the nearest five minutes, if *crontab* is set up to execute *atrun* only at five minute intervals.

Dumps and backups

One of the most important aspects of system management is taking regular backup copies of the files on disk. If the data on the disk is lost or corrupted — by hardware failure, program error, or human incompetence — it can be recovered, provided you have kept a backup.

Effective backup means making a copy of the various files on some medium — tape or removable disk — which can removed from the computer and kept in a safe place. On older mainframes and minicomputers, backup media included big removable cartridge disks, and reel-to-reel magnetic tape. On today's microcomputer systems reel-to-reel tapes are still sometimes used, but the main media are floppy disks and cartridge tape.

Floppy disks are mainly suitable for small systems only: the typical capacity of a diskette on UNIX systems is 720k. Backing up a full hard disk of 70 megabytes or more on floppies can therefore be a little tedious, and tape is much more convenient.

A number of programs are supplied with UNIX to look after the backing up (or 'dumping') of files, and their subsequent restoration from the backup medium.

Perhaps one should distinguish two rather different concepts. On the one hand we have backing up and restoring, at the system (or filesystem) level. This is essentially a system administrator function, and can be done without any detailed knowledge of the actual applications. The system manager may well do backups without any reference to the users. On the other hand we have the archiving of specific files and directories. This is a function to be carried out by a user, or at least at user request: a user may be conscious of the need to keep a copy of the latest version (or indeed a particular version) of a specific file which he is continuing to work on, or he may take an archive copy prior to removing the file from the disk, since it is now of historical interest only.

UNIX has programs to provide for both types of backing up.

The *dump* and *restore* programs can be used on either the entire contents of disk, or a specified filesystem. There are a series of 'levels' available. For instance, if you do a level 3 dump, it will contain all those files which changed since the last level 2 (or lower level) dump.

For file archiving purposes, many versions of UNIX have a program called *tar* (short for 'tape archive', but also available for use with diskette). Unlike *dump* and *restore*, *tar* can be used with specific files and directories.

Another program of the same class, but available as part of standard System V, is *cpio*; it performs much the same sort of functions as *tar*, but its command options, and the format of the files it creates, are quite different. *Cpio* files are the generally preferred way of exchanging software and data on tape or diskette.

Taking backups to tape is one aspect of system management which does require physical intervention by the system manager to load and change the tapes. Moreover, if the speed of the tape is insufficient for the purpose, it may well take an excessive length of time. A number of organisations have therefore adopted the policy of having an additional disk used only for backup purposes and doing regular disk to disk copies automatically, with tape dumps used occasionally as a further safeguard. Provided you can afford the extra disk, this is quite a satisfactory solution.

System management with AIX

One of the novel features of IBM's AIX is its approach to system management. Most system management functions, as we have seen, require the use of super-user privileges, and this can be dangerous for the system and daunting for the system managers themselves. In AIX, a number of the more common functions are reserved, not to the super-user but to a special *system* group, which is allowed a number of special privileges. This is all the more convenient because AIX allows multiple concurrent groups.

Chapter 19
Getting More from the Shell

In Chapter 6 I described a few of the things that the shell — the UNIX command processor — can do. But the shell is really quite a sophisticated programming language in its own right, and you can use it to do a lot of things that would otherwise require a traditional language such as COBOL or BASIC.

How the shell fits in

First of all, it should be noted that the shell is not a specially privileged program. In most respects it is just like any other program that one might write to run under UNIX.

Some people picture the shell as a sort of outer husk surrounding the kernel, and therefore coming between the kernel and the user. In fact, this is not entirely accurate. In a sense the kernel comes between the shell and the user, since (on systems without separate i/o processors) the terminal handling routines in the kernel examine what you type, character by character, looking for backspaces and so on, and only when you hit Return does the complete line get passed on to the shell. The shell thus does not have to cope with the more technical aspects of keyboard handling, and can concentrate on interpreting a complete command line. This has also made it much easier for various people to write alternative shells.

The shell and its environment

You may recall from Chapter 6 the 'environment variable' PATH, which is used to instruct UNIX where to look for programs. Actually, there are a number of such variables, as shown in Table 19.1.

If you wish, you can change the settings of any of these variables, by typing, for instance:

TERM = vt100

Actually this command as it stands will probably not achieve what you

Table 19.1 Selected Bourne shell environment variables.

Name	Meaning
HOME	the default directory for the *cd* command
LOGNAME	your login name
PATH	the search path for commands
CDPATH	the search path for the *cd* command
MAIL	the name of a mail file: if this variable is set, the shell will inform you of any mail arriving in that file
MAILPATH	a list of file names; if this variable is set, the shell informs you of the arrival of mail in any of the files listed
MAILCHECK	this determines how often the shell checks in the files specified in MAIL or MAILPATH for the arrival of mail; by default every 600 seconds (ten minutes)
PS1	primary prompt string; by default the $ sign
PS2	secondary prompt string – used if you have entered a shell command but the shell considers that more input is needed to complete it; by default the > sign
TERM	the type of terminal you are using
TZ	the time zone (for instance GMT)

intend; the setting of TERM that you have specified will be remembered by the shell, but not passed on to any program that you may run from the shell. To get the shell to pass the information on, you additionally need to use the *export* command:

TERM = vt100
export TERM

You can create your own variables with your own names, if you wish, for instance:

count = 10

To find out the current setting of any variable, the easiest way is to use the *echo* command:

echo $TERM

or

echo $count

Note that when referring to a variable as opposed to setting it, you have to precede the name with a dollar sign.

Some variables are set up automatically when you run a shell script.

The variables *$1*, *$2*, and so on are 'positional parameters', and represent the various arguments used when calling the shell script. For example you might write a shell script called *save*, to make backup copies of files, and containing the following text:

cp $1 $HOME/$1.saved

You can use this shell script by typing

save afile

This will then substitute the argument *afile* for the positional variable *$1*, and the pathname of your home directory for the HOME variable. So if your home directory is */usr/fred*, it would be as if you had typed

cp afile /usr/fred/afile.saved

There is an additional positional variable *$0*, referring to the name that the shell script was called by — in this case 'save'.

Startup files

If your login program, as specified in the password file, is the Bourne shell, the first thing it does is to look for two shell scripts — one of them a system file called */etc/profile*, the other a file called *.profile* in your login directory. Together these two scripts determine your 'profile' for the session.

In a profile script you would normally set (and export) environment variables, for instance to tell UNIX what type of terminal you use, to add extra directories to your search path (if you regularly use special software packages, with their own directory structure), or to change the shell prompt from the plain $ sign to something more informative.

You might also get the system to give you some extra information at login time, for instance how many other users are logged on.

Built-in commands

The shell has built into it a number of commands that you might have thought were ordinary programs. Indeed, some of them used to be separate programs and are now built in — as far as the user is concerned, it makes very little difference. In addition, there are some other built in commands specifically concerned with the flow of logic within a shell script. Table 19.2 gives the built-in commands in a typical version of the Bourne shell.

Table 19.2 Bourne shell built-in commands.

Command	Meaning
cd	change working directory
echo	echo its arguments
pwd	display working directory
test	evaluate an expression
umask	set permission bit mask for file creation
break	exit from a *for* or *while* loop
continue	go to the next iteration of a *for* or *while* loop
eval	execute commands given in arguments
exec	execute command in place of this shell
exit	terminate the shell
export	mark environment variables for exporting to subsequent commands
hash	remember search path of command
read	read a line from standard input
readonly	mark names as not to be changed
return	exit from a function
set	set various conditions
shift	renumber the positional parameters
test	evaluate conditional expression
times	display amount of time used
trap	execute a command when a signal is received
type	indicate how a command would be interpreted
ulimit	set limit on size of files to be created
wait	wait for a process to terminate

Advanced shell programming

Using the shell, you can specify quite complex series of commands to be carried out. Moreover, you can control the way in which the shell will move from one statement within your shell script to another, using statements such as *if*, *case*, *for*, and *while*. You can also define your own subroutines or functions.

In Chapter 6 I mentioned the use of wild cards in a command line, to allow the command to apply to a selection of files within the current directory. So

rm *.tmp

would delete all files in the current directory with names ending in *.tmp*. Sometimes, however, you may need to specify a list of files constructed in a less obvious fashion — for instance, to get a full directory listing of all files belonging to a specific user. You may remember the *find* command, which can be used to list the files in question; but how can such a list be incorporated into a shell command? The answer is as follows:

find / -user joe -print > joelist
rm -l `cat joelist`

The thing to note here is the use of 'command substitution', denoted by the pair of left hand quotation marks ` ` otherwise known as backquotes or grave accents. If you include a command (such as *cat joelist* in our example) within backquotes, UNIX will execute the command, and then use its output (in this case the contents of the file *joelist* — that is, the list of files previously collected using the *find* command) to complete the command line that it is to execute. Strictly speaking, the example just shown will not work if *joelist* is too long, as there is a limit to how many arguments the shell can deal with.

Speaking of backquotes reminds me to mention the use of ordinary (right hand or double) quotation marks within a shell script. The shell has as we have seen its own conventions for interpreting special characters within a command line. Sometimes one needs to include such characters within a shell script or command line and have them passed on to the actual program being called, rather than interpreted by the shell. Surrounding the expression in question by quotes could have this effect. For example, if two words need to be passed together as a single argument to a program, they should be surrounded by quotation marks, so that the shell will not treat the space character separating the words as special. This sort of technique arises quite often in shell script construction; however, it is best learnt by studying actual examples that you may find in your installation.

The C shell

So far the examples given have covered the standard UNIX shell, known as the Bourne shell, since this is the only shell that you can be sure of getting on all UNIX systems. However, the C shell, *csh*, is almost as widely distributed, and many people prefer to use it.

The C shell has a number of features not in the Bourne shell. For the casual user, the most useful of these is the history facility. The C shell always remembers the last command you typed in, and you can always repeat it by typing

!!

If you want, you can get the C shell to remember additional commands, not just the last one. The *set history* command is provided for this purpose. If you type

set history 12

the shell will start remembering the commands you type from here on, and will store the twelve most recent ones. At any time you can use the *history* command, which will show you the last twelve on your screen, each with its own 'event number'. To repeat a previous command, just type ! followed immediately by the event number in question.

If you prefer, you can dispense with event numbers and use the initial letters of the commands instead. For instance, the C shell will interpret

!c

as referring to the most recent command that you typed in which started with 'c'.

Other features of the C shell

Another useful feature of the C shell is its alias mechanism. You can use this to define shorter or more convenient ways of referring to files or commands. For instance, suppose you are familiar with MS-DOS or VMS and hence with the DIR command. It may annoy you that the UNIX equivalent is called *ls*. Moreover, whenever you get a directory listing you always use the *-l* option, to show the file sizes, permissions, and so on. You can use the *alias* command as follows:

alias dir ls -l

So from now onwards you can type *dir* at the C shell prompt, and the shell will automatically interpret this as meaning *ls -l*.

If you use aliases regularly, it is worthwhile putting them in a startup file, so that they will be available whenever you log in.

The feature of the C shell that gives it its name is the use of syntax and operators based on the C programming language. I mentioned previously that the Bourne shell has its *if*, *while*, and other statements for control flow, just like a programming language. Of course the C programming language has equivalent statements, but the format and rules for using them are different from the shell. Such differences are confusing for programmers, and the C shell therefore largely follows the C rules.

Relationships between the shells

Most implementations of UNIX have two or more shells available, and some users may switch from one to another. Some shell scripts may be written for the Bourne shell, others for the C shell, and it is necessary to have some means of distinguishing between them, as a Bourne shell script would often not work under the C shell, and vice versa. Many of the common UNIX utilities are in fact implemented as shell scripts — that is, Bourne shell scripts, since the Bourne shell is the one shell common to all UNIX installations. A user running the C shell must still be able to use these commands, and should not have to know that they are Bourne shell scripts. The convention is that the C shell treats all shell scripts as Bourne shell scripts unless their first line starts with a # (indicating that the line in question is a comment). So if you are in the C shell, and execute a shell script without this character at the start, the C shell will start up an instance of the Bourne shell and pass it to your file to interpret.

Obviously, a Bourne shell script should not start with a comment character: if it does, the C shell will interpret it as a C shell script, and it will probably not work correctly. The Bourne shell, by the way, knows nothing abut C shell scripts.

The Korn shell

The C shell is one of the 'Berkeley enhancements' that never made its way into standard UNIX as offered by AT&T. However, AT&T have produced a very much extended version of the Bourne shell, called the Korn shell (*ksh*), which could in due course supersede both the Bourne shell and the C shell, since it includes the functionality of both, while making very good use of the resources of System V.

Like the C shell, the Korn shell has a history facility. This is invoked using *r* for repeat. Thus you would type just

r

to repeat the last command,

r 76

to repeat command number 76, or

r c

to repeat the last command starting with c.

This notation is probably easier to remember than the C shell's exclamation marks, and the comparison is even more pronounced if you want to correct errors in your last command. Suppose you had typed

lx -il /usr/fred/letters/abc

when what you really meant was

ls -il /usr/fred/letters/abc

In the Bourne shell you would need to type the whole line again. In the C shell you can use the ^ character to change one or more characters. In this case you would type

^x^s^

and this would have the result you originally intended. In the Korn shell, however, you would merely type

r x=s

The Korn shell, moreover, allows you to extend this notation to correct lines other than the immediately preceding one. For instance, to change 'x' to 's' in the last command starting with 'l', you would type

r x=s l

Unlike the C shell, moreover, the Korn shell remembers your command history, even though you log out and then log in again subsequently.

The Korn shell provides another method of repeating and editing previous commands, using *vi* (or another editor such as *emacs* or *gmacs*, if preferred). When you are at the shell prompt, you type normally. Hitting Escape will take you into the *vi* command mode, and you can then move up and down within the history file, using the various *vi* commands to move around and edit text. The main difference from the standard use of *vi* is that you can only see one line of text displayed at a time. When you have finished editing a line, you can hit Return, and the line as modified will be executed.

Vi and the shell behave very differently in respect of terminal handling. The shell uses canonical processing − in other words it does not get handed the input a character at a time, but is only woken up when the kernel has assembled a complete line. This is very efficient, but not flexible enough for a program like *vi*, which needs to consider each character individually. The Korn shell gets the best of both worlds, by starting off in canonical mode, and then switching to raw mode when you hit Escape.

More features of the Korn shell

Another major innovation in the Korn shell is that it uses 'jobs'. When you start off a background process, using the & symbol, the other shells respond by giving you a number, which is the process ID of the background process, for instance

1234

In the Korn shell, however, you get given two numbers, for instance

[1] 1234

The number in square brackets is a job number. You can control jobs in various ways, particularly if you have job control in the form of the *shl* command, allowing you to switch back and forth between them. Clearly at any one time you can have several jobs running in the background, each of them possibly comprising several processes.

Like the C shell, the Korn shell has an alias facility. In fact this is used by the Korn shell itself to implement certain common commands. For example, the *echo* command is built into the Bourne shell. In the Korn shell the equivalent built in command is a more generalised one called *print*, and *echo* is implemented as an alias for *print*, using the appropriate option.

Like the C shell, the Korn shell has tilde substitution. In other words the ~ or tilde symbol is used to mean a particular user's home directory. So for instance ~*mary* would be a more reliable way of referring to the directory that is probably, but not necessarily, called /usr/mary.

The Korn shell has some other useful features. When you change directories it will remember the previous one, so that you can switch back and forth between two directories as you wish. There is also a time-out facility, so that if you leave your terminal unattended (that is you don't use any shell commands for a specified period) you will automatically be logged off – a useful security measure.

Other shells

A number of other shells have appeared over the years. One that is well within the AT&T canon is the restricted shell, *rsh*. This is, in fact, the same program as the normal *sh* or *ksh*, but with some of its facilities disabled. In particular, *rsh* users cannot change directories, cannot use the / character in a pathname when issuing commands, and cannot change their command search path. This means that they can only run programs which are in their own directory, or in directories specifically included in the path that the system administrator has set up for them. This is quite an effective way of putting restrictions on what such a user can do, without denying them the facilities of UNIX altogether.

Another class of shell that has recently become popular is a visual shell — in other words one designed to use the full vdu screen, in the same way that *vi* is a visual editor. XENIX includes a visual shell, called, not surprisingly, *vsh*.

IBM's AIX has two additional shells. One is the DOS shell, which has been tailored to look as nearly as possible like the PC-DOS command interpreter, for those who are familiar with this environment. The other is a visual, window-driven shell, called the Usability Package.

When to use shell programming

The decision as to when to use a shell script, and when to write a program, depends to a great extent on convenience and speed. A shell script, if one can be written to carry out the command, is very quick to write, and needs no compilation, but may be slow in operation. Conversely, if you need to set up a standard procedure to be used very often, perhaps involving a fair amount of processing, it can often be better to write a program, using one of the programming languages discussed in the following chapter.

Chapter 20
Writing Your Own Software

Today there is a vast amount of software available for running under UNIX. And by using the shell and the various standard utilities, you can very often achieve results in UNIX without programming that would have certainly involved writing a program in many other operating systems. But sometimes it may become necessary to write a program yourself — or more likely have one written for you by an experienced programmer.

UNIX was originally designed to be good for programmers to use, and it is still so good in this respect that some organisations write programs under UNIX, even though they will eventually be used under a totally different operating system.

The C programming language

UNIX is very well supplied with programming languages, but there is one language — C — that has a very special status. Whatever language a programmer may work in, it is hardly possible for him to understand how to use the facilities of UNIX without some knowledge of C. This chapter will not, of course, attempt to teach you how to program in C, but merely to give some idea of the flavour of the language.

C was invented in the early 1970s by Dennis Ritchie, specifically as a vehicle for rewriting UNIX so that it could be portable between one machine and another. The origins of C, however, go back further than this, to a language called CPL, short for Common Programming Language.

CPL developed into BCPL, which is still in use today in certain academic environments. One of the most striking points about BCPL is that it recognises only one data type — a machine word, used for characters, numbers, or indeed pointers to other data items. Ritchie developed B from BCPL, and C from B. In the process, additional data types were provided for. C and its ancestors also have some family likeness to Algol, which has given rise to other languages such as Pascal and Ada.

The basic building block of any C program is the function — a mathematical concept which has been taken up in a number of programming languages. In mathematics a function is a relationship between two variables. For instance one can define a square root function, since (considering positive numbers only) you can supply any number as an 'argument' to the function, and another number is then defined as the result of the function. The use of functions in programming starts from this principle; for example, in writing a program you might want to make it find the square root of a number. There are various ways of finding square roots, but they are all rather complicated – certainly you would not want to write out the full formula or 'algorithm' every time a square root is needed.

Probably, you would use a statement such as

y = sqrt(x)

which takes the square root of some variable called x, and stores the result in another variable called y. In the above statement, the word *sqrt* is the name of a function, the variable x is an argument or parameter to the function (the input to it in a sense) and the output of the function, its return value, gets stored in y. Notice the brackets (parentheses) following the function, and surrounding the argument. Brackets are the essential distinguishing mark of a function in C.

Of course our statement will only work if the function *sqrt()* has been defined in advance – a very common function such as a square root is likely to be provided with the programming language, but other functions we would need to write ourselves. Actually, C comes with a big library of standard functions, and *sqrt()* is one of these.

Functions in C are more generalised than our example might suggest. They do not necessarily return a value, and they can have several arguments, or indeed none at all – but the brackets are still put after the function name to show that it is a function. A function, in fact, is equivalent to what in another language might be called a subroutine. Every C program consists of at least one function: there is always the function called *main()*, which may in turn call as many other functions as required.

C is an essential part of UNIX, but its use has spread far beyond UNIX itself, and it is now a very well established language in other operating systems. C is often used for writing 'system software' – that is operating systems, database managers, and other tools that need to work closely with the operating system, or where efficiency at run time is the prime requirement. The key to the success of C is its special combination of 'high level' features with the ability to get down to the bits and bytes that the hardware is actually dealing with, and thus produce (in skilled hands) a program that will run very efficiently.

'Standard' C was long defined by the book, *The C Programming*

Language, by Brian Kernighan and Dennis Ritchie. A more formal definition has now appeared in the XJ311 standard. Programming languages do not stand still, however, and an extended version called C++ is becoming popular.

Program development with C

Writing a program in C requires the use of a number of UNIX utilities. Once you have worked out the structure of your program — that is, broken down the task into a number of separate logical steps, each of which can be coded as a separate function — you write the actual 'lines of code' for each function, probably using a text editor such as *vi* to input the program into the machine. You will also need to call upon quite a number of the standard UNIX functions, representing standard subroutines and system calls. For instance, every program will need to do some form of input and output, and all this is accomplished by means of functions, since C has no input/output statements as such. Fortunately there are a large number of such functions available, grouped in a standard C library, and some other more specialised libraries. I have listed some of the more common library functions in Appendix C.

When your program is ready, you 'compile' it, using the *cc* command, which takes your source program, and converts it into object code.

The compilation process checks your program to make sure that its syntax is correct, and returns you an error message if you have got it wrong. But the amount of checking it does is somewhat limited, and you may decide that you want it checked out more thoroughly — for instance, to make sure you are not using constructs that may work differently on different machines. The *lint* utility is provided for just this purpose — its name apparently arises because it can pick out the fluff in a program!

If the compilation is successful, it produces an executable file which by default is called *a.out*, although you can call it something else if you wish. You can now try the program out by typing the name of this executable file as a command.

Actually, the compilation is done in several phases — a pre-process phase, a compilation phase, an optimisation phase, and a link edit phase. If necessary, you can suppress one or more of these phases. If you have a big program, it may be convenient to split up the source code into several different files. If you want to change only part of the program, you can run the pre-process and compilation phases for just that one file, and combine the output at link edit phase with the previously compiled versions of the other files.

Library functions

The link edit phase takes one or more object files and links them to form *a.out*. It is at this stage that libraries come into play: UNIX has a very large number of library subroutines that are defined as functions and can be linked in as necessary.

Many library functions are self-contained, since they include within them all the local variables that they need for their internal processing, and pass data to and from the main program merely by the function arguments and return value. However, certain functions will not work unless you have specific data structures set up in your main program which the function can then refer to. The standard input/output functions are a good example – they require a table of (typically) 20 entries to be set up in the main program, each entry containing information about a file or 'stream'.

To get this table included in each program in a standard fashion requires the use of the C preprocessor, which is normally invoked automatically at the pre-process phase of compilation. At the start of your program you need to include the statement:

#include <stdio.h>

where the # is a standard way of indicating that a statement is intended for action by the preprocessor. The above statement will incorporate a special 'header file' into the source code, and thus cause the table in question to be set up for you, together with various definitions needed by the i/o routines.

Just as UNIX provides a number of libraries of compiled functions for inclusion at the link edit stage, it also provides a variety of standard header files (or 'include files') for inclusion at the pre-process stage, many of them related to particular function libraries.

The UNIX programming environment

If your program consists of a number of different files, it may be difficult to remember which files are included in a particular program, and which ones have changed recently. For instance, you may have a number of programs under development, any of which use a selection of various common subroutines that you have written. Maybe you have a team of programmers, each of them working on different aspects of an overall suite of programs.

To keep track of what needs to be recompiled and linked in which program, you can use the *make* utility. This keeps track of which files are needed in which program, and what has to be done with them. By noting the dates when the various files were last altered, *make* can work out which of them need to be reprocessed to produce the new version of the complete program.

Sccs

Another useful utility is the source code control system (*sccs*): a series of utilities for keeping your source programs up to date, and at the same time enabling you to get back to an earlier version if you want, by noting all the differences (the 'deltas', to use the *sccs* terminology) between one version and the next.

An *sccs* document has its own special format, incorporating a history of all the various changes that have taken place. However, you can use the *get* command to produce from it an ordinary text file representing the latest version (or a previous version if required). *Get* with the *-e* option produces a text version that you can edit in the ordinary way with a text editor such as *vi*; the edited version can then be used to update the master *sccs* document, using the *delta* command.

Debugging

With modern high level languages, writing a program is not too difficult. The difficult part is getting from the first draft of the program to one that actually works and does what its specification says it should do. The most time-consuming activity in program development is testing, or debugging: running the program and seeing what it does, then finding out why what it does is different to what you intended, and putting it right.

There are various techniques for debugging. The most productive method is to examine your source program very carefully, checking precisely what each statement will do with the test data that you fed into it. Sometimes, however, this does not seem to produce the right answer – particularly with a language like C, which sometimes interprets statements in rather subtle ways that it is easy to overlook.

For example you may want to test for two variables being equal, and write

 if (a = b) ...

Now this is a perfectly good statement in C, but does not do what you intended. You should have written

 if (a == b) ...

with a double equals sign (studying the standard C documentation will explain why this is) but it is an easy mistake to make. There are a number of similar traps for the unwary, some of them a lot more obscure.

Debugging can be made easier by various facilities provided with C. For instance, there is a conditional compilation facility in the preprocessor, using #*if*. A useful method of debugging is to get the program to print out the contents of important variables at specified points, so that you can check whether they have been set to the right values. But you would obviously want to suppress this printing when the program is complete and running correctly. So you include in your program some coding such as:

#ifdef DEBUG
   printf("Count is %d", count);
#endif

The *printf()* statement here will display the value of the variable *count*; but if you compile the program without setting the DEBUG flag, the statement will not be compiled, and hence will be omitted from the executable program. So you can have debugging statements like this included in your program source code, but when you have finished debugging, and compile the program in its final version, the statements will disappear from the program.

Another useful feature of C under UNIX is the *assert* statement. If you know that a particular variable must have a certain value for the program to work correctly, you can include a line such as:

assert (count == 1);

When the program comes to this statement in the course of execution, it checks that the assertion is true; if it fails (in other words *count* is not equal to 1) the program will terminate with an error message.

Sometimes, when you can't work out what has gone wrong just by debugging at source code level, it may be necessary to delve into the executable program, and examine the state of the process when it terminated. UNIX systems generally include some special utilities called 'debuggers', which can help with this. The standard debugger, called *sdb*, can look at the object code of a program, together with a core dump, if you have one, that is the image of the memory contents of a failed process, which will have been copied out to a special disk file called *core* at the time the program terminated.

The debugger makes use of a special part of the compiled program called the 'symbol table', which contains the names of functions and variables, and can relate them to particular addresses in the program.

There is a utility called *strip*, which can remove the symbol table, when you are sure that you are finished with it.

Sdb (unlike the older *adb* program) can also examine the source files. I say 'files' deliberately — remember that a C program is often made up of a number of source files, containing functions which it was convenient to put into separate files and compile separately. *Sdb* can identify a particular line of code in the source and relate it to the object program. You can execute the program under *sdb*, producing various diagnostics, or even step through it an instruction at a time to see what happens at each step, as a way of tracking down an elusive error.

Sdb works with C programs, but some UNIX systems include another debugger, *dbx*, which can work with Fortran and Pascal as well. Some proprietary language compilers come with their own debugging tools.

Other languages

C is not the right language for every purpose. It can enable you to carry out very 'low level' programming, but at the same time it can be dangerous. To use it effectively requires considerable skill on the part of the programmer.

There are a number of other programming languages which may be more suitable for certain kinds of programming. Apart from C, COBOL and Fortran are still the most widely used of the traditional languages, for commercial and scientific applications respectively. It is interesting that IBM have specified C, COBOL, and Fortran, as the three languages supported in their new System Application Architecture (SAA) in preference to IBM-originated languages such as PL/I and RPG III; C, COBOL, and Fortran have also had special attention from the X/Open Group.

COBOL

COBOL is short for 'COmmon Business Oriented Language'. It is one of the oldest languages still in existence, but still very widely used for business-type applications such as sales ledgers, payrolls, and the like. For instance, the popular SunAccount packages are written in COBOL.

Compared to C, COBOL is much more 'English-like', not to say verbose, and you can write statements such as

MULTIPLY PRICE BY QUANTITY GIVING AMOUNT.

If you use meaningful variables ('data-names' in the COBOL terminology) such as PRICE and QUANTITY, COBOL can be made to a large extent self-documenting, and certainly a well-written COBOL program should be much easier to understand, and therefore to change if necessary, compared to the average C program.

A COBOL program is divided into a number of main 'divisions', the most important of these being the DATA DIVISION, in which all the data-names used in the program must be defined, and the PROCEDURE DIVISION, containing all the actual processing. The DATA DIVISION in turn includes a WORKING-STORAGE SECTION, containing variables in the usual sense, and a FILE SECTION defining the format of the various data files which the program uses as input or output.

COBOL programs have sometimes suffered from the lack of structure in the language. COBOL is not organised on the basis of functions, like C. Most COBOL programmers, however, divide their PROCEDURE DIVISION up into SECTIONs, and make each SECTION carry out one well-defined task. They have one MAINLINE SECTION, which controls the overall flow of the program, and calls the other SECTIONs one by one to carry out the detailed processing.

This structure can be extended to several levels as required, and certainly helps to reduce programming errors, and facilitate subsequent changes, but it has one severe limitation: all variables are global, and apply to the program as a whole. Some COBOL programmers like to define a working-storage variable with a generalised name like FLAG2, and use this for different purposes in different parts of the program. If one piece of code has a bug, and sets the variable to an unexpected value, this can upset other parts of the program in ways which are difficult to track down. By contrast, a language in which variables can be declared local to a particular subroutine keeps the problems local if the variable takes on unusual values, and the program is thus easier to debug.

COBOL for UNIX is supplied by a number of different software houses under different brand names, of which Level II COBOL from Micro Focus is perhaps the best known. Some versions are fully compiled, others interpreted, and others again are 'semi-compiled' – that is the compiler produces a special intermediate language, which is then interpreted. Even fully compiled COBOL programs are not necessarily totally stand-alone object programs like those produced by the C compiler, but may need a special run-time file.

COBOL has throughout its history been controlled by committees, and is thus fairly well standardised. A new version, COBOL 85, will give much better structured programming facilities than before.

Fortran

Fortran has been around even longer than COBOL. Its name is short for 'formula translation' and you program it by writing expressions in a sort of algebraic syntax. Its main use has always been for scientific and mathematical processing, and it comes with a variety of special mathematical functions. Fortran 77 is a common version, and many UNIX systems include the *f77* command to run the Fortran compiler.

In UNIX, there is probably little to choose between C and Fortran for purely scientific processing – C has access to essentially the same basic subroutines. The reason that Fortran is still popular, despite its age and the old-fashioned nature of the syntax, is that there are a large number of specialised libraries available from third party suppliers, for particular types of scientific and technical computation.

There have been a number of moves to smarten up Fortran, and UNIX systems often provide pre-processors such as EFL (Extended Fortran Language) or Ratfor (Rational Fortran).

BASIC

For those people whose experience of computers is limited to home computers, BASIC is the most familiar computer language. Some of the computer studies taught in schools also gives the misleading impression that BASIC is what computing is all about. In fact BASIC is a rather unusual language. Vaguely derived from Fortran, it was originally developed for teaching purposes, as a 'beginners' all-purpose symbolic instruction code', but it is often regarded as very unsuitable for beginners, since it encourages them in bad habits. BASIC is also a very non-standardised language; there is an ANSI standard, but many of the commercial versions bear little resemblance to it or to each other.

BASIC is very often an interpreted language: rather than having to compile your program, you can execute the source code, each statement being translated by the interpreter as it is reached. This makes it much quicker to get something running, since the compilation phase is avoided, but the performance of the program itself is usually much slower than if it had been compiled.

There are quite a number of BASIC compilers and interpreters for UNIX. With all the other excellent languages available, and with the shell taking the place of an interpreted programming language, it is difficult to see why anyone would want to use BASIC with UNIX, but if you want to you certainly can.

Still more languages

Much better than BASIC for teaching purposes is Pascal, which is rather like a friendlier and more elegant version of C, without C's power for low-level manipulation. Modula 2 is an updated version of Pascal, while another language from the same stable is ADA, which has been widely adopted for military purposes but also widely criticised for having far too many facilities, so that it is difficult to learn and the programs are difficult to debug.

Those who are interested in 'artificial intelligence' applications will want to use Lisp or Prolog, while some other still more specialised languages are also available.

A special case – PL.8

The PL.8 language and its compiler deserve a mention in any book on UNIX, even though they are not commercially available. PL.8 is the language used by IBM to write system software for the 6150's ROMP microprocessor. It is a variant of the PL/I language as used on IBM mainframes, but it is similar to C in being a high level language with low level capabilities. In fact one of the design aims of the ROMP chip was that it should be suitable for programming in such a language rather than in assembler.

The PL.8 compiler is remarkable in that it can take source code in three different languages – C, Pascal, and PL.8 itself – and produce object code for four different processors – IBM mainframes, the 801 mini, the Motorola 68000, and the ROMP.

Assembler languages

C, COBOL, Fortran, and so on, are all 'high level languages'; that is, the structure of the language relates to the type of problems to be addressed using it, rather than the detailed structure of a particular computer or microprocessor.

The language that any particular microprocessor understands – its machine code – is quite unintelligible to most human beings. It can be made slightly more intelligible if the numeric operation codes representing the various instructions are replaced by mnemonics such as MOV (move), CMP (compare) and ADD (add), and the numeric memory addresses are replaced by meaningful names. The program needed to translate the mnemonic language into machine code is generally referred to as an assembler (as distinct from a compiler, used for high level languages) and the language itself is an assembler language. Often it includes 'macro' facilities, whereby a commonly used sequence of machine instructions can be represented by a single assembler statement.

Assembler languages by their nature are specific to one type of machine or another, and can be very difficult to use. Nowadays they are only used where it is impossible to use a high level language. For instance, in any UNIX system a small part of the kernel has to be written in assembler, the rest being of course written in C.

Fourth generation languages

The term 'fourth generation language', or '4GL', has become very fashionable over the last few years. Interestingly enough, no-one ever talked very much about first, second, or third generations of languages. The idea is supposed to be, however, that machine code is the first generation, assembler the second, and high level languages such as C and COBOL the third.

Fourth generation languages are different from the first three, in being non-procedural. In each of the first three generations, a program consists of a procedure − that is, a series of steps that the computer must go through one after the other in order to achieve the desired objective. In a true 4GL, however, you specify the objective, and leave the system to work out the steps. As an example, let us take a program to print a sales analysis report by region. If you were to write this in C or COBOL you would need to think of all the steps the program would have to go through − for instance:

- read the next record from the file;
- if there are no more records, print final totals;
- if the current record is for a new sales region, print subtotals, reset the subtotals to zero, print headings for the new region;
- print out the various fields;
- add them into the running totals and subtotals;
- add 1 to the line count;
- if the line count is greater than 60 set it back to 1, add 1 to the page number, advance to the next page, and print page headings;
- and so on.

In a 4GL you would merely state what fields were to appear on the report, with what totalling, and leave it to the 4GL software to work out the actual steps involved.

The SQL query language, which we looked at in earlier chapters, is a prime example of a 4GL − you specify what you want to achieve, and not how the program is to set about it. In packages such as Ingres, the software uses sophisticated optimisation techniques to decide what records it shall access in which order to carry out a complicated SQL query. The basic principle of being able to carry out operations on whole sets of records chosen from the database is far removed from the pedestrian approach of languages such as COBOL and Fortran.

However, SQL is not a complete language for business applications − it deals only with the database side of an application, and does not cater for screen handling, or the general flow of the logic within a program. To build a complete system, therefore, SQL needs to be used in conjunction with another language. There are two main ways in which this can be done − by embedding SQL into a language such as C, or by using it as part of a special-purpose 4GL.

Embedded SQL

SQL is often used, as we saw in Chapters 11 and 12, for interactive enquiries on databases − you type SQL statements at the keyboard, and have the results displayed on your screen. But a lot of computer processing today uses a database not just as a source of information, but as part of a complete application such as order processing, stock control, and so on. Clearly if data entry clerks are keying in large numbers of repetitive transactions, they should not be expected to compose SQL statements − they need to have a form displayed on the screen so that they can input data by filling in the blanks.

Often, such an application can be put together using a database package, with very little actual programming. If the processing required is at all complex however, it may well be necessary to have a special program written − but still making use of the database facilities.

Embedded SQL is often the answer. Packages such as Ingres, Oracle, and Informix allow you to embed SQL statements within a program in C or sometimes other languages such as COBOL, so you get the flexibility of the traditional language combined with the strength of SQL for database handling.

When SQL is embedded within a C program, it needs additional features to cope with the difference between fourth generation techniques of SQL, and the third generation techniques of C. The main problem is with the SELECT statement. An SQL SELECT statement can return any number of records, which is fine if you are having them displayed on your screen. A third generation language on the other hand cannot cope with more than one record at a time. The answer is to use a 'cursor', to enable a number of records to be SELECTed together, but then taken into the program one at a time for processing.

So retrieving records from a database in embedded SQL takes a number of steps. The program needs to include a DECLARE CURSOR statement, giving each cursor a name, and specifying the selection criteria to be associated with it. An OPEN CURSOR statement is used at the point where the selection is to take place. This defines a subset of the database, satisfying the specified criteria, but does not yet return any data into the program. Finally the FETCH statement is used to retrieve each of the selected records one by one.

Other special SQL statements are required to enable the program to interrogate the database manager, and find out how many records were returned by a selection, and whether an error occurred.

Embedding SQL in C is generally quite straightforward; you insert the SQL statements at appropriate points in the program, each prefixed by '*exec sql*'. The database package provides both a pre-compiler and a subroutine library. The source program is passed through the pre-compiler, which basically transforms the *exec sql* statements into a series of subroutine calls, incorporating error checking as appropriate. At the link stage, the various subroutines are called in from the library supplied.

Building on SQL — today's 4GLs

Embedded SQL thus enables the programmer to solve the database access parts of an application very easily, but it does nothing for the presentation of data on the screen, which is the major part of many programs in today's computing environment.

Some database managers and other packages provide solutions to the screen handling problem along the lines of embedded SQL. For instance, Ingres provides embedded calls to FRS (the Forms Runtime System); you can have *exec frs* statements intermingled with your *exec sql* statements, so that the user interface is catered for as well as the database handling, but still within the overall flow of a C program.

A logical extension of this approach is to do away with the C framework, and provide a complete fourth generation language, incorporating SQL and screen access commands. Ingres provides OSL (Operation Specification Language), and other database packages provide equivalent languages, such as Informix-4GL.

Why use a 4GL?

A 4GL has a number of distinct advantages over traditional programming:
- it is much quicker to program;

- there is much less opportunity for logical errors;
- more attention can be given to what is really required, since it is less laborious to work out how to provide it;
- expensive programming staff may not be required.

The whole method of developing software can change. Using previous generations of programming languages, the working out and coding of the logic is so laborious that it should only start when there is a very clear definition of what needs to be done: a detailed specification needs to be written, embodying the users' requirements, before programming can really start. Unfortunately, the specifications produced by systems analysts are often difficult for users to understand; they may think the specification has described what they want, but it is difficult to be sure until they have seen the final product. The systems analyst may have missed some basic point that is so obvious to the users that they did not bother to mention it. And the whole business of analysis and programming may take so long that the requirements have changed by the time the system is ready.

Using a 4GL, the whole process can be speeded up dramatically. Moreover, it is much less expensive to make changes to the system, so development can take the form of 'prototyping' – you can try something out and have a running application very quickly, which you can demonstrate to the users and get their comments on whether it is really what they want, before spending time and effort refining the design and producing a finished product.

Actually, a 4GL in the usual sense (that is a series of lines of text which you edit and then submit to a compiler or interpreter) is not the last word in development tools. Modern database systems often allow you to develop applications by 'painting' screen and report layouts, and filling in the blanks in a series of menus and forms. Such products may be considered not so much a 4GL as a 4GE – a Fourth Generation Environment.

Chapter 21
Networking

What is networking?

Networking is one of the most talked about and least understood subjects in the whole field of information technology. Basically, networking means the connecting together of two or more computers (the 'nodes' of the network) so that they can work together.

There are two types of networks:
- local area networks (LANs) in which the nodes are in the same building, or at least on the same site;
- wide area networks (WANs) in which the nodes are not all on the same site, so that the cables need to cross public roads.

The difference between LANs and WANs is extremely important. A WAN normally involves the use of communication lines provided by British Telecom or its equivalent — maybe lines permanently leased to the organisation, or public dial-up or packet switching services. In either case the network must adhere to the standards that the telecommunications authority has laid down.

A local area network on the other hand is not obliged to follow any external standards. All the cabling and the devices attached to it are under the user organisation's control, so it can adopt different standards, which generally allow transmission of many more bits per second. The other important point about a LAN is that it assumes, and generally relies on, close co-operation between the various stations on the network. The techniques generally used will only work if a packet of data is sure to reach all the stations on the network within a defined timescale. Even at electronic transmission speeds (nearly the speed of light) this imposes a maximum length on the network cable.

A node to be connected to a network needs some hardware and some software. It is possible, for instance, to connect dumb vdus to a LAN, but only by attaching to each an intelligent network interface device, which can almost be regarded as a computer in its own right. So when we talk about networks, we are fundamentally thinking of connecting one computer with another, rather than a computer with its terminals.

The hardware required for local networking and for several kinds of wide area networking generally involves high speed synchronous communication. It is not a case of attaching devices externally to the normal serial ports, as one would attach a modem, but of inserting special cards into the computer, connecting them to the system bus. Some computers are indeed sold with appropriate networking hardware already included. Moreover, a single physical network connector may correspond to several logical devices as understood by UNIX: if a UNIX host computer is acting as a 'file server', connected via a network to many local computers or workstations, the host often has a single physical connection to the network, but shared or 'multiplexed' by hardware or software, so that it can serve multiple users.

Open systems

Connecting one computer to another can be a difficult matter. Certainly it will only be successful if standards are defined that both computers can work to.

The International Organisation for Standardisation (confusingly abbreviated to ISO) has defined a seven layer model for Open Systems Interconnection (OSI). The model is not a standard itself, but a framework within which detailed standards can be gradually accepted. The aim is that eventually computers from any manufacturer will be able to interact fully without difficulty.

The seven layers are shown in Table 21.1 (in their logical order, with Layer 1 at the bottom). To describe the seven layer model in detail would require an entire book to itself. However, a brief description of each layer should do something to illustrate the complexity of modern data communications standards.

The Physical Layer

This is concerned with such things as the shape of the plug and socket, the number of pins in the plug and what they are used for, the type of cable, and the voltages used to represent data.

The Link Layer

The Link Layer is concerned with 'data link control' between two communicating devices. Typically the data is grouped into packets of a number of bytes each, with additional bytes added to indicate the start and end of the packet, its destination, and an error checking facility. Note, by the way, that the entire OSI setup assumes that we are dealing with synchronous communications, rather than asynchronous (byte by byte) as used with most UNIX terminals.

Table 21.1 The OSI seven-layer model.

Layer	Description
7	Application
6	Presentation
5	Session
4	Transport
3	Network
2	Link
1	Physical

The Network Layer

This (like several other layers) is rather confusingly named. If you are connecting one computer or device directly to another (even via a network) the Network Layer is not really relevant. It applies when the connection needs to be made via some intermediate point, so that two or more separate communication paths are involved, one from the source to the intermediate node, and one from there to the destination. Network Layer services are concerned with routeing, to ensure that each packet is sent on its way correctly.

The Transport Layer

The Transport Layer builds on Layers 1 to 3 to provide a complete end to end service; for instance, it checks that the various packets in a message all arrive once only and in the correct order, and puts them into order if they should happen to arrive out of sequence.

Alternatively there is a simplified version using 'datagrams', in which each packet is treated in isolation.

The Session Layer

The Session Layer is responsible for setting up process to process connections, managing them, and subsequently closing them down.

The Presentation Layer

This is concerned with matters such as data formatting and code conversion (between ASCII and EBCDIC, for instance).

The Application Layer

This is the most diverse of the layers, and is concerned with the way one computer system interacts with another. A few Layer 7 standards have been defined so far, but many more will certainly follow. The SQL query language is a good example, and there are standards for file transfer and manipulation (FTAM) and terminal emulation (Virtual Terminal Protocol). X.400 provides a standardised electronic mail service, while POSIX itself may become a Layer 7 standard in due course.

OSI implementations

The general idea of OSI is that of allowing many different types of physical connection and lower-layer protocols to serve many different ways of using systems; in other words an 'hour-glass' shape, with multiple standards at Layers 1 to 3 serving multiple standards at Layers 5 to 7, with Layer 4 as a common standard in all cases. In practice things have not worked out so neatly, as there are the two types of Layer 4, connectionless (datagram) and connection-oriented.

It should be pointed out, by the way, that in many circumstances some of the layers are irrelevant − for instance, within a single LAN there is no need for a Network Layer, or (probably) for a Presentation Layer.

Looking at the bottom half of the hour-glass (Layers 1 to 3) there are two main types of OSI network: local area networks on the one hand, and X.25 on the other.

Local area network standards

There are three main LAN standards, defined by the IEEE 802 Committee. They differ in the network topology (whether the network is a ring, or a 'bus' with two ends) and in the method of controlling access if two stations want to transmit at once. The two access control methods are: 'token passing', in which a special packet is sent round the network − any station which picks it up has the right to transmit; and 'CSMA/CD' (carrier sense, multiple access, with collision detection) in which each station waits until the line is clear, then sends its message and takes corrective action in the few cases where it detects that another station has transmitted simultaneously.

The three IEEE standards are given in Table 21.2.

Table 21.2 Local area network standards.

Standard	Topology	Access control method
802.3	bus	CSMA/CD
802.4	bus	token-passing
802.5	ring	token-passing

The 802.3 standard is based on the very widely used industry standard called Ethernet; 802.4 is used in the MAP standard for factory automation; 802.5 is the LAN standard promoted by IBM.

X.25

X.25 is the main OSI standard for all communication except where one of the LAN standards is used. In its latest version it is a complete standard covering Layers 1 to 3 of the OSI model. X.25 can be used for wide area networks within organisations (linking different branch offices together) and a version of X.25 is used by public packet switching data services.

In the future, X.25 will clearly be one of the most important standards for networking; already it is available on a wide range of UNIX systems.

TCP/IP

Of the various network software products under UNIX, TCP/IP is very widely used. TCP/IP was adopted for ARPANET, the wide area network originally developed by the US Department of Defense, which links many universities and other organisations together, in Europe and North America.

In terms of the OSI model, TCP/IP relates mainly to the upper layers; it is generally implemented on top of some lower-layer standard such as Ethernet or X.25. However, TCP/IP itself is not an OSI standard.

TCP/IP is not just a UNIX standard; many of its components work on other operating systems as well – for instance, VMS on DEC VAX computers. It comprises a number of different protocols, all of them designed to allow two or more host computers to communicate.

Being specifically designed for wide area networking (although it can be used for local networking as well) TCP/IP needs to provide resilience: it does not rely on any one 'master node' controlling the network. In fact, each computer connected to a TCP/IP network has a number of 'daemon' processes, which broadcast to the rest of the network the address and status of the machine, and the identity of logged on users, so that the other nodes can pick up this information and use it to route messages. The main TCP/IP protocols are as follows:

Internet Protocol (IP)

This is a Network Layer protocol for the routeing of data (without validation checks).

Internet control message protocol (ICMP)

This looks after error messages if data is found to have been corrupted in transmission.

Transmission control protocol (TCP)

TCP, together with IP, gives the name of the entire package, although the two protocols are only part of the picture. TCP is a Transport Layer service. It provides for flow control, acknowledgement of data, and retransmission of bad data.

User datagram protocol (UDP)

This is a 'connectionless' equivalent of TCP. It would typically be used over Ethernet, which provides its own checking facilities, so that they do not need to be duplicated here.

Telnet

This and the following protocols are all at Application Layer in OSI terms, Telnet itself being similar in function to the OSI Virtual Terminal protocol. Telnet provides remote login: if you are connected to computer A you can ask it to act as a terminal, and log you in via the network to computer B. Telnet can work between UNIX and non-UNIX systems, and does the necessary conversions so that the host can treat all users identically, whether logged in locally or remotely.

File transfer protocol (FTP)

FTP allows files to be sent or retrieved between computers, and can also provide directory listings. The OSI equivalent would be FTAM.

Simple mail transfer protocol (SMTP)

This allows reliable transmission of electronic mail, and thus corresponds roughly to X.400.

TCP/IP commands specific to UNIX

These include:
- remote login (*rlogin* − similar to Telnet but used between UNIX systems only);
- remote shell (*remsh* − allowing execution of commands on a remote system);
- remote copy (*rcp*);
- remote who (*rwho* − allowing you to find out who is logged on to the various computers on the network).

Accessing remote files

Many large companies are finding it necessary to link their computers together in a network, perhaps spanning countries and continents. If such a company has standardised on UNIX, it is now becoming possible for a user to treat an entire network as if it were a single UNIX computer, accessing files on any machine as if they were on a local filesystem.

Obviously a networked system must give you some means of accessing remote files, and be able to know where to look for them. Basically there are two ways this can be done − by special conventions in filenames, or by special directories that are 'mounted' in the same way that a local filesystem is mounted.

The *uucp* utility (UNIX-to-UNIX copy) allows you to copy files between one computer and another. It uses the exclamation mark as an extension to the conventions of directory pathnames. For instance, if you are connected to a machine known to the network as *vax1*, and want to access a file on it called */usr/fred/letter3*, you would specify the pathname as *vax1!/usr/fred/letter3*.

Obviously *uucp* will only work if you have previously set up the name *vax1* in your own machine. The *uuname* command will list all system names that have been defined for this purpose. It may be that *vax1* is connected in turn to another machine, which it knows as, say, *argus*. In this case you can send a message to a directory on the further machine, for instance *vax1!argus!/usr/john*. This system can be extended even further, provided all the computers in the chain are willing to co-operate.

Uucp uses tilde substitution, as in the C shell and Korn shell; so if the remote machine has a user whose login name is *mary*, you could send her a message by typing for instance

uucp myletter vax1!~mary/letters

The Newcastle connection

The Newcastle connection is a system developed at Newcastle University for allowing UNIX machines to communicate with one another.

It uses a special convention in filenames. Remember that / at the start of a pathname means the root of the directory structure, and .. means the parent of a particular directory. So what does /.. at the start of a pathname mean? Logically it should take you still higher up the hierarchy, above the local root, in other words into a network.

The Newcastle connection can be implemented without changing the kernel. What it does require, however, is a change to the standard library routine for opening files, to detect that the file is remote, look up a table to find out where it is located, connect you to the remote machine, and start up a 'stub' process there to handle the file access for you. Thereafter, any accesses you make to the file in question are redirected to the remote machine, where the stub process will carry them out.

What you can actually do on the remote machine depends of course on your access permissions. But in principle you can read and write data files, and even execute programs.

Obviously a scheme like the Newcastle Connection will only work if each of the various computers knows about the others. Login names need to be set up for the various remote users, and as you might imagine the security aspects need to be carefully thought out.

RFS

When UNIX System V Release 3 was announced in 1986, one of the most interesting new developments was Remote File Sharing (RFS) and the various extensions to the operating system which are required to support it.

RFS aims to give you access to remote files and directories just as if they were on your own local machine. To achieve this, it makes use of several new features of System V.3, particularly Streams and the file system switch. The new facilities do not come for nothing, however – System V.3 with RFS is said to require at least 2 megabytes of main memory just for the operating system.

RFS is an Application Layer protocol in OSI terms, and therefore requires suitable support from lower layer services. This is provided by TLI (Transport Layer Interface) and TPI (Transport Provider Interface) which provide an OSI-compatible Transport Layer service.
The initial implementations of RFS were on local area networks, including Ethernet (with part of TCP/IP running on top) and AT&T's own low-speed network, Starlan. It has subsequently become available on wide area networks, using X.25.

Streams

Standard protocols for RFS are designed to use Streams. The Streams concept was not officially included in System V until Release 3, but it had been invented by Dennis Ritchie some years before, and implemented on internal AT&T versions of UNIX.

Streams is a new way of implementing character special files (such as terminals). In System V (unlike the earlier internal versions) it does not replace the existing terminal handling routines in the kernel, but is used only when required – for instance, to communicate using RFS. Using Streams, a process can control the various 'modules' required to act on the data passing through – for instance, if a terminal uses a line discipline to deal with canonical erase and kill processing, a line discipline module would be brought into play; in other cases this module would not be required.

File system switch

The file system switch is essentially a new layer of the kernel, which separates the input/output system calls from the actual file system. This enables the same system call to access either the actual UNIX filesystem, or a distributed RFS filesystem.

Access to remote files in RFS does not rely on special conventions in the pathname, as with *uucp* or the Newcastle connection; the remote directory hierarchy (or part of it) is 'mounted' in an appropriate place on the local directory structure. First of all, the remote machine needs to 'advertise' part of its filestore as available, using the *adv* command. The local machine can then issue a *mount -d* command effectively to incorporate the remote files as part of its own filestore.

Using RFS

Using RFS, you can treat files on a remote UNIX machine very much as if they were on your own local disk. You can even lock files and records, which other networking systems find difficult.

RFS requires one UNIX machine on a network to act as a network master, and set up the connections between the various computers. However, once this has been done, the network master can be disconnected, and connections between the other machines will still operate.

As part of the RFS package, AT&T provides a recovery mechanism to cope with failures of the network. This is obviously essential, as otherwise you might lock an area of the remote file and then lose the connection. Without some means of recovery the file might stay locked indefinitely, preventing access by other users.

Another feature of RFS is a name server, which will translate a file name you give it to a location on the network.

UNIX can even recognise the problems that occur with networks spanning time zones. Sometimes it is important to know, for instance, which of several files was updated last. UNIX with RFS has the ability to work out that an update which took place in San Francisco at 10 a.m. (according to the time zone, as defined by the TZ environment variable on the local computer) was later than one at noon the same day in London.

Competitors to RFS

The main competitor to RFS is NFS, developed by Sun Microsystems. It is implemented in a somewhat different way from RFS, with a 'virtual file system' in place of the file system switch. The main outward difference is that NFS is not limited to talking to UNIX systems. The *exportfs* system call is used to make a filesystem (or part of one) available to remote users, in a similar way to the *adv* call in RFS.

A somewhat similar system is 6150 Distributed Services, offered by IBM. This is implemented in the kernel of the AIX operating system, and uses a client/server model. The protocol used is LU6.2 – a standard within System Network Architecture (SNA) which IBM are promoting in parallel to OSI as the interconnection standard for IBM machines of all types. Like RFS, Distributed Services will allow one computer to use files on another, transparently to the user.

Distributed databases

Networking can be approached from a different angle – as part of a database management system rather than as an operating system function. Some of the main database packages are being developed into 'distributed databases'. RTI, for instance, offer a distributed system called Ingres/Star.

Ingres/Star was launched in July 1986. The ultimate aim is for a system which will allow 'transparent simultaneous access to data on multiple dissimilar systems'.

The product is designed to allow the user to access and update data on remote databases. Neither the user nor the application program need to know where a piece of data is physically stored. There is a 'distributed query optimiser' which uses a global data dictionary, and takes network costs into account when deciding among the many options available to achieve a distributed relational join. Remote updates are supported, but a transaction can only update data at a single remote site. Multiple-site updating will be introduced later, but will only be feasible when the 'two phase commit' procedure is available.

The initial version also has a facility for 'deferred copies'. In other words you can keep two copies of the database in different locations, for reasons of resilience and performance. The host updates its own files, then transmits the updates to the remote site to be actioned there. If the data link goes down, the host will store up the updates, and transmit them when communication is restored.

Part IV
UNIX Today and Tomorrow

Chapter 22
Varieties of UNIX Systems

UNIX has been evolving within AT&T ever since it first appeared. However, the appearance of System V in 1983 was a major watershed, not so much for any technical features of the system as for the commitment it represented on the part of AT&T. System V was special because of the support that AT&T began to give it as *the* standard, which all other versions would have to fall in with. However, one should not minimise the technical improvements in System V, some of which were very significant.

The evolution of System V

Previous AT&T versions had always supported disk block sizes of 512 bytes, which is rather small for today's larger memories and faster disks. From System V onwards, a particular filesystem can have blocks of either 512 or 1024 bytes, with an indicator in the superblock to show which it is. System V also included a more reliable method of writing data to disk, and various innovations aimed at speeding up access to the data.

Also geared to performance improvements were changes to the size of kernel tables. Much of the memory occupied by the kernel is actually taken up with tables, for processes, files, buffers, and so on. In previous versions the sizes of these tables were fixed; in System V the size can be tuned to give a trade-off between memory usage and speed. Later versions have allowed still more tables to be variable in size — for instance, the maximum number of open files per process, previously limited to 20, is now a parameter that can be tuned as necessary.

A major improvement in System V was the introduction of various inter-process communications facilities (IPC for short). Previous versions allowed one process to communicate with another by means of pipes, which are easy to use, but not fast enough for certain purposes. System V adds messages, semaphores, and shared memory.

Another innovation was the *terminfo* database of different types of terminal and their characteristics, optionally replacing the *termcap* file developed by Berkeley.

Print spooling was much improved, with the *lp* command offering much better facilities compared to *lpr* in System III.

Also new in System V was the 'common object file format' (COFF), intended to bring some standardisation into the format of object and executable files, which previously differed considerably between different implementations. Of course the *contents* of an object program — that is the actual machine language code produced by a compiler — must be specific to a particular processor; but at least the surrounding data, telling UNIX how to load the program and so on, is now standardised. An immediate benefit of this was the provision in System V of a number of utilities enabling you to manipulate object files.

System V.2

System V Release 2 had a number of new features, some of which had previously appeared, not always in quite the same form, in Berkeley UNIX; for instance, the *shl* command gives 'job control' facilities for rapid switching between shell layers.

Other new commands in Release 2 included *mailx*, giving many new options compared to the existing *mail* program, and *pg* to display file contents a page at a time (similar to the Berkeley program *more*).

The *cron* command was changed to allow users to schedule their own jobs for execution at regular times; previously a single system-wide *crontab* file was used, which could not be updated by ordinary users. The *at* command was introduced into standard UNIX from BSD.

A major enhancement in Release 2 was advisory record and file locking; a very important facility for proper multi-user working, and one which had already appeared in many commercial UNIX-based systems. Release 3 added mandatory locking.

System V.3

The major innovation in System V Release 3 was the Streams I/O system, together with RFS (remote file sharing) as described in Chapter 21.

Release 3 also provides for shared libraries. The final stage in compiling a program and making it executable is the link edit phase, bringing various compiled object modules together, to form a single executable file. Some of these object modules may be standard UNIX subroutines, contained in the various libraries. Consequently, even a rather small C program can end up quite large, if it has had the standard i/o or maths routines linked in. In Release 3, libraries can be shared: library routines do not need to be included within each executable file, but can be dynamically linked into the program at run time. This typically reduces the size of object files by about half, and speeds up loading.

A very important innovation in Release 3 was demand-paged virtual memory, providing considerable performance improvements on suitable hardware. Actually, demand paging, like a number of other features, appeared in an interim version, Release 2.1.

The importance of System V for AT&T

For AT&T, released from its legal constraints, and set free to pursue commercial ventures, UNIX System V has been a key factor in its assault on the computer market. Other aces in AT&T's hand are its reputation within the USA, its partnership with Olivetti in overseas markets, and its ability to design and build its own hardware, from the microprocessor upwards. AT&T's own computers, including the 3B2 range, are now the first computers on which new UNIX versions appear, and therefore have a very special position in the UNIX market. It will be interesting to see how AT&T/Olivetti continue to balance the somewhat conflicting interests of supplying a manufacturer-independent operating system, while themselves being a major hardware supplier.

But AT&T is today only one of many companies tackling the UNIX market — a market that began with minicomputers, but is now dominated by the 'super-micro'.

UNIX hardware — the minicomputer background

When UNIX was first invented, microcomputers did not exist, and even microprocessors had not yet been invented; the mainframe computer was king, and minicomputers were relatively new. In its first few years, UNIX was a system exclusively for minicomputers from Digital Equipment Corporation (DEC) — particularly the PDP-11.

The position of DEC in the minicomputer world is similar to that of IBM in mainframes. Indeed DEC, from small beginnings, rose in a few years to outstrip all the traditional mainframe companies except IBM itself in terms of sales.

DEC, like other manufacturers, offer their own proprietary operating systems on all their machines. There were various operating systems on the PDP computers, and VMS is the main system for the

32-bit VAX range. UNIX's place in the DEC world has been a minority operating system, used by those who for one reason or another were not satisfied with the proprietary offerings. DEC themselves played an ambiguous role, offering UNIX implementations without particularly pushing them. DEC's own version of UNIX, known as Ultrix, is based on BSD 4.2. However, as a member of the X/Open Group, DEC is now officially committed to support for System V.

Berkeley UNIX

Since about 1981 there has been a second influential strand of UNIX development, parallel to AT&T's System III and system V − the University of California at Berkeley (UCB) have issued their 'Berkeley Software Distributions' − BSD 4.1 (1981), 4.2 (1983) and 4.3 (1986).

Of course there has been considerable cross-fertilisation between Berkeley and AT&T − the C shell has been ported to nearly every version of UNIX, and another Berkeley innovation, the *vi* text editor, has become a standard feature. Nonetheless, there are still substantial differences between Bell and Berkeley UNIXes. The BSD versions, for instance, have their filesystems organised differently for faster performance, their own method of inter-process communication using signals, and a system of 'sockets' for pipes and networking. BSD UNIX is a very powerful operating system, especially suitable for larger machines and scientific applications. However, it lacks some of the newer features of System V, such as inter-process communication by means of semaphores, shared memory, and message passing, not to mention the networking facilities of System V.3.

Graphical and CAD workstations

UNIX is commonly thought of as a multi-user system, but some UNIX machines are specifically designed as powerful single-user computers for graphics and computer-aided design.

Sun Microsystems are a leading maker of high resolution graphics workstations. They have pioneered several innovations such as the NFS networking system, and the NeWS windowing standard. Sun are also working with AT&T to bring the System V and BSD versions of UNIX closer together.

Sun's own operating system, SunOS, is based on BSD 4.2, but also has a number of System V features. Different users who are used to System V or to BSD can have their environment configured so that the operating system appears to be the one that they are used to.

The Pyramid solution

The principle of providing Bell and Berkeley systems side by side has been taken still further by Pyramid, whose operating system, OSx, provides two UNIX 'universes' in one.

Under OSx, you can use the *att* command to change to the AT&T version of the operating system, or the *ucb* command to change to the Berkeley version. If you're not sure which you are currently in, you can type

universe

and the system will tell you which it is. You can also use the other universe just for one command. For instance, if you're currently in *ucb* you can type

att cpio

to run the *cpio* tape archiving utility, a specifically AT&T program, without leaving the Berkeley universe.

The design of OSx shows a great deal of ingenuity in providing every detail of each version of UNIX. For example, the *ls* command works in slightly different ways, listing the filenames across the screen in one type of UNIX, down the screen in the other. OSx, therefore, provides two versions of the program. If you type *ls*, the system appears to run the program */bin/ls* as usual. In reality, it gets the program either from */.ucbbin/ls* or from */.attbin/ls*, but this is totally transparent to the user.

A different approach — the Torch TripleX

The British company Torch first entered the market with systems based around the BBC Microcomputer, but in recent years they have concentrated on UNIX. Their TripleX range represents a very different approach from the traditional UNIX system with its host machine and dumb vdus. The TripleX range, like all UNIX machines, can be used as multi-user computers, but they are specifically designed to bridge the gap between the true multi-user system on the one hand and a network of micros on the other.

A typical TripleX installation would comprise a number of UNIX machines linked together by the Ethernet local network. Some of these machines would be traditional small micros with their own winchester disks and diskette drives; others could be diskless workstations, running UNIX in their own right, but sharing a disk with one of the other machines in the network. This approach, in which the workstations are computers rather than just terminals, so that every user has his own processor and a memory-mapped display, permits a much more sophisticated user interface than usual. In the case of the TripleX, the result has been the OpenTop user interface, described in Chapter 16.

XENIX

Of all the proprietary versions of UNIX, none has had more success in terms of numbers sold than XENIX.

XENIX was first developed as a way of making UNIX acceptable to business users. At that time AT&T was still subject to legal constraints, and only grudgingly allowed outside organisations to use the system — with no guarantees that it worked, and no support. Nonetheless, the basic flexibility and openness of UNIX made it a good starting point, and a number of organisations recognised its potential. One of these organisations was Microsoft, who produced XENIX as a modified version of AT&T UNIX Version 7, bundled it together with a variety of useful features, and offered it as a supported package.

XENIX thus began as a commercial implementation of UNIX for minicomputers. In this role, however, it has been largely superseded by 'straight' versions of UNIX, although some manufacturers — Altos, for example — still offer XENIX as the main operating system for their 16-bit machines.

Many of XENIX's distinctive features have been whittled away over the years, as standard UNIX has caught up and overtaken it. Standard System V is definitely a serious commercial offering, so there is seldom any obvious reason for choosing XENIX in preference to a more generic UNIX system.

The main selling point today for XENIX is as a version of UNIX specifically adapted to personal computers, and it is generally provided with some special features for this purpose. For instance, it can coexist with other PC operating systems such as MS-DOS: using the standard FDISK utility you can divide up your hard disk into separate DOS and XENIX partitions, and re-boot from one operating system to another without too much difficulty. Some versions have utilities for copying files from one partition to the other.

XENIX has been upgraded to give compatibility with System III and subsequently System V, but still has some features showing its separate ancestry. For instance, it has its own standard object file format, which differs from the System V COFF standard.

XENIX itself comes in several different flavours. Microsoft do not sell it directly, but via software houses such as the Santa Cruz Operation (SCO), or hardware suppliers such as IBM. SCO, besides inheriting

Logica's XENIX business, have long-established versions of XENIX for IBM PCs and other machines, and have also launched a range of application software, much of it intended to bring the PC type of package into the UNIX market.

PC software for UNIX

One area in which personal computers running MS-DOS/PC-DOS have scored over UNIX systems is in terms of the application software. Programs such as the Lotus 1-2-3 spreadsheet, the dBase II and dBase III data managers, and the WordStar word processor, account for much of the success of the IBM PC and its rivals. Few such programs were available under UNIX, until SCO provided some very similar programs to run under XENIX.

SCO Professional is a '1-2-3 lookalike', providing all the functionality of the Lotus product, but with a larger maximum spreadsheet size, and file locking to allow it to be used on a multi-user system.

SCO Foxbase is a data management package compatible with dBase II. If you have written programs for dBase II you can run them on Foxbase, and they will run in full multi-user mode without any special modifications.

SCO Lyrix is a word processor for UNIX or XENIX systems. It can be made to emulate the WordStar user interface, which, although not exactly user-friendly, is at least very familiar to many people, your author included. But Lyrix can do much more than WordStar, and has advanced features such as automatic footnotes, tables of contents, and windows. It creates text files in full 8-bit ASCII, whereas WordStar works on 7-bit characters, using the eighth bit for its own purposes.

UNIX and the IBM PC

The IBM Personal Computer was undoubtedly the most successful of all 16-bit microcomputers – particularly if you include the 'clones' produced by other manufacturers – and it is not surprising that a number of UNIX implementations appeared for this type of machine, even though the hardware was really too restricted to support a serious UNIX system.

The first PC able to be considered for UNIX was the 8088-based PC-XT, in its hard disk version. Several versions of UNIX appeared for this machine, including Venix (from Venturcom), XENIX (the SCO version), and PC/IX from IBM themselves.

These versions appealed to the specialist market of users wanting a

UNIX machine on their desk, but they all had severe performance problems. Even in single-user mode, PC UNIX systems are decidedly slow compared to MS-DOS, because of the enormous difference in the complexity of the operating system. Probably most PCs with UNIX ran it as a single-user system; indeed PC/IX was only available with a single-user licence.

A slightly more satisfactory PC UNIX system became possible with the advent of the IBM PC-AT, whose Intel 80286 was specifically designed for multi-tasking systems. IBM themselves offered a version of XENIX for this machine, but again it had limited success: the machine was still not really powerful enough, the potential users (for instance very small businesses) failed to appreciate the benefits of multi-user systems, there was little in the way of packaged software, and it was tiresome to switch between XENIX and DOS, because of the limitations of the 80286.

The next generation of 32-bit personal computers have overcome the major limitations of the PC-AT. The 80386 is a true 32-bit processor, with the features and performance that a UNIX-type system needs. Whereas XENIX on the PC-XT and AT can merely coexist with DOS, 80386-based systems should allow UNIX and DOS to work side by side, running DOS as a task in a UNIX environment, rather than having to reboot the machine to switch from one to the other.

Microsoft were continuing to develop XENIX for the 80386, in parallel with development by AT&T of standard System V for the same chip. But the differences in functionality between UNIX and XENIX were disappearing, and there seemed little point in both developments continuing side by side. In 1987 it was announced that Microsoft and AT&T will be pooling their efforts, and a single system will emerge, with XENIX elements, but sold officially as UNIX System V.

The new UNIX for the 386 will be sold by different suppliers and probably with some competition on prices and additional features. But at last the product will be sold under a single name, ending the confusion that has bedevilled the UNIX market for so long. An exception to this unified approach, however, will be IBM.

Extending the IBM PC (1) — the Personal System/2

The original IBM PC, slightly extended in its XT and AT models, lasted quite a long time by computer industry standards. The replacement range arrived in 1987, in the shape of the Personal System/2. The range includes a number of new features such as $3\frac{1}{2}$ inch diskettes (720k or 1440k) and new display standards, but it is more interesting because of the operating systems supported. All models support PC-DOS (version 3.3) and all but the low-end Model 30 support OS/2, the multi-tasking replacement for PC-DOS.

OS/2 is somewhat more UNIX-like, compared to PC-DOS or MS-DOS. It is designed to use the features of the 286 processor, and also to allow a single standard DOS program to run in parallel with multiple OS/2 tasks. However, it is noticeable that even the version offered on the top-end model 80 will use none of the special features of the model 80's 80386 processor.

XENIX is not part of the new IBM offerings. Instead, on the PS/2 model 80, IBM are offering AIX, their proprietary version of UNIX, which first appeared on the 6150. No doubt AIX will take full advantage of the 80386, and will thus be the only IBM-supported operating system to do so.

The PC market place now looks much more fragmented than for a number of years. The old IBM PC and its many compatibles running

Fig. 5. The IBM 6150 in its desktop version. (Courtesy IBM (UK) Ltd.)

DOS will be one strand, the new OS/2 will be a second, the Apple Macintosh perhaps a third, and UNIX (either standard UNIX or AIX) will be the fourth. In this four-horse race, UNIX looks to have a very good chance of establishing itself as a personal computing standard.

Extending the IBM PC (2) — the 6150 (RT PC)

Both AIX and the 6150 were introduced in 1986. Both are of considerable importance for the story of UNIX.

AIX is a relatively new name as a version of UNIX, but it is one which we will be hearing more and more of in the years to come. It was developed for IBM by Interactive Systems, who had produced a number of other versions of UNIX, particularly PC/IX for the IBM PC-XT, and IX/370 and VM/IX for the IBM mainframes. Clearly IBM have learnt more about UNIX as a result of these developments and AIX is a much more solid and strongly marketed product than its predecessors. Prior to AIX, IBM had given UNIX only rather hesitant support; but the 6150 was announced with AIX as the main operating system — the first time an IBM machine has featured UNIX in this way.

The 6150 is a good illustration of the dual nature of UNIX; on the one hand a powerful single-user system, suitable for computer-aided design and other applications which require a powerful workstation; on the other hand a multi-user system suitable for commercial as well as scientific applications. In fact the machine was originally launched as a CAD and technical/scientific machine, but IBM soon changed the marketing to concentrate on the commercial side.

Despite being known in the USA as the 'RT PC', the 6150 is not really a personal computer. It could well be the start of a new range of more powerful mid-range UNIX machines from IBM. The potential of the machine is enormous — the 700 people employed in developing AIX in Austin, Texas, together with IBM's very highly automated and low cost production facilities, could make it a world beater. But as always with IBM, it is marketing considerations that will determine its future role.

UNIX lookalikes

At various times there have been 'UNIX-lookalike' operating systems, with names such as Idris, Cromix, Coherent, UNOS, uNETix, and QNX. Some of these have been quite close to UNIX, others have only a passing similarity. Few, however, have had any real success in the market, and today the demand is clearly for systems that are fully compatible with standard UNIX, which has meant being derived from System V source code.

One area where a lookalike may still have some place is the very cheap imitation, to run on personal computers. The best-known example is probably PCNX. This is designed to give much of the outward appearance of UNIX, and was even called 'PCUNIX' when it first appeared. The name soon changed, no doubt at the insistence of AT&T.

Another product in the same class is Minix, designed for educational purposes, and functionally almost identical to the old Version 7 UNIX. The system has, of course, been written entirely from scratch, and the source code is freely available. Like PCNX, Minix makes use of the MS-DOS filing system.

Systems of this nature can be useful for people who just want to learn how to use a UNIX-like environment, but they are not a substitute for the real thing in commercial applications.

True lookalikes could become more important, when non-AT&T standards such as POSIX have become well established. A fully POSIX-compatible operating system could be produced without using a line of AT&T source code. Before long such a system is almost bound to appear, and there would be no reason to regard it as inferior to an AT&T UNIX.

Chapter 23
Standards and the Future

Standardising UNIX

A major problem with UNIX at one time was its lack of standardisation, as different computer manufacturers supported different and incompatible versions. A program might be written for one version, but with no guarantee that it would work on another version. 'Standard' UNIX lacked such essential features as record locking, inter-process communication and indexing, and these were implemented in one way in XENIX and in a different way in other versions. Realistically there were two main families of UNIX systems, the AT&T versions and the Berkeley versions, with XENIX as a further complication.

One of the main benefits of UNIX is its availability over a wide range of machines. This benefit was, of course, not fully realised as long as each supplier went his own way, and so there was a call amongst the users of UNIX for greater standardisation. In the USA, the UNIX user group (called */usr/group* in UNIX's typical abbreviated manner) pioneered the standardisation process, but it has gathered momentum considerably in recent years, and other groups have taken part in setting standards, particularly AT&T themselves with their System V Interface Definition (SVID), the IEEE with POSIX, and the X/Open group of manufacturers.

The System V Interface Definition

The SVID (Volumes 1 and 2) corresponds to System V Release 2, and is divided into a specification for a 'Base System', and the following areas of 'Extensions':
- kernel;
- basic utilities;
- advanced utilities;
- software development tools;
- administered system;
- terminal interface.

The third volume relates to Release 3. It covers additional base level functions, and extensions to cover some of the important innovations of Release 3, namely network services and shared libraries.

Altogether these various parts of the SVID standard cover most of the current UNIX product from AT&T, but omitting certain implementation-specific features, even those specific to AT&T's own 3B range of computers.

POSIX

The work of the /usr/group standards committee led to a still more important venture, by the IEEE (Institute of Electrical and Electronic Engineers) in their standard 1003, 'Portable Operating System for Computer Environments', generally known as POSIX.

The major part of the initial POSIX definition covers system calls, and the data structures needed to support them. A future version will include sections on terminal control, as well as a number of optional extensions such as multiple groups and job control.

The aim of the 1003 standard is thus to produce a standardised UNIX for which programs can be written, so that a conforming program will be sure to work correctly on a conforming operating system. This does *not* imply compatibility at the object code level; a program may need to be recompiled to run on a new machine, but once compiled it should run without modification.

POSIX differs in several ways from the SVID, but in 1987 it was announced that the two would be brought into line.

In addition to the main IEEE group working on POSIX (1003.1) there are two other groups: Group 1003.2 is looking at the shells and other utilities (remember, 1003.1 deals mainly with system calls); Group 1003.3 meanwhile is working on testing methodologies, and is making use of the experience of AT&T in creating the SVVS.

In due course, POSIX could become the most influential of all standards for UNIX, as it becomes first an IEEE 'full use standard', and is then (as its proponents hope) taken up by ANSI (the American National Standards Institute) and subsequently by the international standards bodies. Ultimately, it may well become an Application Layer standard as part of OSI.

POSIX is also becoming a standard which purchasing authorities such as the US Government can insist on in inviting tenders for computer systems, and it is therefore a standard which all suppliers, even AT&T themselves, will be forced to comply with. In the UK, the Central Computer and Telecommunications Agency (CCTA) has advised all government departments that following the finalisation of

POSIX as a standard, all government computer systems where portability is important should insist on POSIX compatibility.

The POSIX standard needs to be read in conjunction with the X3J11 draft standard for the C programming language. This is based on the original Kernighan and Ritchie standard, but with some extensions such as the 'void' data type. X3J11 covers not only the syntax of the language itself, but also a standard library of input/output and other functions.

The X/Open Group

The other main body seeking to standardise UNIX is the X/Open Group of computer manufacturers. The original members were a European club, referred to as the 'BISON' group:
- Bull;
- ICL;
- Siemens;
- Olivetti;
- Nixdorf.

They were soon joined by:
- Digital Equipment Corporation (DEC);
- Ericsson;
- Hewlett Packard;
- Philips;
- Sperry (formerly Univac);
- AT&T.

Subsequently, Bull merged with parts of Honeywell and NEC to form Honeywell Bull, and Sperry merged with Burroughs to form Unisys. Thus most of the major computer manufacturers are now represented, with the one notable exception of IBM.

The aim of the group is not to set formal standards (they leave this to bodies such as the IEEE) but to work together, adopting such standards as exist, to define a Common Applications Environment (CAE) which will increase the number of application packages available, and provide a better return on investment for software development by users or independent software houses.

The CAE is based on the SVID, but goes considerably further in adopting 'industry standards'. For instance, SVID does not yet include data management: the CAE has adopted C-ISAM (as used in Informix) as the basis of a standard for indexed sequential files, and takes 'an extensive subset of SQL' as the standard query language.

There are standards for C, and advice on how to write truly portable C programs. Additionally, the group has adopted standards for other languages — FORTRAN-77, ISO-Pascal, and COBOL (the 1974 COBOL standard, extended to include the ACCEPT and DISPLAY statements from Micro Focus Level II COBOL).

The five volumes of the X/Open Portability Guide thus address the main issues of *practical* standardisation, as opposed to the theorising of standards-making bodies. Their contents are shown in Table 23.1. Note that the Group have invented the term 'XVS' to refer to the X/Open System V standard. The word 'UNIX', with its proprietary overtones, seldom appears in the Guide.

Table 23.1 Contents of the X/Open Portability Guide.

Volume	Contents
1	XVS Commands and Utilities
2	XVS System Calls and Libraries
3	XVS Supplementary Definitions: • internationalisation; • terminal interface (the *curses* library); • inter-process communication; • source code transfer, by tapes, diskettes, or *uucp*.
4	Programming Languages
5	Data Management: • indexed sequential access method (ISAM); • structured query language (SQL).

Future areas to be looked at include local area networks, distributed filesystems, the GKS graphics standard, transaction processing, and windowing.

UNIX across the frontiers

Being partly a European group, X/Open have concerned themselves particularly with the internationalisation of UNIX — that is, extending it to cover the various European languages with their special accented letters. The 127 combinations that make up the 7-bit ASCII code do not provide for accented letters as such (although to some extent you can make do with backspacing and over-striking). To cover all the European languages, extended versions of ASCII have been devised, using 8 bits per character, which doubles the number of combinations to 256. This ought to present no problem — virtually all computers today work internally on 8 bits to a byte. However, 7-bit ASCII is still often used in data communications; moreover some of the standard UNIX utilities assume that text will only come as 7 bits, and have used the eighth for their own purposes, so that if you use these programs with true 8-bit data the text will come out mangled.

Actually, internationalisation as defined by the X/Open Group goes well beyond character sets. The narrow American viewpoint of many of the originators of UNIX meant that they failed to provide for the complexities of European languages. For instance, in German there is a lower case letter (the 'sharp s') which has to be converted to two letters ('SS') when the word is put into upper case, while in Spanish the alphabetic sequencing of words puts 'ch' as if it were a separate letter following 'c', and 'll' following 'l'. Add to this the need to have error messages and other text in an appropriate language, as well as the different ways of expressing numbers, dates, and currency, and the size of the problem may become apparent.

The X/Open standards (based on some pioneering work by Hewlett Packard) provide an additional environment variable called LANG which defines the language, the territory, and the character set to be used. The Portability Guide gives some advice on writing programs for use in more than one country. In particular you should not include any plain language messages in the program itself, but use a separate 'text source file' for each language, which can then be compiled by a standard utility into a message catalogue. At run time, selecting an appropriate value of LANG will make the program speak the appropriate language.

The real-time issue

Despite the increasing use of UNIX, it is still not the answer to every computer requirement. There are some sorts of computing for which UNIX is not very suitable, although the number of such areas is much less than it would have been a few years ago. In several areas, UNIX is being adapted to overcome its current limitations.

Many computers today are used for real-time applications. This is one area where UNIX has made little headway – and UNIX would need to change quite considerably before it could become a satisfactory real-time system. First of all, however, what does this phrase 'real-time' actually mean?

A real-time system is one designed to respond to an external stimulus within a clearly defined (and often short) timescale. The most extreme example, perhaps, is an on-board computer controlling a missile or a spacecraft. The computer is being fed all the time with information about the position and speed of the vehicle and its environment, and responds by turning motors on and off, or adjusting the direction controls. If the time it takes to respond is not constant, the adjustments may not have the required effect. A literally down-to-earth version of the same thing is a flight simulator, in which the displays and instruments which the pilot sees must respond to the controls in exactly the same way as if he were really flying the aircraft. A more trivial example is a video game: it is no coincidence that all the best arcade type games (as opposed to adventure games, which are well established under UNIX) are written for single-user computers, thus avoiding the problems of real-time processing in a multi-user situation.

Real-time systems are also used extensively for process control in factories, turning machines on and off, or maybe directing robots. Another example might be a power station, with measurements being supplied constantly to the computer, of water level, steam pressure, and the electrical output.

In all these cases co-ordination is very important — the computer has to respond very quickly, and — still more important — its speed of response must be very predictable.

Most UNIX systems are not predictable in this way. If you have used a multi-user UNIX system you will know that sometimes the machine seems to react instantly to what you type in, but at other times you are kept waiting for what may seem an age. The reason for this is fairly obvious — UNIX is a time-sharing system which needs to allocate time to all the processes that happen to be running. There is no effective control over the creation of new processes, and the more of them there are the less processor time any one of them is given.

In some operating systems, particular processes can be guaranteed to override everything else, so that multi-user facilities can coexist with a guaranteed response for a particular critical process. This is quite different to UNIX, which attempts to share the available time 'fairly' amongst the competing processes. Admittedly you can use the *nice* command to assign higher or lower priorities to particular processes, and a high priority process will then get more of the time available, but whatever its priority a process will still experience a degraded response when usage becomes heavy.

Real-time operating systems

Operating systems designed for true real-time work have to respond very quickly to interrupts: an event such as completion of input/output activity on a device, or a signal from a sensor, can interrupt the current process and immediately cause a special interrupt handling routine to be called. In UNIX, if an interrupt occurs while a process is running in user mode, the system can suspend the normal running of the program and put the user process into kernel mode to deal with it. But when it comes to processes currently running in kernel mode, UNIX is 'non-preemptive' — it cannot interrupt such a process to schedule a real-time process instead. This is acceptable for the sort of processing that UNIX is designed for — after all, most processes stay in kernel mode only for a short time — but it effectively rules out real-time processing.

The problem really is that the length of time a process can stay in kernel mode can be excessively long by the standards of real-time systems. Some versions of UNIX have been devised to minimise this problem by providing 'preemption points' in the kernel, so that if a kernel process is interrupted it can continue as far as the next preemption point, and then give way to the real-time process, which thus gains control far sooner than it would in a normal UNIX system.

There are other reasons why response in UNIX is unpredictable. One is that the time needed to obtain data from a file can vary considerably — if the data in question is currently in a buffer in memory, the program will retrieve it far more quickly than if it needs to be fetched from disk; the loading of the machine will affect this, since the more disk activity is going on, the less likely it is that a block of data used a while ago is still in memory. Moreover, different parts of the same data file may take different times to fetch.

The piece of program that actually handles a real time event such as an interrupt is normally compiled in with the kernel, and executed in the same way as any other piece of kernel code. It may even be possible to have this interrupt handling dealt with by a special front end processor, and thus not have to bother the central processor at all. But in either way the interrupt handler itself will probably do the absolute minimum necessary, and produce output for a user program to handle. In UNIX, this user program may need to be loaded in from disk; or it may be resident in memory, or may have been temporarily swapped out. These three situations have drastically different effects on the time needed to get the program running.

Actually, judicious use of some of the features of UNIX can mitigate this problem. For a start, there is the 'sticky bit' which can be set for the program in question. If this bit is set on, then the program code will be retained when the process using it terminates, so that the next time it is used it will not have to be reloaded. For real-time purposes it may be better in any case to have the process remain active, thus also avoiding the necessity for a *fork*. Even so, the process may find itself swapped out in the normal way; but here again UNIX provides an answer, in the shape of the *plock* system call, which effectively locks a process in memory to prevent it being swapped out at all.

Many real-time systems need to carry out certain functions — perhaps checking the status of an external sensor – at very regular intervals. UNIX is not very suitable for this purpose; the *alarm* system call can schedule an alarm a given number of seconds later, and the *cron* and *at* facilities can schedule programs to run at times expressed in minutes, but neither is any use for a function which must be carried out reliably at intervals expressed in fractions of a second.

Many real-time systems involve a number of concurrent co-operating processes, and hence need a fast and effective method of communicating between one and another. Pipes are the most commonly used type of inter-process communication in UNIX, but their use is restricted: the processes in question need to have inherited the file descriptors from a common ancestor (named pipes are now available, however, to avoid this restriction). Moreover pipes are slow, in that they use·the file system. Of course, in most cases the data transfer takes place through buffers in memory rather than being actually written to disk, but even so the data needs to be physically moved twice – from the sending process's data area to the buffer, and from there to the receiving process's data area. Fortunately, System V now offers greatly improved means of inter-process communication, including semaphores for synchronisation, and shared memory for exchange of data.

Hewlett Packard, in particular, have implemented a number of real-time features in their own version of UNIX, called HP-UX. In addition, a number of UNIX look-alike operating systems have appeared designed for real-time use. Indeed, AT&T themselves have produced a UNIX-like real-time system called MERT. Other systems such as D-NIX have been developed from scratch as real-time systems, but with System V compatibility.

Transaction processing

UNIX is often said to be unsuitable for transaction processing. This is much less clear-cut than the position with real-time processing. First, however, some explanation is probably required.

Transaction processing generally refers to the input of commercial transactions. For instance, in an order processing system, customers may be making orders by telephone which need to be keyed in straight away to the computer, so as to update the various files. Such a system could be regarded as 'real-time' in a sense – after all, if the customer is waiting for confirmation, some degree of delay will be unacceptable – but the problems which arise are more to do with overall throughput levels, and the ability of the system to cope with failures. Hardware features, such as intelligent i/o processors, or the design of the disk channel, can make a great deal of difference to a system's performance.

Throughput can be a problem when there are very large numbers of users on-line at once. UNIX was not designed to give high performance in this situation; the design of the filestore, and the amount of disk handling involved in the general running of the system, mean that a heavily used system is often slowed down by its disks more than anything else. Another potential problem is in the loading of programs; if a new transaction means *fork*ing a new process, this in itself will slow the system down.

Actually, a lot of UNIX-based systems are used for transaction processing, at least on a small scale. Moreover, UNIX itself is being improved continually in ways which address some of the main objections to it in this area. The introduction of locking in System V Release 2 is an obvious example. On the performance level, UNIX is in many ways better than it used to be. For instance, Release 3 includes a 'virtual *fork*', which avoids the need for a new process to copy its parent's data area, while AIX has a similar feature.

Demand paging should provide important performance improvements, particularly on heavily used systems, while shared libraries will help by reducing the space that programs take in memory, and the time needed to load them. Most important of all, perhaps, 32-bit microprocessors are being designed specifically to cater for UNIX-type systems, and should give still further improvements in performance.

Data management and the UNIX filestore

UNIX is increasingly used for data management applications, typically using a database management system and often an associated 4GL. In many ways, UNIX is a good environment for this sort of system. However, performance is again a problem, partly because of the design of the UNIX filestore, partly because of the inner complexity of a relational database system. In fact, some of the DBMS suppliers claim to have to have improved their performance so substantially that the original versions of their products must have been extraordinarily slow!

The buffer cache mechanism used by the standard UNIX system calls for reading and writing disk files is intended to improve performance, but may cause problems if a disk failure occurs. A process doing a normal write to a data file does not access the disk directly, but merely updates the contents of the appropriate buffer. If the buffer in question needs to be released to make room for new data being read in, the kernel writes it back to disk. Otherwise, physical writing occurs as a result of the *sync* system call, which flushes all the buffers to disk. Most UNIX systems have a background process which issues the *sync* call every thirty seconds or so.

Standards and the Future

This means that the application program has no knowledge of whether a physical update has taken place, and no control over when it happens; moreover, physical updates do not necessarily take place in the order which the application program might expect.

None of this matters in the normal case, since UNIX takes care of the writing to disk. However, if a hardware failure occurs during the course of a transaction, the database may be left in an indeterminate and inconsistent state. This problem has, of course, been recognised by AT&T, and has been partly addressed by the 'filesystem hardening' of successive versions of System V, but it can be avoided altogether by database products which avoid using the standard UNIX disk i/o.

Use of raw disk

In UNIX it is quite permissible to bypass the standard UNIX filing systems, and read and write raw disk − in other words, treating a partition of the disk as a device rather than a structured filesystem. This, after all, is the way that the UNIX swapper works.

A database management system often handles much bigger files than those UNIX was designed to cope with, and could sometimes benefit from using raw disk − for instance, enabling a single file to span more than one physical device or filesystem. With very large files it may also be helpful to bypass the indirect block addressing provided by the UNIX inodes and address blocks, thus giving faster access; moreover the files can be organised in a less fragmented fashion. Using raw disk also means that the UNIX buffer cache is bypassed; the database manager must provide its own buffering, but can use larger than normal buffers for improved throughput.

The Unify database management system uses raw disk, and it has also been adopted in the 'Turbo' version of Informix. Other database products may follow suit. However, the advantage is not all one way. For applications which do not have extremely large tables, use of the UNIX file system may still be appropriate, and is essential if one is to take advantage of the various UNIX file handling utilities or features such as RFS. Ingres uses the UNIX file system, and is nonetheless regarded as a high performance product. No doubt, in the future, the dilemma will be resolved by further improvements in UNIX's own file handling.

Chapter 24
UNIX in the Wider Context

Many companies and organisations are now adopting UNIX as a standard operating system, to provide a common approach to computing, so that machines from many different suppliers can work together. In other companies, UNIX is an important part of the whole picture, but needs to coexist with machines running other operating systems.

Some organisations, both private and governmental, have actually specified UNIX as a standard for the 'middle level' of computing, alongside some proprietary system on the mainframe and MS-DOS or PC-DOS (or in the future OS/2) on the PC. In this chapter I hope to clarify a little how UNIX can fit into an overall company policy of this nature.

UNIX and the proprietary systems

Industry-standard operating systems such as UNIX will increasingly dominate the smaller computer scene. However, there are still a number of proprietary operating systems in existence. Most of the big mainframe suppliers have their own operating systems; in particular two IBM mainframe operating systems − MVS and VM − are now so well established that they have effectively become industry standards themselves. On minicomputers there are also a number of proprietary operating systems; VMS, running on DEC's VAX range, is the most important.

Compared to UNIX, the proprietary operating systems may offer better performance − after all, they were designed specifically for the machines they run on, and should fit very closely with the hardware. They may also have benefited from a great deal of 'polishing' to make the various parts fit together and appear as a consistent whole. By contrast, UNIX, being the product of so many different organisations at one time or another, sometimes does not seem to hang together very well. However, System V is acquiring a more and more 'professional' image with each new release.

UNIX on the mini and the mainframe

This book has been concerned mainly with UNIX as a system for microcomputers — but UNIX is well established on minis as well, and there are UNIX implementations on mainframes, including IBM's own IX/370 and Amdahl's UTS. UNIX actually has a place on the very biggest computers of all — the so-called 'supercomputers' made by Cray and others — but the mainframe is still largely the province of proprietary operating systems.

Mainframe versions of UNIX are often 'hosted' on top of a proprietary operating system such as VM, and run alongside non-UNIX applications. The hosted approach treats UNIX as a special service for those who require the UNIX tools and facilities, while keeping the proprietary operating system for general purpose computing.

As interest in UNIX grows, many mainframe installations are likely to make some provision for UNIX, but there is something of a culture barrier to be overcome. Mainframes are run by data processing departments, with their own peculiar mentality and their own closely guarded skills. A job that would be quite easy to do on a UNIX system can sometimes take months of work by highly paid 'systems programmers' on a mainframe system. No wonder the users in so many companies have been turning their back on the corporate mainframe, and finding their own solutions to computing needs, either individually with PCs, or on a departmental basis with UNIX.

Mainframes in the UNIX era

Mainframe computing will not disappear overnight, but it is beginning to look very expensive compared to the UNIX approach. Replacing a mainframe with enough microcomputers to give each user the equivalent performance would often be a very much cheaper option. The logic of the technology is inescapable: since the invention of the micro, processing power is cheap, and there is no point whatever in having a big machine just so that processing power can be shared amongst many users. Mainframes should be used where nothing else will do — for instance, centralised accounting or order processing systems, where it is vital to have all users on-line to a single computer.

Many organisations, in the course of evaluating UNIX, have asked the question: how will this fit in with our policy of being an IBM user (meaning an IBM mainframe user) or a user of ICL, Honeywell, and so on? The fact that this question is asked at all reflects the undue prominence given to the mainframe in the company's thinking — not surprisingly, perhaps, since the mainframe is the pride and joy, or, perhaps the constant headache, of the data processing department, who are regarded as representing computing expertise within the organisation. Mainframes from now on will be a diminishing proportion of any company's computing resources, even if they continue to absorb more than their due share of money and expensive manpower. The centre of gravity in computing is moving towards the micro, and in this context a company policy of preference for UNIX can well make sense.

Linking PCs to a UNIX system

The typical terminals attached to a UNIX system have changed over the years. Originally there was the teletype, with its keyboard and printer: some of the UNIX utilities such as *ed*, and the shells themselves, would still be happy in that environment. Then came the vdu, and with it new programs such as *vi*, written to take advantage of the screen. Today's vdus are becoming increasingly sophisticated, with their own microprocessors, and one make of vdu is often able to emulate another. The gap is closing between the plain vdu and the personal computer.

With the prices of personal computers dropping all the time, there is now little difference in cost between the cheapest microcomputers and standard vdus.

Of course a vdu terminal often has things that a cheap micro may not have – a more extensive keyboard, a better screen display, and the communications software already built in – but a PC has the great advantage of its own processing power, and this can be used to lighten the load on the UNIX host.

The widespread use of PCs has left its mark on users' expectations as to the user interface. If they are used to colour and slick presentation techniques on their PC, they may expect the same from multi-user systems, and be dissatisfied with the poor image of much UNIX software. But the more sophisticated the screen display, the more demand it makes on the central processor. Really good screen displays are much easier if the controlling software is running in the workstation or PC rather than the host.

You can now buy a variety of software for personal computers that enables them to act in this way as terminals to a host computer.

PC Works

PC Works is a terminal emulator package which runs in a PC, emulating various terminal characteristics, and allowing you to change

UNIX in the Wider Context

terminal settings by means of a setup screen. You can have preprogrammed login sequences, available from the main PC Works menu. The UNIX machine sees the PC as an ordinary VT100 terminal.

PC Works can also be used for file transfer. In this case it requires a second piece of the package to be running in the UNIX host, to cooperate with the PC, and set the correct protocols,

PC Interface

PC Interface is a more ambitious product than PC Works, although as yet not quite so widely available. It includes three modules:
- an interface package;
- an emulation package;
- a context switch facility.

The interface package treats the UNIX machine as a shared resource for file storage. Part of the UNIX filestore is used as a virtual PC disk drive, which can be referred to in the standard DOS fashion as 'C:' or 'D:'. All the ordinary DOS commands can be used in connection with this disk, but the UNIX permissions and locks apply in addition. Some special commands are available from within DOS, including copy programs (DOS2UNIX, UNIX2DOS), commands to deal with locks and permissions and to see a UNIX-style directory listing (LOCKS, UCHMOD, UDIR), plus a PRINTER command to direct printing to the printer on the UNIX machine.

The emulation package allows you to log in to UNIX directly, and you can additionally send, receive, and store files.

The context switch allows you to switch immediately between DOS and UNIX. The task you have left remains frozen, and you can pick it up later where you left off.

PC Interface is available for use over an RS232 connection, just as would be used to connect an ordinary vdu, or alternatively over a local area network (for instance, Ethernet). Of course, the difference in transmission speed is considerable: typically 9600 bits per second using RS232, 10 megabits using Ethernet. The Ethernet connection would be far preferable in most cases, although obviously more expensive. Also, using Ethernet but not RS232, you get the full benefit of the context switch utility – your DOS application can be using the host as a file server, so that effectively you have two lines open to the host, one for DOS and one for UNIX.

UNIX-PC co-operation

The idea of the PC and the UNIX host working together is very attractive – ideally each doing what it is best at. The UNIX machine would give multi-user access to the database, and the PC would provide a user interface of the quality that has become commonplace for PC software. To get the full benefit from such an arrangement, however, the UNIX application software needs to be designed with PCs in mind. A few examples are now emerging – for instance, the Informix and Ingres database packages.

Informix and Ingres are each designed as a two-process system, on the client/server model. Each user who is accessing the database has two processes running simultaneously. One of these runs the user program with all the details of the particular application; it handles the formatting of the vdu screen and prompts the user for input. The other process runs in the background and handles all the actual searching and updating of the database. The two processes communicate via standard inter-process communication facilities, using SQL, the standard database language. Informix and Ingres now run not only on UNIX but on PCs, and can enable the two types of machine to work very closely together, with the front-end application process on the PC, the back-end process on the host.

This arrangement has several advantages from the point of view of performance. For a start the host is doing much less work than normally, since all the work of translating formatted input into SQL has been done elsewhere; moreover, the kernel is not having the overhead of dealing with raw terminal input. It should thus be possible to have more users running on the same machine without degradation. Also, the 'front end' application process will have a processor to itself, handling the user interface, the formatting of the screen forms, and so on, and should be able to react much more quickly to the user's input.

UNIX as a file server

Many organisations provide multi-user computing by means of a network of single-user micros. This can be a cheap alternative to a true multi-user system such as UNIX, and is particularly appropriate for tasks such as word processing and office automation. Most systems of this nature have a mixture of 'workstations' – that is personal computers – and 'file servers' with large hard disks which users at the various workstations can access.

File servers on a network need special multi-user software, to allow files to be owned by particular users, to set access permissions, and so on. This is not catered for at all well by MS-DOS/PC-DOS, so the software needs to be provided either as a package running on top of DOS, or as a specialised operating system such as Novell Netware. But of course UNIX has all the multi-user facilities required, and much more besides. For those companies who need a network of PCs, but also have true multi-user applications, a UNIX host as a network file and print server could be just the answer.

The job of the systems integrator

Throughout this book I have been attempting to describe how a user or a systems administrator can use a working UNIX system. But how does a system get set up in the first place? If you are a company about to purchase your first UNIX computer, how do you ensure that it will all work correctly, that the software that looks so attractive can actually drive the terminals and printers you have chosen, that the disk will be big enough to hold your files, that the machine will be powerful enough to support the transaction load, that all your users will have directories set up for them, that your systems administrator will know where to start?

The answer to all these questions is that you should choose very carefully not only what system you buy, but who you buy it from. The purchase of a UNIX system is not like buying a car, or even a personal computer — in these cases the supplier will expect you to know precisely what you want and how to use it. A UNIX system, on the other hand, needs care in configuration, so that the complete package you end up with hangs together. It also needs care in installation, so that the hardware and software will all work correctly.

In buying a UNIX system, you should go to an established systems house with a track record in supplying and supporting UNIX. They will be able to help you consider the various options, and make up your mind precisely what sort of system is best suited to your business requirements. If your needs are at all out of the ordinary, it may be best to start by commissioning a short consultancy study, which will result in a recommendation and the outline definition of a system.

These days most requirements can be satisfied by means of a standard application package, possibly with a little 'programming' or setting up, to make it do what you want. Some requirements, however, still need actual programs to be written in a language such as C or COBOL, or perhaps in a 4GL. Obviously programming in a conventional language will be by far the most expensive option, but sometimes there is no realistic alternative. Again, a reputable systems house should be able to advise you.

Having decided on the hardware and software required, and placed the order, you can begin preparing to receive the new machine. A room may have to be set aside for the computer, cables laid for connecting the terminals, maybe desks purchased or at least moved around to take the terminals themselves. More important still, you will need to prepare the staff for the new system: telling them what is going to happen, reassuring them if need be that their jobs are not threatened, and organising training for those who will be using the system directly or indirectly.

The importance of training

Training is essential if you or your company are to get the best from your machine. Everyone needs training if they are to drive a car, and a computer, while not so dangerous to life and limb, is far more complicated in what it can do than a motor vehicle. So anyone setting out to use a computer must have a certain amount of instruction.

As with vehicles, different levels of training are appropriate for different classes of computer. Just because you have passed your driving test does not make you competent to drive a bus or a heavy lorry; similarly the fact that you know your way round a single-user computer does not mean that you should be entrusted with looking after a multi-user system. For UNIX in particular, the scope for unfortunate mistakes if you're not sure what you're doing is quite large.

With UNIX systems, moreover, there are different classes of user. Some need to be able to control the system as a whole, adding users, doing backups, and so on; others will be using particular application software, and need only a rudimentary knowledge of UNIX itself.

Whatever their level, however, users need some training. Even if you think you know how a particular piece of software works, there are probably some finer points that would come out in a training session. And if you are just starting out, you may totally fail to appreciate some important point that would make the system so much easier to use.

There is an obvious temptation to cut corners, and go for cut-price options, or try to get by just by reading the manual. Beware that computer manuals, while better than they were, can still be difficult to follow, even for the computer professional. And UNIX manuals typically tell you about the facilities of the software but do not suggest what you could use them for.

What training do you need?

The first stage in UNIX training — at least for those who have not used computers before — should be some background education as to the nature of computers and how they fit into modern business life. The next stage is learning to use the terminal, and an overview of the main concepts and commands of UNIX itself. Even those who only ever use a particular word processor or accounting package should have some understanding of concepts such as directories, as otherwise they may be unable to locate particular files and think they have lost them, or fail to understand the need for good practices in allocating filenames and carrying out the various 'housekeeping' procedures.

The next stage is learning the actual software package. If people are going to use several packages, do not try to instil them all at once: the students will end up totally confused, especially if the different packages use different command structures, as is quite likely.

Once users have had basic training in the use of the chosen package, they should get started right away in using it, and thus build on the knowledge obtained from the course. After using it for a month or two, they may be ready to benefit from one of the advanced 'workshop' courses that some training houses offer.

Finally, users may need training in the specific application. Even if this has been built for you using one of the standard packages such as Informix, Uniplex, and so on, training in that package generally is no substitute for training in the application that has been developed. Your systems house should be asked to provide such training as part of the overall solution.

Training is in many ways the key to UNIX. The operating system, and the packages it supports, have enormous potential to serve the needs of the organisation. If you fail to take advantage of the resources available, and join the ranks of those who are disillusioned with computers, you have only yourself to blame. Given careful planning, professional advice in devising a solution, adequate training of your staff and commitment on the part of management, you can join the ever-growing ranks of those who have tried UNIX and found it gave them exactly what was required.

Appendices

Appendix A
Keyboards and Characters

The basic unit of information in a UNIX file is the 'byte', made up of eight bits. In text files, there has to be some convention as to which combination of bits forms which character. On most UNIX systems – and indeed on most computers of all types – the convention used is ASCII (American Standard Code for Information Interchange), also known as International Alphabet Number 5. A different convention called EBCDIC (Extended Binary Coded Decimal Interchange Code) is used on IBM mainframes: it is a true 8-bit code, with no 7-bit version, and quite different to ASCII in the actual codes used.

ASCII is fundamentally a 7-bit code – some communication protocols use the eighth bit of the byte for parity checking – so it gives a basic repertoire of 2^7 combinations, or 128 different characters.

The seven-bit ASCII code is sufficient for the English language, but to cater for all the other European languages with their special accented characters, eight bits are required. Extensions to the ASCII code have therefore been devised and recent upgrades to UNIX have been 'internationalising' various of the utilities, for example, to ensure that they do not use the eighth bit for their own purposes. For Japanese, two bytes are needed per character, but that is another story.

In English, 52 of the 128 basic ASCII codes are obviously needed for the letters of the alphabet (upper case and lower case), one for the blank space character, and 10 for the digits 0 to 9. A further 32 are taken up by punctuation marks, and a rather odd collection of special symbols, as will seen from the table that follows.

The punctuation signs have some peculiarities. In normal typesetting there is a distinction between left and right hand quotation marks, in both the single and the double forms. In standard ASCII the single forms have left and right versions but the double forms do not. The shell, the C programming languages, and other UNIX utilities tend to use right hand single quotes (or apostrophes) in pairs, rather than one right and one left. Additionally, the shell uses pairs of left hand quotes (or backquotes) to denote command substitution.

Some of the traditional typewriter keys are not provided and hence are difficult to use in computer systems – particularly the °, also $\frac{1}{2}$, $\frac{1}{4}$, and $\frac{3}{4}$. Note also that there is no £ sign, although in practice most keyboards and printers allow for £ signs in one way or another. On the other hand, such symbols as \, |, ^, and ~ have little use outside computers.

So far we have accounted for 95 characters out of the 128. All the above are 'printable' characters – they can be printed directly on a normal computer printer, and entered directly into the computer by pressing the appropriate key on the keyboard (with a few possible exceptions, e.g. the backquote is sometimes omitted from the keyboard).

In addition, the ASCII code provides for 33 control characters, used for 'data link control' and other purposes in data communications, making up the total of 128. The control characters are generally referred to by abbreviations such as EOT (end of text), BEL (sound the bell or bleep on the terminal), and so on. By definition these are all 'non-printable' characters, although some of them may in fact control the working of a printer, and they generally do not appear on the keyboard. However, all keyboards seem to provide for ESC (escape) and CR (carriage return), and most also have BS (backspace) and HT (horizontal tab).

All normal keyboards have fewer keys than the number of different characters that need to be input. As on a typewriter, you can input an upper case rather than a lower case letter by holding down the shift key while pressing the letter key in question. Computer keyboards have an additional key similar to the shift key, marked Control or Ctrl. Holding down the Ctrl key while pressing a letter key gives you a further range of input possibilities. These may vary with the application but by default they give you 26 of the 33 special control characters. Six of the other seven are obtained by combining Ctrl with other keys, in the following range:

@ [\ ] ^ _

Fig. 6. The standard IBM keyboard.

Keyboards and Characters

The combination of holding down Ctrl and pressing (say) A is generally printed as ^A or Ctrl-A. Some keyboards also provide an Alternate (Alt) key to provide still further combinations.

Newline characters

Two different control characters are sometimes involved in starting a new line of text: CR (carriage return), and LF (line feed). Strictly speaking, carriage return means going back to the left hand position, and line feed means going down one line. Both movements are involved in starting a new line of text; some operating systems (such as MS-DOS) generate both control characters, and some printers expect to receive both. In UNIX, by convention, only the LF character is stored in text files, and is interpreted as doing the combined function of CR and LF. To insert a new line in text you can input an LF, by hitting Ctrl-J. Generally speaking, however, you hit the Return key and thus generate a CR (an alternative way of doing this is Ctrl-M), and UNIX will convert this to LF (depending on the *stty* settings).

Referring to binary numbers

In referring to the various ASCII codes, one can obviously use the decimal equivalent of the binary number (that is, a number between 0 and 255). But it is sometimes convenient to use a representation more closely aligned with the underlying binary representation. If you divide a byte into two groups of four bits, you can represent it as two 'hexadecimal' digits (in the range 0 to 15). For convenience, 10 is represented in hexadecimal as A, 11 as B, and so on up to F for 15. Thus a byte can have any value between 00 and FF.

A further representation sometimes used is 'octal', in which groups of three bits are each represented as a digit between 0 and 7. A byte in octal representation can have values between 000 and 377.

Table A.1 gives the basic 7-bit ASCII codes and their meanings. The first three columns of the table show the numeric value of the character in octal, hexadecimal, and decimal respectively. The 'Ctrl char' column shows the combination of a control key and an ordinary key that you can use to generate certain ASCII codes from the keyboard. The next two columns show the printed version of the character (if any) and the standard ASCII names for those that are not printable. The 'Description' column gives further information.

Appendix A

Table A.1. ASCII codes and their meanings.

ASCII value						
Oct	Hex	Dec	Ctrl char	Print char	Name	Description
000	00	0	^@		NUL	null
001	01	1	^A		SOH	start of heading
002	02	2	^B		STX	start of text
003	03	3	^C		ETX	end of text
004	04	4	^D		EOT	end of transmission
005	05	5	^E		ENQ	enquiry
006	06	6	^F		ACK	acknowledge
007	07	7	^G		BEL	bell
010	08	8	^H		BS	backspace
011	09	9	^I		HT	horizontal tab
012	0A	10	^J		NL	newline (line feed)
013	0B	11	^K		VT	vertical tab
014	0C	12	^L		NP	(FF) new page (form feed)
015	0D	13	^M		CR	carriage return
016	0E	14	^N		SO	shift out
017	0F	15	^O		SI	shift in
020	10	16	^P		DLE	data link escape
021	11	17	^Q		DC1	device control 1; start (xon)
022	12	18	^R		DC2	device control 2
023	13	19	^S		DC3	device control 3; stop (xoff)
024	14	20	^T		DC4	device control 4
025	15	21	^U		NAK	negative acknowledge
026	16	22	^V		SYN	synchronous idle
027	17	23	^W		ETB	end of transmission block
030	18	24	^X		CAN	cancel
031	19	25	^Y		EM	end of medium
032	1A	26	^Z		SUB	substitute character
033	1B	27	^[		ESC	escape
034	1C	28	^\		FS	file separator; quit
035	1D	29	^]		GS	group separator
036	1E	30	^~		RS	record separator
037	1F	31	^_		US	unit separator
040	20	32				space
041	21	33		!		exclamation mark
042	22	34		"		double quotation mark
043	23	35		#		hash
044	24	36		$		dollar
045	25	37		%		percentage
046	26	38		&		ampersand
047	27	39		'		right quotation mark (apostrophe)
050	28	40		(		left parenthesis

Table A.1 *Continued*

051	29	41	)	right parenthesis
052	2A	42	*	asterisk
053	2B	43	+	plus
054	2C	44	,	comma
055	2D	45	-	minus (hyphen)
056	2E	46	.	full stop
057	2F	47	/	slash
060	30	48	0	zero
061	31	49	1	
062	32	50	2	
063	33	51	3	
064	34	52	4	
065	35	53	5	
066	36	54	6	
067	37	55	7	
070	38	56	8	
071	39	57	9	
072	3A	58	:	colon
073	3B	59	;	semicolon
074	3C	60	<	less than
075	3D	61	=	equals
076	3E	62	>	greater than
077	3F	63	?	question mark
100	40	64	@	at sign
101	41	65	A	
102	42	66	B	
103	43	67	C	
104	44	68	D	
105	45	69	E	
106	46	70	F	
107	47	71	G	
110	48	72	H	
111	49	73	I	
112	4A	74	J	
113	4B	75	K	
114	4C	76	L	
115	4D	77	M	
116	4E	78	N	
117	4F	79	O	
120	50	80	P	
121	51	81	Q	
122	52	82	R	
123	53	83	S	
124	54	84	T	
125	55	85	U	
126	56	86	V	

Table A.1 *Continued*

127	57	87	W		
130	58	88	X		
131	59	89	Y		
132	5A	90	Z		
133	5B	91	[		Left square bracket
134	5C	92	\		backslash
135	5D	93	]		right square bracket
136	5E	94	^		circumflex
137	5F	95	_		underline
140	60	96	`		left quotation mark (grave)
141	61	97	a		
142	62	98	b		
143	63	99	c		
144	64	100	d		
145	65	101	e		
146	66	102	f		
147	67	103	g		
150	68	104	h		
151	69	105	i		
152	6A	106	j		
153	6B	107	k		
154	6C	108	l		
155	6D	109	m		
156	6E	110	n		
157	6F	111	o		
160	70	112	p		
161	71	113	q		
162	72	114	r		
163	73	115	s		
164	74	116	t		
165	75	117	u		
166	76	118	v		
167	77	119	w		
170	78	120	x		
171	79	121	y		
172	7A	122	z		
173	7B	123	{		left brace
174	7C	124	|		vertical bar
175	7D	125	}		right brace
176	7E	126	~		tilde
177	7F	127		DEL	interrupt

Appendix B
Standard Commands and Utilities

In this Appendix I have attempted to list the main commands and utilities that you can expect to find in any modern UNIX system. Such a list can never be definitive, because suppliers are constantly adding new commands to their versions of UNIX, and the standards-making bodies are following on behind. However, published standards such as the System V Interface Definition (SVID) and the X/Open Portability Guide today provide a much more reliable list of what is included in UNIX than was possible before they appeared.

Most of the commands and utilities listed below are programs, and they will mostly be found as executable files in the */bin* directory of a typical UNIX system. Some, like *cd* and *echo*, are built in commands which come as part of the shell. Others, again, are not programs in themselves, but merely additional names for programs. For instance, *ln* and *mv* are often the same program as *cp*, and *rmdir* the same program as *rm*; in each case the ability of UNIX processes to know by what name they were invoked allows a single program to serve for several quite different commands.

For each command I give a brief indication of what it does; this will not always correspond with the established descriptions in the UNIX manuals, which are sometimes meaningful only to the initiated. Unfortunately, in a few cases it seems impossible to give a readily understood explanation in a few words, and the reader is referred to the standard UNIX manuals for a fuller description.

Lists of commands and utilities

Table B.1 gives the most common standard commands that are generally available to users. I have explained most of them in more or less detail earlier in this book.

Table B.1 Standard user commands and utilities.

ar	file archiver
at	executes commands at a later time
awk	scans text file for patterns
banner	outputs big letters
basename	gives all but the last element of a pathname
batch	executes a batch job now (see *at*)
cal	prints a calendar

Table B.1 *Continued*

calendar	lists your appointments
cancel	cancels line printer requests (see *lp*)
cat	copies a file or files to standard output
cd	changes your working directory
chgrp	changes the group owner of a file (see *chown*)
chmod	changes permissions on a file
chown	changes the owner of a file
chroot	changes root directory for a command
cmp	compares two files
col	deals with reverse linefeeds
comm	finds lines common to two sorted files
cp	copies a file
cpio	copies file archives in and out
crontab	controls user level *crontab* files
csplit	reads a file and splits it into sections
cu	communicates to another UNIX system
cut	cuts out selected fields from a text file
date	displays the date and time
dd	copies a file and converts it to a new format
df	reports free disk space
diff	finds the differences between two text files
dircmp	compares files in two directories
dirname	gives the last element of a pathname (see *basename*)
du	reports disk space used by directory
echo	sends its parameters to standard output
ed	line editor
egrep	searches a file for a pattern
ex	line editor
expr	evaluates an expression
false	returns a non-zero exit code (see *true*)
fgrep	searches a file for a pattern (see *egrep*)
file	determines file type of a specified file
find	searches the filestore for files
grep	searches a file for a pattern
id	prints user and group id
join	joins two files on a specified field
kill	sends a signal to a process
line	copies one line from standard input to output
ln	makes a new link to a file
logname	displays your login name
lp	print spooler
lpstat	tells you the status of line printers
ls	lists the files in a directory
mail	electronic mail utility
mailx	enhanced electronic mail utility

Table B.1 *Continued*

mesg	permits messages to be sent to your terminal
mkdir	makes a new directory
mknod	creates a special file (device or FIFO)
mv	moves (renames) a file
newgrp	changes to a new group
news	prints news items
nl	adds line numbers to a file
nohup	runs a command to continue after you log out
od	octal dump of a file
pack	packs a file to make it smaller
passwd	changes your password
paste	combines text files together
pcat	unpacks files and outputs them (see *pack*)
pg	shows you a file a page at a time
pr	formats a file and prints it to standard output
ps	reports status of current processes
pwd	tells you your working directory
rm	removes a file
rmdir	removes a directory
sed	stream editor
sh	runs the shell
shl	manages shell layers
sleep	does nothing for a specified time
sort	sorts a file to specified sequence
spell	checks spelling
split	divides a large file into smaller chunks
stty	changes terminal settings
su	changes your effective user id
sum	generates checksum and block count for a file
tabs	sets tabs on a terminal
tail	outputs the last part of a file
tar	tape archiver
tee	diverts copy of standard input to a file
test	checks various conditions
touch	changes access date on a file
tr	translates characters
true	returns a zero exit code
tty	gets the name of the terminal
umask	controls permission bits when creating files
uname	tells you the name of the current UNIX system
uniq	strips out duplicated lines of a file
unpack	unpacks a file (see *pack*)
uucp	copies files to another UNIX system
uulog	queries a uucp log file (see *uucp*)
uuname	lists names of remote UNIX systems (see *uucp*)

Table B.1 *Continued*

uupick	accepts transmitted files (see *uuto*)
uustat	status and control utility for *uucp*
uuto	sends files using *uucp*
uux	executes a command on a remote system
vi	screen editor
wait	waits until processes are complete
wall	sends a message to all terminals
wc	counts words in a file
who	shows who is logged in
write	sends a message to another user

Table B.2 gives some commands and utilities that are mainly applicable for programming and software development.

Table B.2 Software development utilities.

admin	creates and initialises *sccs* files
as	assembler
bs	compiles and interprets modest-sized programs
cb	C beautifier for source code
cc	C compiler
cdc	changes comments in an *sccs* file
cflow	generates a C flowgraph of external references
comb	combines *sccs* deltas
cpp	C language preprocessor
cxref	C program cross reference
delta	creates a delta (change) in an *sccs* file
dis	disassembler
env	sets the environment for execution of a command
get	creates a specified version of an *sccs* file
ld	link editor for object files
lex	generates a C program to analyse text
lint	checks C programs for potential problems
lorder	finds best order for files in an object library
m4	macro processor
make	maintains up-to-date versions of programs
nm	displays symbol table of an object file
prof	displays program profile data
prs	displays an *sccs* file
rmdel	removes a delta from an *sccs* file
sact	displays current *sccs* file status
sdb	symbolic debugger
size	displays section sizes of object files
sno	SNOBOL interpreter
strip	removes symbolic information from an object file

Standard Commands and Utilities 261

Table B.2 *Continued*

time	times the execution of a command
tsort	sorts a list of ordered pairs (for use with *lorder*)
unget	cancels a previous *get* command
val	validates *sccs* files
what	displays identifying information in *sccs*
xargs	constructs argument lists and runs a command
yacc	compiler-compiler

Many of the commands in Table B.3 are not intended for ordinary users.

Table B.3 System management commands.

acctcms	produces command usage summaries
acctcom	displays accounting record summaries
acctcon1	connect-time accounting
acctdisk	disk-usage accounting
acctprc1	process accounting
config	extracts system configuration information
crash	examines system images
cron	runs commands at pre-set times
dcopy	copies file systems for the best access time
devnm	names a device
diffmk	mark differences between files
errdemon	starts the error-logging daemon
errdead	extracts error records from dump
errpt	report of logged errors
errstop	stops the error-logging daemon
ff	file system statistics
fsck	file system consistency check
fsdb	debugs file systems
fuser	identifies processes using a file
fwtmp	manipulates connect accounting records
getty	invites a user to log in
hyphen	finds hyphenated words
init	initialises the system
killall	kills all other processes
link	performs the *link* system call
mkfs	makes a filesystem
mount	makes a filesystem available for use
mvdir	renames a directory
ncheck	generates pathnames for inode numbers
nice	runs a command at lower priority
nroff	typesetting program
prfld	gives a profile of the operating system
pwck	checks password file for inconsistencies

Appendix B

Table B.3 *Continued*

runacct	daily accounting
sadc	system activity report package
sag	displays a graph of system activity
sar	collects system activity information
shutdown	closes the system down
sync	updates superblock and writes buffers to disk
tbl	formats tables
tic	compiles *terminfo* entries
timex	times a command and reports system activity
umount	unmounts a filesystem
unlink	performs the *unlink* system call

Table B.4 lists the standard graphics commands, including those included in the *stat* package, and available only via the graphics shell (see Chapter 13).

Table B.4 Graphics commands.

abs	absolute value of an expression
af	arithmetic function
bar	generates a bar chart
bel	sounds an audible tone
bucket	breaks a range into intervals and counts elements in each
ceil	ceiling function
cor	correlation coefficient
cusum	cumulative sum
cvrtopt	reformats arguments
dtoc	directory table of contents
erase	erase display screen
exp	exponential function
floor	floor function
gamma	gamma function
gas	generate additive sequence
gd	prints a listing of GPS
ged	graphical editor
graph	prints a straight line graph
graphics	calls the graphics shell
gtop	transforms GPS into *plot* format instructions
hardcopy	generates a copy of the screen on a printer
hilo	outputs high and low values of input vector
hist	generates GPS for a histogram
hpd	displays GPS on a Hewlett Packard plotter
label	prints labels on a graph
list	lists contents of input vectors
log	logarithm function
lreg	linear regression

Table B.4 Continued

mean	arithmetic mean (average)
mod	modulo function
pair	group vector elements in pairs
pd	prints a listing of *plot* format
pie	generates GPS for a pie chart
plot	generates GPS for an xy graph
point	empirical cumulative density function point
power	power function
prime	generates prime numbers
prod	calculates product of input elements
ptog	transforms *plot* format to GPS
qsort	sorts elements of vector
quit	ends the session
rand	generates random numbers
rank	outputs number of elements in each vector
remcom	removes comments
root	calculates roots
round	calculates rounded values
siline	generates line of given slope and intercept
sin	calculates sines
spline	generates smooth curve
subset	selects elements from the input
td	displays GPS on a Tektronix 4014 terminal
tekset	clears and resets display screen
title	appends a title to a GPS
total	calculates total of input elements
tplot	reads plotting instructions
ttoc	generates textual table of contents
var	finds difference between slope point and outer point
vtoc	outputs visual table of contents
whatis	gives descriptions of graphics commands
yoo	deposits output of a pipeline into a file

The utilities and programs listed in Table B.5 are commonly found in UNIX systems, but are not included in the X/Open Portability Guide.

Table B.5 Some other common utilities.

atrun	runs commands scheduled using *at*
csh	the C shell
crypt	encrypts a file
more	a page output program; superseded by *pg*
lpr	a print spooler; superseded by *lp*
bc	interpretive calculation utility
cw	prepares constant width text for *nroff*

Table B.5 *Continued*

dc	desk calculator
deroff	removes special characters from *nroff* files
eqn	formats mathematical text
factor	factorises a number
head	outputs the first part of a file
man	displays entries from the UNIX manual
mmcheck	checks usage of *mm* macros
mmt	typesets documents using the *mm* macros
prep	prepares text for statistical formatting
quot	reports disk usage by user
soelim	copies included files within a text file
tbl	formats tables
troff	prepares text for typesetting
units	converts feet to metres, etc.
wrap	removes special characters from a file
zap	kills off a user

Appendix C
System Calls and Library Routines

This Appendix lists the various system calls and other standard subroutines that a programmer can call upon in UNIX. Some of these are true system calls, some are subroutines (of which some include system calls within them, others do not), others still are merely 'macros' which the C pre-processor will convert before compilation. However, as far as the programmer is concerned, they are all included in a C program in just the same way.

Table C.1 gives a list of the most usual UNIX system calls. Note that some of them (for instance *exec*) can be called from a program in slightly different ways, and therefore have several different names for basically the same function.

Table C.1 System calls.

access	check whether the process has access to a named file
acct	enable system accounting
alarm	schedule an alarm signal after a specified time
chdir	change current directory
chmod	change access permissions of a file
chown	change owner and group of a file
chroot	change root directory
dup	duplicate a file descriptor
exec	execute a program. Also *execl, execle, execlp, execv, execve, execvp*
exit	cause the process to terminate
fork	create a new process
getpid	get the process id. Also *getpgrp* (process group id) and *getppid* (parent process id)
getuid	get the real user id. Also *geteuid* (effective user id) *getgid* (real group id) and *getegid* (effective group id)
ioctl	various operations on a device
kill	send a signal to another process
link	give another name to a file
mknod	create a special file
mount	mount a filesystem
msgctl	message control
msgget	get message queue
msgop	message operations; comprising *msgsnd, msgrcv, msgsz*
nice	change priority of a process

Table C.1 *Continued*

pause	wait until a signal is received
pipe	open a pipe
plock	lock process region in memory
profil	give an execution time profile of the process
ptrace	trace the execution of a child process
semctl	various semaphore operations
semget	create an array of semaphores
semop	do semaphore operations
setpgrp	set process group id
setuid	set user id. Also *setgid* (group id)
shmctl	shared memory control
shmemget	get shared memory segment
shmop	shared memory operations
signal	control the processing of signals
stat	return status information for a file. Also *fstat*
stime	set system date and time
sync	flush file buffers
time	return the current time
times	return the elapsed time
ulimit	set maximum file size etc
umask	set file mode creation mask
umount	unmount a filesystem
uname	return various system information
unlink	remove a directory entry
ustat	return statistics about a filesystem
utime	set access and modification times of a file
wait	sleep until a child process exits

Table C.2 includes two types of input/output routines – the basic routines (*close, open, creat, lseek, read, write*) and the more standard routines such as *fopen* which make use of the basic routines.

Table C.2 Input-output routines.

clearerr	reset error and end of file indicators
close	close a file
creat	create a new file
ctermid	generate a pathname for the terminal
fclose	close a file
fcntl	various file operations
ferror	test the error indicator for a file
feof	test end of file indicator for a file
fflush	write out buffered data to a file
fileno	return the file descriptor for a file
fopen	open a file. Also *fdopen, freopen*

System Calls and Library Routines

Table C.2 *Continued*

fread	read from a file
fseek	move the read/write pointer. Also *ftell*, *frewind*
fwrite	write to a file
getc	get a character from a file. Also *fgetc*
getchar	get a character from standard input
getw	get a word (integer) from a file
gets	get a string from a file. Also *fgets*
open	open a file
lseek	change the position of a read/write pointer
pclose	close a pipe
popen	open a pipe
printf	formatted output to a file. Also *fprintf*, *sprintf*
putc	output a character to a file. Also *fputc*
putchar	output a character to standard output
putw	output a word (integer) to a file
puts	output a string to a file. Also *put*
read	read from a file
scanf	read formatted input. Also *fscanf*, *sscanf*
setbuf	assign buffering to a file. Also *setvbuf*
system	issue a command to the shell
tmpfile	create a temporary file
tmpnam	create a name for a temporary file. Also *tempnam*
ungetc	push character back into an input stream
vprintf	formatted output of an argument list. Also *vfprintf*, *vsprintf*
write	write to a file

The general routines in Table C.3 appear in either the SVID or the POSIX standard.

Table C.3 General library routines.

abort	cause abnormal termination of a process
abs	return absolute value of a number
assert	test a condition, and abort with an error message and program line number if not true
bsearch	binary search on a sorted table
clock	report usage of CPU time
conv	translate characters; a set of routines including *toascii*, *tolower*, *toupper*
crypt	encrypt a string of characters, using the DES algorithm. Also *setkey*, *encrypt*
ctime	convert date and time. Also *localtime*, *gmtime*, *asctime*, *tzset*
ctype	classify characters; a set of routines including *isalpha*, *isupper*, *islower*, *isdigit*, *isxdigit*, *isalnum*, *isspace*, *ispunct*, *isprint*, *isgraph*, *iscntrl*, *isascii*
cuserid	get user name

Table C.3 *Continued*

drand48	generate random numbers. Also *erand48, jrand48, lrand48, mrand48, nrand48, srand48, seed48, lcong48*
dup2	duplicate a file descriptor
directory	a library of directory operations: *closedir, opendir, readdir, rewinddir*
ecvt	convert floating point number to a string
end	last locations in program
frexp	manipulate floating-point numbers. Also *ldexp, modf*
ftw	traverse a directory tree
getcwd	get working directory
getenv	get an environment variable
getlogin	get user name
getpass	read a password
getpw	get login name from uid
getut	access *utmp* file entry
getopt	get option letter
group	a library of group database access routines: *endgrent, getgrent, getgrgid, getgrnam, setgrent*
hsearch	manage hash search tables. Also *hcreate, hdestroy*
isatty	find out whether a file descriptor relates to a terminal
l3tol	convert between 3-byte integers and long integers
lockf	lock region of a file
logname	get login name of user
lsearch	linear search of a table. Also *lfind*
malloc	allocate areas of memory. Also *calloc, mallinfo, mallopt, free, realloc*
memory	memory operations, including *memccpy, memchr, memcmp, memcpy, memset*
mkdir	make a directory
mkfifo	make a fifo special file
mktemp	make a unique filename
monitor	prepare execution profile
password	a library of password database access routines: *endpwent, getpwent, getpwnam, getpwuid, setpwent*
perror	output system error message. Also *errno, sys_errlist, sys_nerr*
putenv	change environment variable
qsort	sort a table
rand	random-number generator. Also *srand*
regcmp	compile a regular expression. Also *regex*
rmdir	remove a directory
setjmp	jump to distant program location. Also *longjmp*
sleep	suspend operation for a specified time
ssignal	use signals. Also *gsignal*

Table C.3 *Continued*

string	various string operations, comprising *strcat, strncat, strcmp, strncmp, strcpy, strncpy, strlen, strchr, strrchr, strpbrk, strspn, strtok, strcspn*
strtod	convert string to double precision. Also *atof*
strtol	convert string to integer. Also *atoi, atol*
swab	swap bytes
tsearch	use binary search tree. Also *tfind, tdelete, twalk*
ttyname	give the pathname of the terminal
ttyslot	find the slot in the *utmp* file of the current user

A wide range of mathematical functions is provided, some of which will be meaningful only to mathematicians.

Table C.4 Mathematical functions.

bessel	a library of Bessel functions; comprising *j0, j1, jn, y0, y1, yn*
erf	error function of x. Also *erfc*
exp	exponential and log functions. Also *log, log10, pow, sqrt*
floor	floating-point functions. Also *ceil, fmod, fabs*
gamma	log gamma function
hypot	Euclidean distance (hypoteneuse)
matherr	error-handling function
sinh	hyperbolic functions. Also *cosh, tanh*
trig	a library of trigonometric functions, comprising *sin, cos, tan, asin, acos, atan, atan2*

Appendix D
Standard File Formats

It is often said that UNIX knows nothing about the internal format of files. This is only true up to a point. In fact the various UNIX utilities recognise a number of standard file formats, the more common of which are listed in Table D.1.

Table D.1 Standard file formats.

a.out	common object file format (COFF)
acct	pre-process accounting file format
ar	common archive format
checklist	list of filesystems for use by *fsck*
core	core dump of a failed process
cpio	format of archive files produced by *cpio*
dir	standard directory format
filehdr	header of COFF file
fs	format of system volume
fspec	format specification in certain text files
gettydefs	definitions for use by *getty*
gps	graphical primitive string
group	group file
inittab	table for the *init* program
inode	standard inode format
linenum	line number entries in COFF file
mnttab	table of mounted filesystems
passwd	password file
plot	graphics interface
pnch	file of punched card images
profile	system-wide user profile
reloc	relocation information for COFF file
sccsfile	file format for use with *sccs*
scnhdr	section header for COFF file
syms	symbol table for COFF file
system	system configuration table
term	terminal information file (compiled from *terminfo*)
terminfo	terminal information file (before compilation)
timezone	time zone information
utmp, wtmp	user and accounting information

Appendix E
Glossary

This glossary is intended to explain some of the more confusing terms that surround UNIX. It does not, of course include every utility or system call — there are far too many of these — but it does attempt to include all the more important UNIX terms, both those used in this book and those that tend to crop up, unexplained, in UNIX documentation.

& (ampersand): used in the shell to indicate background processing. Used in C for several purposes.
/ (slash): used in UNIX to indicate the root of the directory system, and to separate parts of a pathname.
> (greater than): used in the shell for redirection of output.
< (less than): used in the shell for redirection of input.
\ (backslash): used in UNIX to allow special characters to be input; used in MS-DOS like the / in UNIX.
| (vertical bar): used by the shell to indicate a pipe; used in C as an OR indicator.
~: see *tilde*
4GL: see *fourth generation language*.
2780: an IBM protocol for remote job entry. Also 3780.
3270: a type of IBM synchronous terminal system, and the protocols needed to communicate with it.
6150: a type of IBM computer, known in the USA as the *RT PC*.
8086: a type of 16-bit microprocessor made by Intel. Also 8088, 80186, 80286.
80386: a 32-bit microprocessor made by Intel.

a.out: the default name for an executable file produced by compiling a program.
AIX: a version of UNIX supplied by IBM.
algorithm: a formula or standard method for performing a computation.
ANSI: American National Standards Institute.
application: a program which does a specific task such as accounting or word processing, as compared to a general-purpose program such as an operating system.
argument: a variable supplied to a command, or to a function within a program, when it is called. Also called a *parameter*.
ASCII: American Standard Code for Information Interchange. A standard way of using the eight bits of a byte to represent various characters. In

ASCII (unlike EBCDIC) seven bits are sufficient to represent the letters of the alphabet, numeric digits, and the main punctuation marks etc. The eighth bit is used for different purposes in different types of computer.

assembler: a low-level programming language, in which each statement generally corresponds directly to a machine language instruction.

asynchronous:
(1) a form of data communication in which characters are sent one by one rather than as a frame or block under the control of a clock.
(2) a form of computer processing in which one activity can continue without waiting for another to complete.

AT&T: American Telephone and Telegraph. The owners of UNIX.

attribute: a field or column in a relational database.

awk a UNIX utility providing a special language for scanning text files for patterns and carrying out various operations.

b-tree: a method of implementing an index on a file, using a balanced tree of index records.

BACS: Bankers' Automated Clearing Service. A UK company providing facilities for exchanging credit transfers and direct debits in electronic form.

baud: a measure of communications speed: number of signals per second.

binary: a form of data representation consisting of combinations of the numbers 0 and 1.

beta testing: releasing a software product to a selected number of customers before the official release, so that any bugs can be discovered and corrected.

binary file: a file containing binary numbers rather than ASCII characters. Particularly a file containing an executable object program.

binary licence: a licence to use a binary (object code) version of UNIX, but with no access to the source code.

bit: binary digit, the smallest possible unit of information. A bit can have only two values (0 or 1 if regarded as a number)

block: the smallest amount of data physically transferred to or from a disk or similar device. Generally comprises 512 bytes, 1k, or 2k.

block device: a device such as a disk, in which data is transferred a block at a time. Opposite of a *character device*.

boolean algebra: an algebra dealing in only two values, such as 0 and 1, or TRUE and FALSE.

booting: starting the computer up when it is first turned on, prior to loading the operating system.

bpi: bits per inch. A measure of the capacity of magnetic tape.

BSD: Berkeley Software Distribution. Refers to versions of UNIX issued by the University of California at Berkeley (UCB).

buffer: an area of memory which is used for temporary storage of a block of data being transferred to or from a disk or other *block device*.

buffer cache: a set of *buffer*s maintained by the kernel and used when satisfying i/o system calls.

Glossary

byte: the smallest unit of information that a computer normally deals with, comprising eight *bit*s, or one character.

C: a programming language, used for writing most of the programs making up UNIX.

canonical mode: a type of input processing in which the kernel takes action on backspace and other characters rather than passing them on to the program

cathode ray tube: the 'picture tube' or screen used in television sets and most computer monitors.

CCTA: Central Computer and Telecommunications Agency. A body which makes recommendations to UK government departments on matters concerned with information technology.

character string: a series of ASCII characters, which can be acted on by special string statements in a programming language.

C-ISAM: a package supplied by Informix Software. See *ISAM*.

COBOL: a programming language used for business purposes.

COFF: common object file format.

column
  (1) a vertical array of character positions on a vdu screen or printed page. A vdu screen often consists of 25 lines and 80 columns.
  (2) a vertical array of cells in a spreadsheet.
  (3) in a relational database, the collection of data comprising the corresponding field from every row or record. Synonymous with *attribute*.

commit: to mark a transaction as complete, so that it can no longer be rolled back. See also *two-phase commit*.

compiler: a program which takes a *source program* written in a high level language, and converts it to an *object program* which can then be executed.

console: the primary terminal on a UNIX system. Certain functions can be carried out only at the console.

context switching: switching the processor to deal with a different process.

control flow: the flow of control within a program, as determined by *if* and *else* statements, etc.

CP/M: an operating system invented by Digital Research.

cpio: a UNIX utility used for copying data to and from tape or other devices, in a special format.

cps: characters per second. A measure of the speed of printers.

CRT: see *cathode ray tube*. Also used to refer to a vdu terminal as a whole.

C shell: a shell originated by the University of California at Berkeley. Its syntax resembles the C programming language.

CSMA/CD: carrier sense, multiple access, with collision detection. An access control method used in local area networks.

curses: a library of routines for controlling windows on the vdu screen.

cursor:
  (1) a mark or pointer shown on the screen, which can be moved to an item to be selected.
  (2) in embedded SQL, a pointer to a particular row in a table.

cylinder: the area of a disk pack which can be accessed without head movement, comprising one track for every surface used for recording.

daemon: a background process which handles housekeeping tasks for the operating system.
daisywheel: a type of printer, using a print head shaped like a daisy.
database: a structured collection of data.
database management system: a software package allowing for the manipulation and storage of data in a database.
DBMS: see *database management system*.
DEC: Digital Equipment Corporation. A leading manufacturer of minicomputers.
default: a standard option, which applies if you do not make an explicit selection.
delta: in *sccs*, a record of the differences between one version of a document and the next.
demand paging: a form of virtual memory management, in which pages are loaded into real memory when first accessed by a program.
desktop publishing: using a computer to produce artwork containing both text and graphics.
device: a piece of hardware used for input or output.
device driver: the software included within the operating system to cater for a particular class of hardware device.
DIP: dual in-line package.
directory: a structure in the hierarchy of files on disk; a directory contains a number of files and/or other directories.
disk: normally means a magnetic disk for storing data: either a hard disk or a floppy disk.
disk drive: the machinery for reading and writing data on disks.
diskette: a floppy disk.
distributed database: a database which is partly held on one machine, partly on one or more others.
DMS: Data Management Services. A supplementary product supplied for IBM's AIX.
document: another term for a file, particularly in word processing contexts.
DOS: Disk Operating System. The main operating system used on the IBM PC (also called PC-DOS). Also used generically to include similar operating systems such as Microsoft's MS-DOS.
duplex: able to conduct data communications in both directions. See *full duplex, half duplex*.

EBCDIC: Extended Binary Coded Decimal Interchange Code. A way of using the eight bits of a byte to represent various alphabetic and other characters. It is the standard code used on larger IBM computers. Unlike ASCII, there is no seven-bit version.
environment: a collection of variables making up the context within which the shell interprets commands given to it.

Glossary

exec: a UNIX system call which causes the current process to start running a new program.

expert system: a software package embodying knowledge, supplied by a human expert, together with procedures for making use of it.

Ethernet: a standard for local area networking.

extension: a suffix to a filename, comprising one or more characters preceded by a full stop, and used by certain software to indicate the type of data held in the file.

field: an item of data in a file; for instance an account number, a customer's name, the selling price of a product.

FIFO: first in, first out. A pipe is often referred to as a FIFO file.

file: a collection of data on disk, for instance a word processing document, a file of customer names and addresses, a program.

file descriptor: an integer used to identify one of the open files used in a particular process.

file header: an area at the start of a program or other file containing identifying information.

file pointer:
(1) a pointer in a C program to the data structure associated with a file using the standard i/o library.
(2) an integer giving the byte position which a process has got to in reading or writing a file; also called a 'read/write pointer'.

filesystem: one of the main divisions of the filestore on a UNIX system, comprising a single physical disk, or a partition of a disk.

filestore: the entire set of disk storage on a UNIX system.

filter: a UNIX command or program which receives data on its standard input, processes it, and outputs the results to its standard output.

fixed disk: a disk which is permanently attached to a computer (unlike a floppy disk). See *Winchester*.

floating point: a method of storing numbers, particularly for technical or scientific purposes.

floppy disk: a type of disk which can be removed from the computer, encased in a protective jacket.

flow control: the control of data transmission to prevent data being lost because the receiving device cannot accept it.

font: a typeface, or size and style of printing or text.

footer: in word processing, an item such as a reference which is automatically put at the bottom of every page.

fork: a UNIX system call used to spawn a new process.

Fortran: a programming language used for scientific purposes.

fourth generation language: a 'non-procedural' programming language, in which you define what is to be done, not the processing needed to achieve it.

full duplex: a communications line which can convey data in both directions simultaneously.

function: a basic building block in a C program, comprising a subroutine or set of instructions to be carried out, given a particular argument as starting point.

function key: one of the special keys on a keyboard, generally labelled F1 to F10 (etc.) and used for different purposes in different programs.

GEM: Graphics Environment Manager. A set of programs supplied by Digital Research.

gid: see *group-id*.

GPS: Graphics Primitive String. A standard UNIX format for holding data to generate graphical output.

grep: a UNIX utility for searching a file for *regular expressions*.

group: a collection of *users* who are given certain common access rights to files. See also *process group*.

group-id: a number identifying a particular *group*.

group-name: the name (if any) associated with a particular *group-id*.

hacker: an enthusiast for programming and the internals of computer systems; also, someone who uses ingenuity to defeat the security arrangements of a computer system.

half duplex: a communications line which can transmit data in each direction, but not simultaneously.

hard disk: see *fixed disk*.

hashing: a method of accessing particular records on a disk, by applying a formula or algorithm to the record identifier to find a physical address.

header:
(1) in word processing, constant text printed at the top of every page.
(2) see *file header*

header file: a file (with filename suffix *.h*) to be included in a C source program at the pre-processor stage, using the *#include* statement. Also called an 'include file'.

host: the main computer to which other computers or terminals are connected.

i/o: input/output

IBM: International Business Machines Corporation. The world's leading computer manufacturer.

icon: a little picture on the screen, which you can point at to select the object which it represents.

ID: identification number. See also *uid*, *gid*.

IEEE: Institute of Electrical and Electronics Engineers. An American body who have proposed various standards, most notably the POSIX standard.

implementation: the act of modifying some piece of software to run on a particular machine or operating system.

include file: see *header file*

inode: an area of data giving the characteristics of a particular disk file, and indicating where its data is held.

inode table: a special part of each *filesystem*, containing an *inode* for each file.

Glossary

installation:
  (1) the process of installing software on a computer.
  (2) a particular place or organisation in which a computer is located.
integer: a whole number; also a field designed to hold whole numbers of a particular size in binary form (usually 16 or 32 bits).
interpreted language: a programming language (such as certain versions of COBOL and BASIC) in which each source statement is translated at run time, rather than being *compiled* in advance.
interrupt: a signal sent to a program by the computer representing some event which has occurred outside the program's control.
ISAM: indexed sequential access method.
ISO: International Organisation for Standardisation.

job: in UNIX System V, a process or set of processes scheduled to run in the background.
job control: in UNIX System V, a facility for handling several concurrent shell layers.
job control language: in other operating systems, a language equivalent to the UNIX shell.
join: in relational databases, the operation of combining data from two different *tables*.

kernel: the main controlling program in a UNIX system, which a process passes control to on issuing a system call.
***kill*:** (1) a command which sends a signal to another process, and by default kills it off.
***kill*:** (2) line kill: a feature of *canonical processing* – a special control character used to abandon an entire line that you have just keyed in.

laser printer: a type of printer using print technology similar to a photocopier, but with a laser to build up the image.
library: a collection of object code subroutines, which can be linked into a program as the final stage of compilation.
LIFO: last in, first out. A *stack* operates on a LIFO basis.
line printer: a printer which prints a complete line at a time (as opposed to a character or a page). Also used in UNIX documentation to mean any printer which is used by means of a spooler.
link: an association between a dictionary entry and a file. A file can have more than one link.
linked list: a structure often used in computer systems, containing various items or records, each with a pointer to the one which logically follows or precedes it.
lock: to put a temporary restriction on part of a file, so that other processes are unable to access or modify it.
login: the process of beginning a session at a terminal attached to a UNIX system.

login name: the name by which a user identifies himself to the system, corresponding to a user identification number (uid).
lpm: lines per minute. A measure of the speed of printers.

macro: a statement in a programming language which is translated to a series of other statements before compilation.
mailmerge: a function supplied with a word processor, to produce multiple standard letters to different addressees.
matrix printer: a printer which produces its image in the form of a matrix of small dots. Usually refers to an impact matrix printer, in which the dots are formed by pins striking a ribbon.
memory: see *RAM* and *ROM*.
microcomputer: a computer with a single-chip microprocessor as its central processing unit.
microprocessor: a single-chip VLSI device capable of acting as the central processor to a computer.
modem: modulator/demodulator. A device to allow a computer to send or receive signals using a telephone line.
monitor: the part of a personal computer or terminal containing the display screen.
mouse: a device with one, two, or three buttons, which can be moved about on a flat surface to make a pointer or cursor move on the display screen.
MS-DOS: an operating system produced by Microsoft. Essentially identical to PC-DOS.
multi-tasking: able to process more than one program concurrently for the same user.
multi-user: able to accommodate more than one user of the system at a time.

NFS: Network Filing System. A system used by Sun Microsystems to allow data to be shared between computers on a network.
nlq: near letter quality. An option on certain printers.
NLS: Native Language System. An X/Open standard to allow use of UNIX with different national languages.
normalisation: the process of analysing the structure of data to ensure it is held in the most logical manner.

object program: a program which has been compiled to machine language.
on-line: connected to a computer.
operating system: a set of computer programs which controls the hardware, and provides an environment for the running of application software.
option: a particular way of using a UNIX command, usually indicated by including a single-character option identifier as part of an argument to a command, preceded by a '−' or '+' sign.
OS/2: an operating system produced by Microsoft and IBM.
OSI: Open Systems Interconnection. A framework for standardisation of connection between different computers, drawn up by the *ISO*, and comprising a seven-layer model.

Glossary 279

PABX: private automatic branch exchange. An automatic telephone exchange used within an office.
packet switching: a means of transmitting data by reference to an address held within each packet of data, rather than setting up an actual circuit.
paging: a type of *virtual storage* organisation, in which memory is assigned in small (for instance, 1k) pages, and transferred between memory and disk page by page as required. See *segmentation*.
parallel: a type of connection in which the bits of a byte are sent simultaneously on separate wires.
parameter: an *argument* or option supplied to a command or a subroutine.
path: a series of directory names enabling a specific file to be located within a directory tree.
PC: personal computer; specifically the IBM PC, or one of its 'clones'.
PC-DOS: IBM Personal Computer DOS. See *DOS*.
PICK: an operating system invented by Richard Pick.
pipe: a mechanism for transferring data from one process to another, using the UNIX filestore to hold the data temporarily.
pixel: picture element. The smallest separately addressable element of a graphical display.
POSIX: Portable Operating System. A standard devised by the IEEE, based originally on the */usr/group* UNIX standard.
Postscript: a language used for communicating with laser printers and other graphical devices.
ppm: pages per minute. A measure of the speed of laser printers.
print: to produce printed output on paper. Often also used to include 'printing' to the vdu screen.
Prestel: the UK viewdata service.
process: a task running in a computer. At any one time a task is running a particular program, and generally occupies one or more regions of memory.
process-id: a number uniquely identifying a particular process.
process group: a set of processes belonging to the same terminal session, and having a common ancestor process.
prompt: the character or message displayed at the start of a line by a shell or program which is waiting for keyboard input.
PS/2: Personal System 2. The second generation of IBM personal computers.
PSS: Packet Switching Service.
PSTN: public switched telephone network. The ordinary telephone system.

RAM: random access memory. The main memory of a computer. It loses its data when the current is turned off.
random access: a form of file access in which specific records are retrieved individually, without reading through the rest of the file.
real-time: a type of computer system which can respond in a short and predictable timescale to control external events.
record: a collection of data items treated as a unit.
re-entrant: refers to a program which is loaded into memory only once when

used by two or more processes. Such a program must not be modified in the course of execution.

referential integrity: in a database system, a facility to ensure that changes to one table are not permitted if they would be inconsistent with another table.

region: an area of memory occupied by part of a process. Equivalent to a *segment*.

relation: a table, as used in a relational database.

relational database: a database which consists solely of tables, without pointers or other 'structural' means of holding information.

RFS: Remote File Sharing. A system devised by AT&T for sharing data between computers on a network.

ROM: read-only memory. A special type of memory containing data put there in the course of manufacture, which cannot be changed.

root:
(1) the master node of the UNIX tree of directories.
(2) a name for the super user.

row: in relational databases, a row in a table, equivalent to a record in traditional terminology.

RS232: a standard for serial interface, used between computers and modems, and for other purposes.

RT PC: RISC Technology Personal Computer. Another name for the IBM 6150.

RTI: Relational Technology Inc., the proprietors of the Ingres database management system.

SAA: Systems Application Architecture. An IBM standard for portable software over various machines and operating systems.

sccs: source code control system. A set of programs for keeping track of successive changes to a source program or other text document.

SCSI: small computer systems interface. A standard interface for connecting disks and other devices.

sector: a block of data on a disk, comprising part of a track.

segment: an area of memory associated with a process. See *text segment*, *data segment*, and *stack segment*.

segmentation: a form of swapping in which whole segments, rather than pages, are swapped in and out.

sequential: a form of file access in which records are retrieved in a particular order, corresponding to the values in a *key* field or fields.

serial:
(1) a connection in which each bit is sent one after the other down a single wire.
(2) a form of file access in which the records are retrieved in the order they happen to occur. See *sequential* and *random access*.

shell: a program used as an interactive command line interpreter.

SNA: Systems Network Architecture. An IBM standard defining connections between various types of IBM machines.

Glossary

socket: a type of i/o handling used in Berkeley UNIX systems.
source licence: a licence issued by AT&T entitling the holder to have the UNIX source code.
source program: the original program as written, before being compiled to object code.
spooling: printing a number of documents from a print queue, rather than directly by an application program.
SQL: Structured Query Language. A language devised by IBM for making enquiries on databases.
stack: a structure in memory, in which items are added and retrieved on a LIFO basis. Used for keeping track of subroutines.
stack segment: an area of memory used for the *stack* associated with a particular process
standard error output: an output file (file number 2) to which error messages are sent; by default assigned to the vdu screen.
standard input: the main input file for a process (file number zero); by default, assigned to the terminal keyboard.
standard output: the main output file for a process (file number 1); by default, assigned to the vdu screen.
stderr: see *standard error output*.
stdin: see *standard input*.
stdio: a set of standard routines for input/output processing.
stdout: see standard output.
sticky bit: a bit in the inode, which when set on for a program file causes the file to be retained in memory when its process terminates.
stream: a file, as used by the *stdio* routines.
Streams: a method of organising input/output processing, in System V Release 3.
string: see *character string*.
subroutine: a self-contained part of a program, called to carry out a particular function.
super user: a user with special privileges in a UNIX system.
SVID: System V Interface Definition. A standard published by AT&T.
SVVS: System V Validation Suite. A set of programs supplied by AT&T to test operating systems for being System V compatible.
swapping: removing parts of processes to a special swap area, to make room for other processes in memory.
sync: a system call used to write out the contents of the buffer cache to disk.
synchronous: a form of data communications in which data is sent as frames or packets, under the control of a clock.
system call: an instruction in a program which passes control to the UNIX kernel.
System V: the standard form of UNIX, issued by AT&T.

table: the basic element in a relational database, corresponding to a *file* in other types of system.
tar: tape archive. A program for making copies of disk files to tape or to another disk.

TCP/IP: a set of utilities for networking.
teletex: an electronic mail service similar to telex, but with more advanced features.
teletext: a form of information broadcast using television signals.
teletype: a type of terminal, originally one with a keyboard and printer but no display screen. See *tty*.
termcap: in Berkeley UNIX and other versions, a database of the capabilities of different types of terminals.
terminfo: in System V, a database of the capabilities of different types of terminals. It replaces *termcap*.
text file: a file containing ordinary printable characters, for instance a word processing document.
text segment: an area in memory containing the executable code for a process.
tilde: the ~ symbol, used in the shell to denote the home directory of a particular user.
track: one of the concentric circles containing information on a disk.
tty: Teletype; a terminal attached to a UNIX system.
two-phase commit: a method for ensuring that all resources are available, before proceeding with a transaction. Used in distributed database systems.
tuple: a row or record in a relational database.

UCB: the University of California at Berkeley.
uid: see *user-id*.
UNIX: an operating system invented by AT&T.
user: an individual person authorised to use a UNIX system.
user-id: a number used to identify a particular user.
user name: a name used to identify a particular user. Also called a 'login name'.
utmp: a file listing users currently logged in.
uucp: UNIX-to-UNIX copy. A utility used when communicating between UNIX computers.

VAX: a type of 32-bit minicomputer made by DEC.
vdu: visual display unit.
vi: visual editor. A text editing program.
viewdata: a form of data communication using simple colour graphics.
videotex: a generic term covering *teletext* and *viewdata*.
virtual memory: a technique whereby the memory addresses used within a program are dynamically translated to actual addresses.
VLSI: very large scale integration.

Whetstone: a way of measuring the speed of floating point computation.
WIMP: window/icon/mouse/pointer. A form of user interface.
Winchester: the type of fixed disk used in most current microcomputers. It is sealed to stop dust getting in.

Glossary

window: a rectangular area on the display screen used by a specific file or program.

word: the basic chunk of data handled by a processor — usually 1, 2, or 4 bytes.

worm: write once, read many times. A way of using optical disk.

workstation:
(1) any personal computer or terminal.
(2) a high performance single-user computer for graphics, CAD, etc.

WYSIWYG: what you see is what you get.

X/Open Group: a group of computer manufacturers who have adopted common standards for UNIX

XENIX: a version of UNIX supplied by Microsoft.

x-on/x-off: a simple type of flow control.

XVS: X/Open System V Specification.

X/Windows: a standard method of controlling windows on a vdu display.

Index

16-bit processors, 22, 26
32-bit processors, 22–3, 26–7, 29, 226
3B2, 120, 221
4GL – *see* Fourth generation language
Accell, 117
access control, 101
accounting systems, 133, 138
Acorn, 22
acoustic coupler, 41
Ada, 191, 200
adb (utility), 197
address bus, 21–4
adv (command), 214
AIX, 16, 18–19, 29, 67, 110, 151, 176, 180, 190, 215, 227–8, 238
alarm (system call), 237
Algol, 191
algorithm, 192
alias, 189
alias (command), 141, 186
Altos, 224
Amdahl, 241
Andrew, 151
ANSI, 199, 231
ANSI terminal, 35
answerback, 159
a.out, 123, 193, 194
Apollo, 124
Apple Macintosh, 26, 124, 142, 145, 228
Application Layer, 208, 231
application software, 6
archiving, 179
argument, 47, 192
ARPANET, 209
ASCII, 8, 126, 233, 251–6
ASCII terminal, 35
assembler language, 13, 69, 200
assert (function), 196
assist (utility), 144
asynchronous communications, 126, 127
asynchronous input/output, 162
at (command), 178, 220, 237

atrun (program), 178
AT&T, 10, 12–17, 219, 221, 224, 226, 229–30, 232, 237
att (command), 223
attributes, 102
awk (utility), 84

background processing, 60–1, 146, 161, 188
backquote, 185, 251
backups, 179
BACS, 140
balance forward, 137
BASIC, 81, 199
baud rate, 126
BBC Microcomputer, 223
bc (command), 73
BCPL, 191
Bell Laboratories, 12–13, 15, 90
Berkeley Software Distribution, 15, 222
Berkeley, University of California at, 15–17, 82, 187, 222
binary, 65, 253
  licences, 15
  program, 14
bit, 8, 21, 23–4, 32, 251
BLAISE, 130
block, 68, 219
block mode terminals, 127
boot block, 164
Bourne shell, 59, 182–4, 187
Bourne, Steve, 59
B programming language, 191
break (command), 184
BSD, *see* Berkeley Software Distribution
b-tree, 109, 113–14
buffer cache, 238, 239
built-in comands, 183–4, 257
Bull, *see* Honeywell Bull
bulletin boards, 128
Burroughs, 232
bus, 31

284

Index

byte, 23–4, 251

C++, 193
cache memory, 32
CAD, *see* computer-aided design
cal (command), 93–4
calculation, 73
calendar (command), 92, 94
cancel (command), 52
canonical mode, 157, 188, 213
card indexes, 74
carriage return, 83, 253
cartridge tape, 179
cat (command), 45–6, 48
cc (command), 193
CCTA, 231
cd (command), 56, 184
CDPATH (environment variable), 182
CD-ROM, 34
Central Computer and Telecommunications Agency, *see* CCTA
chgrp (command), 57
chip, *see* silicon chip and microprocessor
chmod (command), 57
chown (command), 57
Cifer, 125
C-ISAM, 109, 232
client/server model, 150, 244
clock speed, 21
COBOL, 100, 101, 133, 136, 197–8, 202, 233
code segment, 28, 159
COFF, 167, 220, 224, 270
Coherent, 228
col (command), 85
colour terminals, 124–5, 148–9, 151
Comet, 129
command substitution, 185, 251
commands, 55, 59, 142, 257–64
commit, 116, 117
Common Applications Environment (CAE), 232
Common Object Format, File – *see* COFF
communications, 126
compact disk, 34
compiler, 14, 69, 123, 193, 198–200
computer-aided design, 124, 222
concurrency control, 101, 116
conditional compilation, 196

configuration, 244
console, 37, 155
consultancy, 244
context switch, 27, 161, 162
  in PC Interface, 243
continue (command), 184
control key, 252, 253
co-processor, 31
cor (command), 121
core dump, 32, 196
core store, 24
cp (command), 65
cpio (command), 179, 223
CPL (programming language), 191
CP/M, 6, 167
C programming language, 13–14, 66, 101, 123, 186, 191–8, 200–3, 232
Cray, 241
Cromix, 228
cron (command), 178, 220, 237
crontab file, 178, 220
csh (command), *see* C shell
C shell, 55, 141, 185, 187–8, 222
CSMA/CD, 208, 209
csplit (command), 85
curses library, 36, 150
cursor
  in SQL, 202, 203
  on screen, 36
cut and paste, 95
cw (utility), 90
cylinder, 33

daemon, 55, 178, 210
daisywheel printers, 38
data, 98
  analysis, 106
  bus, 20, 22
  dictionary, 100
  link control, 206
  names, 198
  segment, 28, 159
database, 80, 94, 96, 98
  management systems, 98–118, 172, 225, 238
  tuning, 172
date formats, 94
dBase III, 225
DBMS, *see* database management systems
dbx (utility), 197
deadly embrace, 116
debugging, 195–7

DEC, *see* Digital Equipment Corporation
delta (command), 195
demand paging, 25–7, 163, 221
deroff (utility), 90
desktop publishing, 40, 123
DialCom, 129
Dialog, 128, 130
diction (command), 85
diffmk (command), 85
Digital Equipment Corporation (DEC), 13, 221–2, 232, 240
Digitus, 19
directory, 45, 49–50, 56, 57
disk, 30, 33, 63–8, 170, 238
diskette, 17, 30, 33, 63, 67, 179, 226
diskless workstation, 223
distributed database, 215
distributed filesystem, 233
Distributed Services, 215
DMS, 110
D-NIX, 237
domain, 102
DOS, *see* MS-DOS
DOS shell, 190
dot commands, 87–9, 129
dump (utility), 179

EBCDIC, 251
echo (command), 182, 184
ed (utility), 84, 242
EFL, 199
egn (utility), 90
egrep (utility), 76
electronic data interchange (EDI), 130–31
electronic mail, 91, 129
emacs (utility), 188
embedded SQL, 202, 203
encryption, 173
environment variable, 59, 182, 183
Ericsson, 209, 213, 223, 232, 243
Ethernet, 209, 213, 223, 243
EUnet, 128
Euronet Diane, 130
European Community, 18
eval (command), 184
ex (utility), 84
exec
 command, 184
 system call, 160
executable files, 69
exit (command), 184

explain (command), 85
export (command), 182, 184
exportfs (command), 214
extension, 167
external databases,

f77 (command), 199
FDISK, 224
field, 99
file, 63–70, 98, 100
file (command), 70
file server, 244
filesystem, 66, 67, 164–5
 switch, 213
filter, 52, 53, 122
find (command), 70, 178, 184, 185
floating point, 21, 66
 processor, 31
floppy disk, *see* diskette
folio, 87, 171
foreign key, 102
fork (system call), 160, 236, 238
Fortran, 197, 199, 233
fourth generation language, 101, 107, 201, 203–4
Foxbase, 225
fread (function), 167
front end processor, 158, 236, 237
FTAM, 208
function, 191–3
function key, 85

ged (command), 121
GEM, 149
General Electric, 12
general ledger, 134
General Motors, 18, 139
getty (program), 55, 155, 156
gigabyte, 24
GKS, 123, 233
GPS, 121, 122
graph (command), 121
graphics, 40, 119–25, 148, 222, 262–3
 command, *see* graphics shell
 library, 122
 shell, 121, 262
grep (command), 75–7, 84
group, 44, 49, 175
group file, 175

hash (command), 184
hashing, 108, 113

Index

head (command), 77
header file, 194
help facilities, 144
Hewlett Packard, 22, 41, 232, 234, 237
   Integral PC, 63
hexadecimal, 253
hist (command), 121
histogram, 119–20
history (command), 186
HOME (environment variable), 182, 183
home computer, 80
home directory, 45, 56
Honeywell Bull, 232
hpd (command), 41
HP-UX, 237
hyphen (command), 85

IBM, 16, 18–19, 36, 111, 197, 200, 224–6, 240–41, 252
   2780, 128
   3270, 127–8
   3780, 128
   6150, 4, 18–19, 22, 28–9, 31, 37, 148, 200, 215, 227–8
   801, 28, 200
   PC, 24, 26, 27, 79, 225–8
   PC-AT, 226
   PS/2, 226
ICL, 128, 232
icon, 145
id (command), 44
Idris, 228
IEEE, 10, 18, 230, 231
   1003 Standard, *see* POSIX
   802 standards, 208, 209
#*if*, 196
#*include*, 194
indexes, 172
indexing, 108, 109
information, 98
Informix, 94, 103–7, 109, 111, 113, 167, 202, 232, 239, 244
Ingres, 113–17, 119, 141, 143, 201–3, 239, 244
Ingres/Star, 215
init (program), 155
inittab file, 155
inode, 67, 164, 168, 239
input-output processor, *see* front-end processor, 237
input-output routines, 266–7
installation, 244

instruction set, 21, 22
integer, 65, 66
Intel
   80286, 226, 227
   80386, 27–9, 226
   8086 family, 26, 27
   8088, 22
Interactive Systems, 16, 228
Interleaf, 124
internationalisation, 233
International Organisation for Standardisation, 206
interpreter, 199
inter-process communication, 219, 222, 237, 244
interrupts, 58, 161–2, 235–6
invoicing, 139
IOS, 149
IPC, *see* inter-process communication
ISAM, 109, 113–14
ISO, 206
IX/370, 16, 228, 241

job, 188–9
job control, 147, 188–9, 220
join, 103, 105, 112
journals, 136
JSB Computer Systems, 149

k, 24
Kermit, 128
kernel, 5, 15, 55, 58, 127, 156–62, 166, 181, 201, 213, 219, 236, 244
Kernighan, Brian, 13, 193, 232
key, 102, 108
keyboard, 36, 86, 97, 251–3
Knowledge-Index, 130
Korn shell, 141, 187–9
ksh (command), *see* Korn shell

LAN, *see* local area network
LANG (environment variable), 234
laser printer, 38, 40, 124, 125
ledger, 133, 136
Level II COBOL, 198, 233
libraries, 69, 194
library functions, 193–4, 265–9
licencing, 14
line
   discipline, 157, 213
   feed, 253
   printers, 39, 52

linear address space, 27, 28
link edit, 69, 193–4, 220
Link Layer, 206
links, 49, 165
lint (utility), 193
Lisp, 200
ln (command), 65
local area network, 205, 208–9, 233, 244
locking, 116, 166, 220, 238
log file, 117
logging
  in, 42, 155
  out, 43
Logica, 225
login (program), 156
login, *see* logging in
login name, 42, 44, 177, 182
logname (command), 44
LOGNAME (environment variable), 182
Lotus 1-2-3, 73, 79–80, 143, 225
lp (command), 39, 51, 220
lpr (command), 220
lpstat (command), 52
ls (command), 44–8, 186, 223
LU6.2, 215
Lyrix, 225

macro, 89–90, 201, 265
  core, 32
  disk, *see* disk
  tape, 179
mail (command), 91–2
MAIL (environment variable), 182
mailbox, 92, 129
MAILCHECK (environment variable), 182
mailmerge, 87
MAILPATH (environment variable), 182
mailx (command), 92, 220
mainframe, 7, 10, 12, 20, 127, 200, 221, 240–1
make (utility), 194, 195
man (command), 61, 90
manufacturing systems, 139
MAP, 209
mathematical functions, 269
matrix printers, 37
megabyte, 24, 32
megaflops, 21
memory, 20–21, 24–6, 28, 32, 163–4
memory management unit (MMU), 26, 28
memory-mapped display, 37, 147
menu, 115, 141, 142

MERT, 237
mesg (command), 93
message of the day, 43
microcode, 22
Micro Focus, 198, 233
microprocessor, 10, 20, 21–3, 26–9, 31, 200, 226–7
Microsoft, 16, 224, 226
Microsoft Windows, 149
minicomputer, 7, 10, 20, 221, 240
Minix, 229
Mips, 21, 28
MIT, 13
mktemp (function), 171
mm (utility), 89–90
mmcheck (utility), 90
mmt (utility), 90
mode independence, 143
modem, 41, 126
Modula 2, 200
more (command), 51, 220
Motorola
  68000, 26, 200
  68020, 27
mount (command), 67, 214
mouse, 36, 145
MS-DOS (PC-DOS), 6, 11, 19, 24, 28, 60, 73, 136, 167, 190, 224–7, 229, 244
Multics, 13
Multiplan, 79
multiplexing, 206
multi-tasking, 6, 9, 25, 146
Multiview, 149
Mumps, 99
mv (command), 65
MVS, 240

named pipes, 167
National Semiconductor, 27
NEC, 232
networking 205–15, 242–4
Network Layer, 207
Newcastle connection, 212
newgrp (command), 175
newline character, 83, 253
NeWS, 150, 222
NFS, 214, 222
nice (command), 235
Nixdorf, 232
Novell Netware, 244
nroff (utility), 88, 89

object code, 14

Index

object files, 220
octal, 256
office automation, 91
Olivetti, 16, 22, 221, 232
One-to-One, 129
Onyx, 26
open item, 137
Open Systems Interconnection, *see* OSI
OpenTop, 148–9, 224
Operating system, 5–6
optical disk, 34
options, 46, 48
Oracle, 80, 110, 117, 119, 172, 202
OS/2, 11, 29, 73, 227, 228
OSI, 117, 206–9, 231
OSx, 223
outer join, 112

Pacific Basin Graphics, 120
packet, 126
packet switching, 127, 209
PAD, 127
page fault, 164
pages, 27, 164
paging, 25, 28
parallel interface, 39
parameters, 47, 48, 192
partitions, 67, 224
Pascal, 191, 197, 200, 233
passwd (command), 58, 177
password, 42, 43, 57, 58, 138, 173, 174, 175
password file, 173–5
paste (command), 85
PATH (environment variable), 181, 182
pathname, 56, 59, 212, 214
payroll, 140
PC, *see* personal computer; IBM PC
PC-DOS, *see* MS-DOS
PC Interface, 243
PC/IX, 16, 225
PCNX, 229
PC Works, 242–3
PDP-7, 13
PDP-11, 13, 24, 33, 221
peripherals, 37
permissions, 49, 50, 165, 175
personal computer, 119, 148, 224, 242–4
personal computing, 73–80
pg (command), 51, 220
Philips, 232
Physical Layer, 206

Pick (operating system), 99, 118
pick and point, 142, 145
pie chart, 119, 121
pipe, 52, 167, 219, 237
pipelining, 21, 28
PL.8, 200
PL/I, 197, 200
plock (system call), 163, 236
plotter, 40–41, 120, 125
port, 30
positional parameter, 183
POSIX, 10, 17–18, 176, 208, 229–30
PostScript, 40, 124, 150
pr (command), 52
pre-emption, 236
prep (utility), 90
presentation graphics, 121
Presentation Layer, 208
Prestel, 129, 131–2
primary key, 102
prime (command), 121
print (command), 189
printers, 37, 40
printf (function), 196
priority, 162
process, 25, 27, 28, 54–5, 159–62
    control, 139, 235
    id, 55
processor cycle, 21
profile script, 183
program, 54, 55, 69
Programmer's Manual, 61
Programmers' Work Bench, 13
programming, 191–204, 244
Prolog, 200
prompt, 43
proprietary operating systems, 240
prototyping, 204
ps (command), 54, 55
PS1 (environment variable), 182
PS2 (environment variable), 182
PSS, 127
PSTN, 127
punctuation, 251
purchase ledger, 134
PWB, *see* Programmers' Work Bench
pwd (command), 45, 57, 184
Pyramid, 22, 223

Q-Office, 74, 96, 97, 158
Q-One, 96
QNX, 228
Quadratron, 96

QUEL, 113
query optimisation, 115
quotation marks, 185, 251

RAM, 32
rand (command), 121
randomising algorithm, 108
Ratfor, 199
raw disk, 239
raw mode, 157, 188
rcp (command), 211
read (command), 184
read (system call), 168
readonly (command), 184
read/write pointer, 68
real-time processing, 139, 234–7
record, 99
redirection, 45
Redwood, 85
re-entrant, 159
referential integrity, 102
registers, 20–21
regular expressions, 75–6
relation, 102
relational database, 98, 101–3
Relational Technology Inc, 113, 215
remsh (command), 211
response times, 144
restore (command), 179
restricted shell, 189
return (command), 184
Reuters, 130
RFS, 16, 213, 214, 220, 239
ring menu, 143
RISC, 22, 28, 29
Ritchie, Dennis, 13, 191, 193, 213, 232
RJE, 128
rlogin (command), 211
rm (command), 50
rollback, 116, 117
ROM, 32, 63
ROMP, 22, 28, 29, 200
root (command), 121
root directory, 56
root filesystem, 66
RPG III, 197
RS232, 30, 40, 243
rsh (command), *see* restricted shell
RTI, *see* Relational Technology Inc
RT PC, *see* IBM 6150
ruler, 85, 86
run-time file, 198
rwho (command), 211

SAA, 19, 197
sales ledger, 134
sales order processing, 138
Santa Cruz Operation, 79, 146, 224, 225
sccs (utility), 171, 195
scheduling, 161, 162
schema, 100
SCO, *see* Santa Cruz Operation
SCO Professional, 79, 225
SCSI, 33
sdb (utility), 197
security, 43, 57, 101, 173, 212
sed (utility), 84
segmentation, 25–8
semaphore, 219, 237
serial port, 30, 39–40
Session Layer, 207
set (command), 184
set history (command), 185
sh (command), 55, 59
shared libraries, 220, 238
shared memory, 25, 159, 219, 237
shell, 5, 43, 54, 59, 142, 147, 181–90
  layers, 147, 220
  script, 50, 69, 77, 182, 183
shift (command), 184
shift key, 252
shl (command), 147, 189, 220
Siemens, 232
silicon chip, 20, 28
single user mode, 37, 155
sleeping processes, 161–2
SNA, 215
sockets, 22
soelim (utility), 90
software development, 219–304, 60–261
sort (utility), 74, 75
source
  code, 14
  licence, 15
  program, 69
Space Travel, 13
spell (command), 60, 77, 87
Sperry, 232
spline (command), 121
split (command), 85
spooler, 39, 51, 52, 92, 220
spreadsheet, 77–80, 225
SQL, 80, 96, 102, 105, 107, 110–13, 115, 201–3, 208, 232, 244
sqrt (function), 192
stack, 28, 159
standard directories:

Index

/bin, 59, 64
/dev, 64, 165
/etc, 64
/tmp, 64, 171, 178
/usr, 56, 64
/usr/bin, 64
/usr/tmp, 64, 171
standard file formats, 270
standards, 7–10, 206–9, 230–34
Starlan, 213
stat package, 74, 121–2, 262
S-Telex, 131
stdio.h, 194
sticky bit, 236
stock control, 139
stream, 194
streamer tape, 35
Streams, 213, 220
strip (command), 197
structured programming, 198
stty (command), 157–8, 253
stub process, 212
style (command), 85
SunAccount, 136–7, 197
Sun Microsystems, 17, 124, 148, 150, 214, 222
SunOS, 222
superblock, 164, 219
supercomputers, 241
supermicros, 11
super user, 169–70, 174
SVID, *see* System V Interface Definition
SVVS, 17
swapping, 162, 163
sync (system call), 238
synchronous communciations, 126, 127, 206, 207
synchronous input/output, 162
system (function), 160
system call, 5, 58, 156, 161, 193, 231, 233, 265–7
System III, 16, 17
system management, 261–2
system manager, 169, 170, 179
systems integrator, 244
systems programmer, 241
system software, 6, 192
System V, 15–17, 219, 221, 224, 240
System V Interface Definition, 17, 109, 230–32
System V Release 2, 166, 220
System V Release 3, 163, 166, 213, 220, 238

tail (command), 77
tape, 30, 34–5
tar (utility), 179
task, 54
tbl (utility), 90
TCP/IP, 128, 209–11, 213
tee (command), 52
Tektronix, 123, 125
Telecom Gold, 129–130
telephone list, 74, 103
Teletex, 132
teletype, 35, 155, 242
telex, 131, 132
terabyte, 24
TERM (environment variable), 159, 181, 182
termcap file, 36, 159, 219
terminal emulation, 242–3
terminals, 30, 35, 172, 173, 157, 242
terminfo, 36, 150, 159, 219
test (command), 184
text processing, 13, 77, 82–3
text region, 159
third normal form, 106
Thompson, Ken, 13
tilde substitution, 189, 212
time-out, 189
time-sharing, 58, 161
times (command), 184
token passing, 208, 209
Torch, 148, 223
touch (command), 48, 49
tplot (command), 122, 123
training, 245–6
transaction control, 101, 116–17
transaction processing, 233, 237–8
Transport Layer, 207
trap (command), 184
Triplex, 148, 223
troff (utility), 88, 89
tuple, 102
two-phase commit, 117, 215
type (command), 184
TZ (environment variable), 182, 214

ucb (command), 223
UCB, *see* Berkeley, University of California at
uid, 177
ulimit (command), 184
Ultracalc, 79
Ultrix, 222
umask (command), 50, 57, 184

uNETix, 228
Unify, 239
Uniplex, 85–88, 94, 95, 117, 141, 158, 171
  diary, 95
  mail, 96
  II Plus, 74, 80
Uniplus+, 16
Unisoft, 16
Unisys, 232
Univac, 232
uniVerse, 118
universe (command), 223
UNIX
  educational use of, 81
  manual, 62
  market size, 19
  nature of, 8
  origins of, 12
  origin of name, 13
  standards, 230–234
  System V, *see* System V
  user group, *see* /usr/group
Unix, varieties of:
  AIX, 16, 18–19, 29, 67, 110, 151, 176, 180, 190, 215, 227–8, 238
  HP-UX, 237
  IX/370, 16, 228, 241
  OSx, 223
  PC/IX, 16, 225
  POSIX, 10, 17–18, 176, 208, 229–30
  SunOS, 222
  Ultrix, 222
  Uniplus+, 16
  UTS, 241
  Venix, 225
  VM/IX, 228
  XENIX, 16–17, 79, 146, 148, 166, 190, 224–226
  see Version 7; System III; System V; Berkeley Software Distribution
UNIX-like systems:
  Coherent, 228
  Cromix, 228
  D-NIX, 237
  Idris, 228
  MERT, 237
  Minix, 229
  PCNX, 229
  QNX, 228
  uNETix, 228
  UNOS, 228
Usability Package, 190
USENET, 128

user interface, 141, 144, 242, 244
user-friendly system, 141–51
users, 174
users, adding and removing, 177
/usr/group, 17, 230, 231
utilities, 257–64
UTS, 241
uucp (utility), 128, 211, 212
uuname (command), 212

V.24, 30, 40
VANs, 130
variables, 198
VAX, 113, 222, 240
vdu, 35, 125, 158, 173
vector, 121
Venix, 225
Venturcom, 225
Version 7, 13, 16
vi (utility), 82–4, 143–44, 158, 188, 222, 242
Victor V286, 135
viewdata, 131
virtual address, 160
virtual disk, 243
virtual *fork*, 238
virtual memory, 25, 28, 164
Virtual Terminal protocol, 208
virtual terminals, 146
visual shell, 190
VLSI, 20
VM, 240, 241
VM/IX, 228
VMS, 113, 221, 240
VRM, 29
vsh (command), 190
VT100, 243

wait (command), 160, 184
WAN, *see* wide area network
wc (command), 52, 77
Western Electric, 27
Whetstone, 21
who (command), 48, 52
wide area network, 205
wild card, 59, 76, 115, 184
WIMP, 145–7
winchester, 33
windows, 145, 147, 149, 233
word, 20, 23
word processing, 82, 83, 86, 225
WordStar, 225
word wrap, 83

workstation, 124, 228, 244
write (command), 93, 168
WYSIWYG, 88

X.25, 127, 208, 209, 213
X.400, 129, 208
X/Open Group, 17, 109, 111, 150, 197, 222, 230, 232−4
X3J11 standard, 232

X/Windows, 150, 151
XENIX, 16, 17, 79, 146, 148, 166, 190, 224−6
Xerox, 145
XVS, 233

yacc (utility), 261

Zilog, 26